CHARLES

CROSSINGS
A SWIMMER'S MEMOIR

Matawan Aberdeen Public Library
165 Main Street
Matawan, NJ 07747
(732) 583-9100

outskirtspress
DENVER, COLORADO

The opinions expressed in this manuscript are solely the opinions of the author and do not represent the opinions or thoughts of the publisher. The author has represented and warranted full ownership and/or legal right to publish all the materials in this book.

Crossings: A Swimmer's Memoir
All Rights Reserved.
Copyright © 2014 Charles Joscelyne
v3.0

Cover Photo © 2014 thinkstockphotos.com. All rights reserved - used with permission.

This book may not be reproduced, transmitted, or stored in whole or in part by any means, including graphic, electronic, or mechanical without the express written consent of the publisher except in the case of brief quotations embodied in critical articles and reviews.

Outskirts Press, Inc.
http://www.outskirtspress.com

ISBN: 978-1-4787-2260-1

Outskirts Press and the "OP" logo are trademarks belonging to Outskirts Press, Inc.

PRINTED IN THE UNITED STATES OF AMERICA

For Marion, Janet, and Clare.

Table of Contents

Preface vii

Chapter 1: Pools 1

Chapter 2: Lake Kashagawigamog 19

Chapter 3: Sources 51

Chapter 4: The Swimmer 75

Chapter 5: Water's Weight 95

Chapter 6: Naiant 117

Chapter 7: Now a Triathlete 140

Chapter 8: A Season on the Farmington River 157

Chapter 9: Walden Pond 192

Chapter 10: Champ 224

Chapter 11: Cayo Hueso 246

Chapter 12: Crossings 273

Preface

When I was in my mid-forties, and after many false starts, I finally learned how to swim. But I should clarify myself. Prior to this I could tread water and propel myself for short distances, but I could not comfortably swim even a single lap in any pool. More than this, the mere thought of swimming any sizable distance was abhorrent to me. Added to this intense distaste for swimming was my mild fear of the water. Perhaps surprisingly for someone middle-aged, water eventually charmed me, and I now view myself as a swimmer.

When I first sat down to record some of my experiences while learning to swim, I had not envisioned writing a book. But my early efforts to write led me to reflect back on my past swimming failures and the idea for this book took shape. Through my writing and my growing confidence as a swimmer I was led to revisit places from my youth inextricably tied to water and swimming. By swimming in pools, lakes, rivers and seaside resorts from my past, I was able look back on my life through what I might call "water's lens." While ostensibly a book about swimming and learning to swim, the following chapters explore, in no small part, my life back on land.

While working on this book, I came to see that water is about loss and I have sought to hold onto my past through my writing. Some of the people and places described have either passed on or vanished to make way for new developments. I have been fortunate to have visited and been able to write about both before they were gone. Surely, the following would best be placed in a postscript, but I feel compelled to note here that the cabins and main building of Birch Point Lodge at Lake Kashagawigamog have been razed. My mother's cousin Jean passed away a few years after the sale of her beloved Birch Point Lodge. John's father died not too long ago, and a few upscale, cookie cutter homes, and their flawless green lawns have replaced the holly trees along with his lap pool. Olympic swimmer Mitja has since retired and I suppose continues on as a swim coach. My daughter Clare graduated college some years ago, and is busy helping animals of all kinds in Texas. My wife Janet continues her experiments in sustainable living, while her health has continued to improve since our swim in Walden Pond. I no longer coach rowing or swimming as my work as a teacher has taken me abroad to China for the last few years.

Since I do not address the question of what attracts certain individuals to water and swimming in the text, perhaps I should reflect some on this question. Freud notes a dream he had "about a kind of swimming-bath where the bathers suddenly separated in all directions; at one place on the edge a person stood bending toward one of the bathers as if to drag him out." He thought dreams about swimming, and I suppose swimming too, tied to bedwetting and predictably enough sexual arousal.

Darwinian is the Aquatic Ape Hypothesis. This theory points to our hairlessness, insulating layer of subcutaneous fat, vestigial webbing between the fingers and mammalian diving reflex as evidence that our ancestors evolved during a time spent near fresh and salt water. According to this hypothesis, those inclined to swim might only be obeying some ancient littoral instinct.

More prosaic reasons why people pursue swimming might include: the vitality that swimming bestows, swimming is a sport for life and swimming skills can save lives. Perhaps it was the physical challenge, the idea of learning something totally foreign, overcoming fear, risk taking behavior, or narcissistic self-absorption for why I finally became a swimmer. I will not speculate here, but instead leave it to the interested reader to form his own opinions.

Unlike most other sports and physical activities, few books have been written on swimming beyond the how to do variety. The books that I came across and found helpful I have acknowledged in the text. I should though point to Charles Sprawson's literate *Haunts of the Black Masseur—the Swimmer as Hero* for the cultural background on swimming his book provided me.

I would like to thank historian Dr. Barbara Anderson for reading some early chapters of the book and providing me with much needed perspective. I also thank linguist Stephen Boeshaar for his critical reading of the manuscript; his suggestions improved the text immensely.

Needless to say my wife Janet, although steadfastly disavowing any editorial skills, has patiently read each chapter with me. Her fine comments, insights and suggestions have immeasurably improved the text. As the reader will comprehend, she is an integral part this book and it would not have been possible to complete without her help.

Should the reader find any amusement, enlightenment, inspiration, or instruction on swimming, I will be pleased.

Charles P. Joscelyne
Mt. Pleasant, Utah

CHAPTER 1

Pools

Indoor pools just don't seem as inviting to me. —Summer Sanders

For years, swimming's exotic and powerful images have appealed to me more than actually swimming. Unlike any land sport, swimming demands that one first overcome a fear of the water—swimming's playing field. A swimmer then must combine a dancer's balance with a gymnast's strength to overcome water's viscous hold. The physiology that swimming requires, to exert oneself while near apnea, makes swimming unlike any other sport.

Swimming's evolution has generated four strokes, and a proficient swimmer must swim all four. Freestyle's windmill, backstroke's paddlewheel circles, breaststroke's undulating advance, and butterfly's sweeping vaults all amaze and confound. Where speeds of more than four miles an hour are blazing, competitive swimmers must endure hours of sensory deprivation to realize an improvement in their times of a mere second.

There is hardly a more daunting challenge than a dawn ocean swim. The king of the beach is not the bodybuilder, but the swimmer who can dive under a cresting wave, surface, and pierce the water with a smooth stroke. Swimming, perhaps more than any other sport, calls the spectator to be first a participant; the soul of swimming is hidden technique, won through practice and toil.

Although I had been lured by these seductive images of muscle and skill, puddle-filled locker rooms, cold water, searing pool decks, sunburn, clinging sand, the reek of chlorine, clogged ears, burning sinuses, and my panicky gasps kept me on land for many years. Happily I have since inured myself to these irritations, and now like—even love—to swim.

I am five or six years old; I face the afternoon sun and thrash the water with a crude stroke while being buoyed by my friend Gary's father. Tired of arching my back to keep my face dry, I am relieved when he moves off to instruct another child.

So ends my first swimming lesson. Other memories are lost, but before this, I somehow learned to float on my back, tread water, and doggy paddle about in squirrel-like starts and stops. But like so many others, in the forty-odd years since that first lesson, I made no progress as a swimmer.

Swimming being motion in all dimensions, it is understandable that there has been a widespread ignorance of its mechanics, but it is also no less remarkable that some continue to see swimming as instinctual. The folk adage "sink-or-swim" dictates that we all know how to swim, though more than a gentle coaxing is needed for some. I once saw a film where a Japanese-American couple, having lost their only son to the Korean War, adopts an orphaned Caucasian infant. To help soothe his loss, the wife begs her husband to raise their new son in the way of the samurai. Before agreeing, the man tests the infant's worthiness by tossing him into a murky pool. When infant drown-proofing became popular, I watched television clips of half-year-olds being dropped into pools, whereupon (I suppose remembering their time in the womb) they cheerfully plied their way back to their mother's arms. Now other than possibly a tortoise, land animals such as dogs, house cats (though they would rather not swim), and horses are all natural swimmers, and as such, are not susceptible to drowning.

Stories and examples like these, along with some fuzzy evolutionary ideas about life beginning in the sea, all tend to support the belief that we, like our animal friends, are born swimmers.

As Mary Oliver recounts in "The Swimming Lesson," this sink-or-swim dictum has had its casualties:

Feeling the icy kick, the endless waves
Reaching around my life, I moved my arms
And coughed, and in the end saw land.

Somebody, I suppose,
Remembering the medieval maxim,
Had tossed me in
Had wanted me to learn to swim,

Not knowing that none of us, who ever came
back From that long lonely fall and frenzied rising,
Ever learned anything at all
About swimming, but only
How to put off, one by one,
Dreams and pity, love and grace—
How to survive in any place.

But trusting Oliver, to believe "the medieval maxim" is to err twice—a dubious method is employed for the wrong goal. Although treading water or splashing across a pool might help survive a drunken pool party or a fall overboard, these presumably inborn skills do not constitute swimming. Swimming is technique following science; the laws of fluid dynamics shape beautiful swimming. Pushing a child into a pool or lake might overcome his or her initial dread of water, but little can be gained from this impatient, ignorant act. I should not be too harsh, for swim instruction is now so much more enlightened, but like with tennis or ballet, swimming progress occurs only after one has achieved a kinesthetic awareness. Although I was fortunate to have never suffered an experience like Oliver's, tips like "kick hard" or "cup your hands" never helped me discover any of swimming's secrets.

Looking like a giant tuna can, the first pool set behind my childhood home holds most of my earliest swimming memories. It must have been a Memorial Day weekend when I helped my father remove a circle of grass, pluck rocks from the dirt, and lay down a cushion of sand. After erecting the frame, my mother and sisters joined us in wrestling the pool's thin steel wall in place. Forever resisting, the wall's warping and buckling filled the air with deep twangs and bangs. Our timely assembly led to a disheartening two- or three-day wait as a submerged green garden hose silently emptied into the pool. Regularly returning to the pool, I gazed into the blue vinyl, wishing the pool filled. Thinking I might speed the process, I would haul the hose out, and covering its metal end with my thumb, spray and lash the water until a painful numbness gripped my hand. There were false hopes: "A fire truck could fill your pool in just a couple hours," said a friend. Upon hearing this, images of glossy red trucks, flashing chrome, lemon-yellow helmets, black coats, and torrents of white water passed before my eyes. Only when I lost interest did the pool finally fill. Little matter, the water came from a cold municipal well, and our pool would need a week or two in the June sun before anyone dared go in.

Too small for real swimming, our pool was mostly used for frolicking, creating whirlpools, or just soaking. Thinking myself clever, I began entering our pool by running across the yard and somersaulting off its top apron. This seemed a great idea until my friends, following my lead, clogged our pool filter with grass carried in by our feet.

No afternoon or evening in our pool seemed to pass without

my mother having boiled hot dogs or watermelon slices waiting for us. Memories of my aunt and uncle and their boys up on a visit from Philadelphia conjure up images of grass, tennis balls, a watermelon, and our collie Goldie all floating about.

All summer long our pool was a great insect trap. A morning's catch might include bees, beetles, gnats, and moths, but not every bug came unwittingly. The hardy and versatile backswimmer, the Navy Seal of its world, I guess mistaking our pool for a pond, would fly in, scull about, and make a few deep dives, all while on its back. Unfazed by the chlorine, it flew off in a few days, hale but probably still hungry. I once grasped one of these gray and white mottled fellows, and ever resourceful, he warned me off with a stinging bite.

Pool cleaning involved two debris zones, the surface and bottom. Although our white plastic pool-skimmer's trickle was an endless fascination, pool vacuuming was a tedious bore. Ever the improviser, my father salvaged and refashioned a five-foot tall commercial dry-cleaning tank to serve as our pool filter. Embarrassed by its extraordinary size and not quite sure what to make of the contraption myself, I was quick to divert questions when friends visited. My spirits sagged whenever my father fogged our pool water with scoops of white diatomaceous earth. "The filter tubes need coating," he said.

During August dog days, our pool was a great place to cool off on muggy, sleepless nights. Like spirits floating above a misty lake, my mother, sisters, and I glided back and forth through the haze.

But summer was all too brief, and Labor Day's inevitable chill signaled the end of our swimming. Abandoned when we returned to school, our pool reverted to its natural state. With an opaque green algae bloom coloring its water, our pool became a frightful place. Maple and sycamore leaves fluttered in and sank out of sight. Winter snows soon followed and covered the last few ice-encrusted leaves. A snowstorm waning, I once trudged over to peer at our pool's snowcap. Standing there in the cold and quiet—a quiet broken only by the clinking and slapping tire chains of passing cars—the previous summer's swims seemed so foreign and forbidding.

When spring came, rains and melting snow created small lakes in the lawn about our pool. Happily, though, longer, drier days prevailed. Balmy air from the Gulf of Mexico greened our grass, and robins arrived to yank worms from the sodden ground.

May's warmth brought the racket of roaring mowers on Saturday mornings, and the light air was filled with the scents of the cut grass and wild garlic. When a pair of crabapple trees in our backyard littered the grass with white and pink petals, my thoughts returned to our pool. Soon reclaimed, our pool was again ready for another summer.

The backyards about my home were all dotted with pools like ours. My friends and I called them "above-ground," as opposed to "dug-in" or "in-ground," pools. Some, belonging to boys with whom I was either not acquainted or at odds with, sat like moored pleasure boats, near at hand, but forever off limits. Several backyards up a shallow rise stood the Brady pool, its pristine blue wall and white frame a match for their son's blond hair and good looks. A few doors over was the Watson pool, an imposing green structure with a lavish, encircling white deck. Friction between my friends and their son kept its waters a mystery. On a whim, we bombarded the pool with dirt clods one Saturday morning. A posse consisting of rival boys, Mr. Watson, and a beagle was quickly formed. Methodically they pursued us along neighboring streets and backyards until Mr. Watson shouted, "If I catch you, I'll put my foot up your ass" and then abandoned the chase.

It was those pools named after friends, that I loved and knew best. There was Robby's pool; high-walled and of a small diameter, its waters were always cloudy. The soil having been excavated from this pool center before the sand cushion was put down made the pool deep in the middle. The water level seemingly always up to my neck, I found swimming exhausting in this pool. A couple peach trees grew nearby. Robby climbed one and scattered peaches about the water on an afternoon. Retrieving a peach, I tried to stay afloat while biting into its hard flesh.

And there was Johnny's pool, by far the largest. Four feet high and twenty-four feet across, its cold, clear waters took my breath away. Pushing off the wall, I would torpedo across its bottom and feel my lungs ache as I neared the other side. Johnny's father had constructed a fine dark-red lacquered deck that I was always afraid of slipping on. W h e n I r o d e home on my bike after an afternoon of swimming, the hunger and the dull pain I felt when taking a deep breath underscored the enormity of Johnny's pool.

Some pools I must have swum in only a few times, for I have few memories. Tommy's azure pool was set in a lush lawn down a short slope from his house. There—with Dasher, his shaggy, black dog paddling about—we spent a happy afternoon before being called in for dinner. Next door to Tommy was muscular George's rusty red pool; a ball of fury, he thrashed the water as he flung my friends and me about. Different was Craig's pool; reflecting his calm nature, my swim there was pensive and serene. Neither friend nor foe, I was uneasy, not sure of my welcome, the few times I swam in red-haired Krissy's and tall Joanne's pools.

My earliest pool memories come from next-door neighbor Gary's pool, only three feet high and no more than twelve feet across. I suffered through my first swim lesson in his pool. Gary was not an easy friend, though, and I took no sides when he and another boy, slinging handfuls of dirt at each other, muddied his pool waters. Offering little information, I maintained my innocence after a phone call to my house later that night. Perhaps it was an act of God that caused my mother to greet me with, "Gary's pool collapsed," when I walked in the door one afternoon. Shocked, I trod across our soggy backyard, all the while feeling his pool waters had violated our lawn. Peering over the red wood slat fence that separated our yards, I gazed at the pool's metal wall, which lay in disarray. On closer inspection, I saw the main seam had given away. Standing before the heap, I imagined, and was sorry to have missed, the moment when the white wave was set loose on the land.

These above-ground pools were seemingly everywhere. My cousins in northeast Philadelphia had theirs set underneath a spreading mimosa tree in their backyard. The asphalt lots outside most toy and hardware stores displayed fully assembled above-ground pools filled with sparkling water. My father later confessed to me that both our pools—our first three-foot-high pool and later a four-foot-high pool—were display models he purchased on discount after the swim season ended in September.

Popular on television back then were men who high dived off guyed towers erected in shopping center parking lots. Death seemed imminent until the water of some high-walled pool broke the diver's fall. The shock wave spreading out, water rocketed out the pool like a heavy wave crashing into a seawall. While watching these stunts, I thought of the opportunities a small maple tree in our backyard might offer me someday.

More startling, though, were the diving horses at the Atlantic City Steel Pier. Risking blindness, these horses dove head first into large above-ground pools. When older, I made light of this schlocky stunt and its commentator, Ed Hurst, while watching the show at a friend's house. My friend's father wasted little time in pointing out to me Mr. Hurst's success as an insurance salesman.

My father maintained our last four-foot pool well into my teenage years, but when its use waned, he either sold or gave it away. The lawn reseeding itself, our pool's circle of sand slowly vanished. In the ensuing years, I kept a vegetable garden where our two pools once stood.

Apparently unaffected by our years of watery fun, tomatoes, squash, green beans, and cucumbers all thrived there for several summers.

Not every pool I swam in was an above-ground pool. Near my home was our township's multi-lane in-ground pool. L-shaped, the pool had a diving well and was probably built with the intention of nurturing future Olympians. Brothers David and Jimmy, without a backyard pool of their own, were pool members. Often their guest, I came to know the pool's frigid waters well. From a recliner, I watched as an endless line of children and adults plunged off the pool's high-dive. Challenges accepted, each of my friends soon fell to the water below. Feeling the high-dive's allure, I occasionally walked over, but sensing my friends' stares, I could never bring myself to grasp the rail and begin the climb.

Associated with status and increased property values, in-ground pools began to appear about my home as I grew older. Across the street, the Barnes had a rectangular pool dug. Guarded by a chain-link fence and a mad German shepherd, I did no more than gaze longingly at their pool's blue waters. Next door to the Barnes, the Darcy pool was well hidden behind a high wood fence. Sadly, my fistfight with the Darcy boy made their pool off limits for me. Beyond our crabapple trees, I followed the construction one summer as our neighbor Martha had a smallish kidney-shaped pool dug in her backyard. Despite my mother's assurances that my sisters and I were welcome, I never swam in that pool.

If I was unable to swim in my neighbors' new pools, there were other, not-too-distant pools to visit. Across the road from my home there was a fenced pasture where a light-colored bay named Buckskin and a chestnut named Gerry would snatch carrots from me with their brownish-yellow teeth. Early in my teen years, the pasture and horses vanished and an expansive apartment complex took their place. Near an old barn, a modest-sized pool was dug for the tenants. My friend Skip was hired as lifeguard, and I had free admission for the summer. Fantasizing the apartments inhabited by wanton single and divorced women, I s p e n t afternoons beside the pool filled with thoughts of sin and licentiousness. As I was arcing off the pool's diving board, the blue bottom met my vacant eyes before I shot below the surface.

Skip and I later visited another swim club one evening where we were pinched, poked, and felt the smooth skin of bikini-clad girls beneath the illumined waters. Back up on the deck, we took in the night air and joked about the sharks in the water.

During the colder months, a neighboring middle school opened its pool for after dinner swims, but the pool's chlorine-choked air and overly warm water limited my visits. There were invitations to other acquaintances' pools. These were mostly languid affairs spent beside upscale pools with slides or diving boards. My high school did not have a pool, and I graduated with few skills and even less interest in swimming.

Commuting for my first few years of college, I learned a pool was hidden somewhere on the campus. Possessed by a vague urge rather than a well-thought-out plan, I set out to become a swimmer. I was away from familiar surroundings, so swimming seemed to me new and approachable. I found the pool one afternoon after classes.

Cramped and painted an unappealing light green, the pool was hemmed in by a narrow walkway and a low ceiling. Leafless trees, visible through windows set high on the wall, hinted at winter's coming desolation. Alone, except for the guard on duty, I felt like a fraud crawling back and forth. Swimming no more than a lap or two before resting to catch my breath, I persisted, hoping to find a rhythm. When the sun's imprint moved higher on the far wall, the guard told me she needed to close for the day. Fatigued and at a loss on how to improve, I hauled myself out onto the concrete and walked off to the locker room. Discouraged, I never went back to that pool, nor would I attempt to swim again for some years.

Upon entering my twenties, distance running supplanted tennis as my athletic passion. Tall and thin, I was well suited for long runs. Moving to central Pennsylvania to finish my degree, I found the terrain and culture ideal for running. A jogging boom had swept the country, and running was no longer the solitary pursuit of those training for track. I entered races, read running books such as Roger Bannister's *The Four-Minute Mile*, and watched every broadcast of the documentary *The Olympiad*.

Spurred on by these words and images, I over trained one spring and developed tendinitis. Lame on land, I visited my school's natatorium, where a twenty-five-meter pool was housed. Harboring no illusions about my swimming skills, I hoped only to stay fit. A few times a week, I side stroked or crawled my way through exhausting laps. The swimmers in adjacent lanes made me envious, as their effortless swimming seemed unattainable. I thought it odd that a few laps of swimming could be as taxing as a mile run. My swimming ended when I returned home for the summer. Combining cycling with easy running, I soon was back on the roads and trails, again renouncing every pool's glassy waters.

I began the decade of the eighties as a student in Manhattan's Upper West Side. New acquaintances likened me to the running obsessed Babe Levy (Dustin Hoffman) from the movie *Marathon Man*. I spent many early mornings and late afternoons traversing the length of Riverside Park, a two-and-a-half-mile narrow strip of parkland paralleling the Hudson River. The closest I came to water back then was running alongside the river near the 79th Street Boat Basin. Tidal, brackish and malodorous, the Hudson is an estuary there. Running in the park, I sometimes raced barges that were being pushed up the river by tugboats. Spying an approaching barge after turning around at

72nd Street, I would slow and prepare myself for the ensuing struggle. Allowing the barge to pull even with me somewhere near 80th Street, I would sprint off and soon pass the Soldier's and Sailor's Monument perched high on my right. Despite running the two miles to the park's end at the 120th Street tennis courts in near five-minute-mile pace, I usually lost these races to the tugboat's relentless diesels. Surprised at the barge-tugboat pair's speed, in time I came to blame the tides or the park's meandering paths for my losses.

On weekends I ran northward, up to the George Washington Bridge. Of the sights I saw, the most puzzling were the dead white chickens that were scattered alongside a lonely stretch of roadway near the bridge's massive base. Perplexed, I later learned animal sacrifices were part of some Caribbean religious rituals.

I remember one cold, clear morning when I paused to stand in the middle of the bridge. Engulfed by the roaring traffic, I felt unnerved by the bridge's quivers and pulses. Gazing south, I saw past midtown's wall of buildings, the World Trade Center, down to the Statue of Liberty. With the statue's patina piercing the morning haze, an aura seemed to surround the statue. To the north, I traced the brownish arc of New Jersey's palisades up to the Tappan Zee Bridge. I felt unburdened and free. I had made my escape from the city. Here at last was open space, a shimmering river, and a rare glimpse of the horizon.

Hovering there, high in a canyon of blue air, I thought of swimming across the Hudson and the consequent need to dodge ships, negotiate tides, and avoid debris. There might be some horrors encountered during such a swim, for I once came across a bloated cow trapped with other flotsam off the rocks on the Manhattan side. Others had made the swim. I had read a story in the *New York Times* about some off-duty cab drivers who, after some drinks, dared a fellow driver to swim across the river. Accepting the challenge, the brave hack jumped into the black night water somewhere around

40th Street and emerged later in Weehawken. And then there was the ambitious English Channel-like swim around the Manhattan Island. Back then competitors received inoculations before entering the Upper New York Bay off Battery Park for their 28.5-mile counter-clockwise swim. My mind balked, and I struggled with this last image. Although I would someday swim down there in the Hudson, I was then only a runner. The morning growing late, I ran on, back across the bridge to Washington Heights and south with the river.

Other than fanciful imagining, I stayed away from water and swimming while I lived in New York. In subsequent years, summer's heat necessitated trips to seaside spots such as Fire Island, Cape May, or Guilford up in Connecticut. But these outings were more for relief, not to swim. A splash of bracing salt water and a cool offshore breeze was what brought others and me.

Away from open water, the odor of pool chlorine hinted that there was an indoor pool hidden somewhere in my university's gym. On rainy or snowy days, I braved the gym's stench to lift weights and run laps on its worn track, but I never tried to find the pool. An acquaintance recounted her swim lessons there, but I met her reports with no more than disinterested nods. I was never deader to water or swimming.

Most of the pools I have swum in over the years have been forgettable motel or campground plashes tucked in behind offices or under shade trees. A few, though, have been more memorable, such as those expansive municipal pools where people mill about tussling or in embrace. Annoyed by the splashing and noise, I pretend to be an apneist in these pools, swimming underwater on ever-changing tacks. Even larger was a wave pool at a water park in Texas, where, like a moth lured to a flame, I repeatedly dove down in search of the waves' source. Water flumes and slides having little appeal for me, I glided past lifeless bodies set on inner tubes in the park's Lazy River. Alluring was a small but deep saltwater pool at a lodge in Quebec's

Laurentian Mountains. After a day of cross-country skiing with my wife Janet, I sounded the pool's depth and torpedoed its length. The high snow pressing against a pair of sliding glass doors seemed incongruous as I bobbed about in the limpid water.

A few years after setting off to become a swimmer, I traveled to Fort Lauderdale to swim in the International Swimming Hall of Fame's Olympic-size pool. Having heard a former collegiate swimmer recall his days swimming "fifties on the fifty" there, I gasped after each lap while watching the pace clock wind down. Afterwards, I toured the hall museum with its varicolored flags and life-sized wax replicas of Johnny Weissmuller and Mark Spitz. The many anonymous Olympic medals, pins, badges, and certificates on display spoke of time passing and that of all types of fame, perhaps athletic fame is the most fleeting.

A year or so later, on a cold and windy January morning, I attended a masters swim clinic at Yale's Robert Kiphuth Memorial Exhibition Pool. The pool's clear water was cold. Resembling an oversize ruler, hash marks on the pool walls marked each yard. After my swim, I stood on the deck and gazed up at imposing steep rows of dark wood seats that encircled the pool. I thought of Olympic great Don Schollander and the countless laps he must have logged in the pool as a Yale swimmer. In his book *Deep Water,* Schollander details the exhaustion and frustration of trying to be both a college student and a world-class swimmer, after winning four gold medals in the 1964 Olympics. Disillusioned with the sham amateurism overseas, mismanagement at home, and corruption of the Olympic ideal, Schollander could manage only a silver medal in the 200-meter freestyle in the 1968 Mexico City Games. Spent, he retired at the age of twenty-two.

From faded kiddie pools to lapis-blue infinity pools, no pool escapes my notice these days. Flying in a jet, I will gaze down, and like a beachcomber hunting shells, appraise each pool before letting it drift off. The backyards of Florida or the Southwest appear flecked with gems of sapphire or aquamarine. Confessing to voyeurism, I spied on the construction of an Olympic-size lap pool during my time living on Florida's East Coast. Via aerial imagery, I have journeyed afar to swim vicariously at Hearst's San Simeon or share a lane with past Olympic heroes in Santa Clara.

Beyond a certain size, a pool's extent has little impact on one's swimming experience; this naturally depends on the swimmer, "because it (water) can be anything–it can be any color, it's movable, it has no set visual description," writes artist David Hockney in his retrospective *Hockney's Pictures*. Pausing from my writing, I turn the pages and study his famous *A Bigger Splash*. The painting is constructed geometrically, with faded blues and pale pinks. Only a blue-white spray breaks the painting's flat monotones. A few pages on, *A Large Diver* uses bright greens and blues and strong flesh tones to depict a swimmer underwater. Hockney's pool pictures lack vigor, though. They would not be my pools. A floating ring, a naked sunbather, and vacant waters hint at listless days beside beautiful but empty pools. "Hollywood is loneliness beside the swimming pool," said actress Liv Ulllmann. Infinitely mutable, each pool awaits each swimmer.

The above-ground pools about my childhood home have all but vanished. A spacious in-ground pool now fills Gary's old backyard. Johnny's, George's, Craig's, and Tommy's pools long ago dismantled, their backyards are empty. Tucked into the far corner of my old home's backyard, the new tenants have erected a small metal above-ground pool. White and smallish, the pool stands where a wisteria vine once grew. This pool is as a connection to my past, and although it is largely obscured from view by new shrubs and bushes, I am always happy to catch sight of it whenever in my old neighborhood.

Although my eldest sister and I have moved away, my younger

sister and her husband are raising their children in a house not far from our old home. Intrigued to swim again in an above-ground pool, I climbed into their blue, bowl-shaped pool one hot August morning. A new concept for me, their pool had no supporting metal frame and its vinyl sides offered a soft cushion. Diving under and gliding to the other side, I wondered how a fifteen-foot stretch of water could have once seemed so large. I was amusing myself by dolphin kicking on my back when my niece and nephew joined me with their blow-up rings. Puzzled as to why their uncle would want to swim in their little pool, they still were happy to paddle about with me.

Janet and I later attended my nephew's birthday party that my sister held at David's and Jimmy's old swim club. Intrigued to be back in the pool again after forty years, I soon realized the pool was twenty-five meters long, what is known as a meter pool. During the adult swim, I churned out lap after lap, all the while recalling the timid boy who swam there years before. After the whistle blew signaling the children's return, I climbed out and walked over to the diving well. The old high-dive, which I could never bring myself to jump off, was gone. A little disappointed, I contented myself with a few jumps off the pool's low board. After drying off, I found the pool manager, and he related that his family had acquired the pool from the township some twenty-five years earlier. He said, "The diving well was too shallow to legally have the high dive."

Wandering about, I studied the club's trees and the pool's concrete walkway; anything that might connect me with my times here. Coming across an elderly couple, I struck up a conversation, hoping they might remember something of the pool's early days. Eyeing the zipper-like scar running down the man's chest, I was let down to hear they "just moved up from Philadelphia." Walking across the deck to the pool's edge, I lost myself in reverie.

Here in the Northeast one must swim indoors most of the year.

POOLS

During the summers, I will usually join an outdoor pool to enjoy for a few months. For the past two summers, I have swum in the choppy waters of a town pool here in mid-state Delaware. This pool's high chain-link fence is menacingly topped with coils of razor wire. It is not a swimmer's pool, as the lifeguards must ask children and adults to vacate the pool's single lane whenever I arrive for a swim.

Today is Labor Day, and it marks the end of another swim season here at the pool. The sky is clear, and although the sun is still strong, there is a chill in the air. Several days of rain a week ago have cooled the pool water. As with most of the summer, the odd child or adult wanders into my lane. Pausing between laps, I watch tennis balls fly and young teens wrestle. Earlier, a half-eaten pizza slice drifted past. Lately though, kids have taken to playing with a garden hose the lifeguards leave running into the pool. Feeling the spray on my back, I will stop swimming and quip, "What are you trying to do, get me wet?"

Today I must ask a lifeguard to speak to a woman who has hauled the hose across my lane. Intent on spraying her daughter and son who stay just out of reach, she snaps, "I'm not bothering you." There is little interest in swimming among those who come here, but I should not complain. I have been for the most part left alone this summer.

I take a meandering route on my bike ride home. The sun setting, I pedal along out-of-the-way roads. I was unaware until moving here that Delaware is in a sense two states— an upper and lower tract separated by the Chesapeake and Delaware Canal. Supported by the industrial giant Dupont and banking concerns in Wilmington, the state north of the canal is home to tony hideouts such as Greenville and Hockessin. Other than resort towns such as Rehoboth, Dewey, and Bethany Beach, most of Delaware south of the canal consists of expansive soybean or cornfields, along with the occasional egg-laying operation. Many of the modest homes along my route have an above-ground pool in their backyard. In no more than a mile, I count seven. None of the pools are being used today and several look in disuse. Tall weeds grow out one pool. Slowing, I stop and gaze at a blue vinyl pool, the same sort as I swam in with my niece and nephew. I recall seeing these pools boxed up, ready for sale in a store last spring. Pictured on the box was a smiling, tow-haired boy filling his pool with a garden hose. The boy reminded me of myself years before. I supposed filling your own pool was still a joy. The day growing late, I ride on, happy to have seen these relics from my past.

CHAPTER 2

Lake Kashagawigamog

We shall not cease from exploration, and the end of all our exploring will be to arrive where we started and know the place for the first time.
—T. S. Elliot

As an American, I am not sure what it means, if anything, to be of Canadian descent. At first glance (French-speaking Quebec excluded), there appears to be little that distinguishes the United States from Canada's bordering provinces. For sure, Canada's colder weather, predilection toward hockey, and curious pronunciations of "eh," "aboot," and "zed" for Z have all been singled out. Their national health care system tags them as socialists, and thus one might imagine them to be a more caring country than the States. But aside from these, most would be hard pressed to come up with anything beyond the "orderly," "courteous", "slower-paced," and even "boring" labels often heard when Canada is juxtaposed with the United States.

Perhaps it is this indistinctness and familiarity bred out of closeness that accounts for the silence and blank looks that greet me whenever I mention my mother is a Canadian. I never hear the "Oh, how interesting," or inquiries such as, "Have you been back there for a visit?" Having almost any other ancestry, even one from the England, would surely elicit more of a response, yet when I was a boy growing up in Pennsylvania's Bucks County, my mother's Canada was anything but a cold, barren annex to the United States. Instead, her Ontario was a watery land for me.

When I was young, no summer seemed to pass without my two younger sisters and me being loaded into our Ford station wagon for the daylong drive north. Toronto, Hamilton, Peterborough, and Windsor, along with lesser-known towns such as Belle River, Halliburton, North Bay, and Powassan were the names of our destinations. Ostensibly to visit my mother's family, our trips to Canada also served as our family's summer vacations.

My mother was born across the river from Detroit in the city of Windsor, but not long after, she moved with her family to Peterborough, a small city northeast of Toronto. I never learned much about Windsor from her beyond that the Canadians who commuted to jobs in the United States were unflatteringly referred to as "nickel immigrants," for the five-cent fee the Ambassador Bridge charged to cross the Detroit River. Rather, it was the stories and memories of her beloved Peterborough that turned this small Ontario city into a magical place for me.

When she reminisced, I marveled with her at the May snows, felt the sting of ice-caked windows, and heard the crowd roar at the Saturday night lacrosse games. I ice-skated with her under the lights, went window-shopping along Peterborough's George Street, and tried to imagine what her city's famed lift lock might look like. I stood with her sister and brothers as they huddled before their kitchen stove on winter mornings. I was there to help nurse her brother Arnold through pneumonia, but too much the self-centered boy, I had little empathy for what my mother must have endured one summer while bedridden in a full leg cast.

As I grew older and began to view the world through my own eyes, our summer trips to Canada began to wipe away some of my mother's misty reverie and brought her Canada into clearer focus.

LAKE KASHAGAWIGAMOG

On what must have been one of my first visits to Peterborough, I remember my father taking me to see the city's lift lock. Knowing nothing then about the couple-hundred-mile- long Trent-Severn Waterway or the lock's claim to be the world's highest hydraulic lift, I stood next to him as we gazed at the lock's concrete walls. Fixing my eyes on what looked like an immense garage lift, I watched and listened as the water rained down from above.

On the same trip, my father drove us by my mother's childhood house on Westcott Street. Here my mother's rosy descriptions stood in stark contrast with the rather ordinary house I saw outside our car.

Maybe more than Peterborough, it was the Haliburton Highlands (or simply Haliburton, as my mother referred to it) that held her fondest memories. The village of Haliburton is a couple hours' drive north of Peterborough, and it was there my mother spent her teen summers working at her aunt and uncle's vacation resort—Birch Point Lodge.

One of several lodges, Birch Point Lodge was set on the southern shore of Lake Kashagawigamog. Getting its start back in the early 1920s, Birch Point catered to those who sought a quiet week or two of canoeing, fishing, swimming, and home-cooked meals.

Kashagawigamog means "long and shady waters" in the native Ojibway First Nations language, and true to its name, nothing more than its long and narrow shape distinguishes it from the countless others lakes that dot the Canadian Shield. For my mother, though, Kashagawigamog might as well have been Canada's only lake, for I never heard her speak of any other.

As a boy, I listened to her tales of long hours of work at the lodge, of being admonished by her brother Arnold for talking while they fished from a boat at dusk, and her night swims across the lake to dances at the Wigamog Inn—another lodge on the lake.

Not particularly interested in the dances, I once asked her, "Did you swim across the lake by yourself?

"No. A bunch of us went together, and we had a rowboat follow along with our clothes and towels," she said.

There was not much lakefront development back then. The Second World War had just ended or was about to end, and Lake Kashagawigamog was largely untouched. I have held onto a dim image of my mother stroking through the lake's dark waters. No light shines from the opposite shore other than Wigamog's lights, and the only sounds heard are creaking oarlocks, some splashing, and laughs or shrieks from the shore up ahead.

When I was about six or seven years old, we traveled to Birch Lodge for a visit. I recall an evening after dinner, when I walked down to the bank and stepped into the lake. My mother watched me from a chair set up on the grassy bank behind me. Like looking through a spotless window, the lake bottom appeared close enough to touch, and I enjoyed feeling the hard-packed sand under my feet. Wading out, I paused to study a large daddy longlegs spider that clung to the undercarriage of the wooden dock on my right. The water deepening, I eventually came to a standstill with the lake up to my chest. Ahead, over a short stretch of water, floated an aqua dive platform. The platform, a rectangular slap on the water, appeared tantalizingly close. I felt an urge to swim out to it, but I remained stuck in place, much too afraid to venture any farther.

In the following days, I would gaze out over the lake and again imagine swimming out to the platform, but the thought of the deep water and what might lurk beneath the platform kept me on land. A cousin of mine, a boy in his early teens, spent what seemed like entire days lolling about on the platform. His dives into the lake impressed me and made me wish I could do the same. Sometimes friends of his would gather on the platform with him, but probably because I was younger, I was never invited to join them.

For years, the thought of swimming out to a dive platform intimidated me. I came to see those capable of making such a swim as accomplished swimmers. Lately, I have noticed inflatable trampolines replacing the platforms along lake fronts. Light, bouncy, and easily maneuvered, they are no doubt more preferred by today's youth.

It must be one of the great joys of parenting—and perhaps why generation after generation chose the same vacation spot—to revisit a favored place with one's own children. With the memories from her teenage years at the lodge intermingling with her gratification as wife and mother, I can imagine no happier time for my mother than the evening she sat and watched me wade into Lake Kashagawigamog.

We made another trip to Birch Point Lodge when I was twelve or thirteen, but perhaps because of some friction between my mother and her cousin Jean, our family never again vacationed there.

Although apart from Lake Kashagawigamog I was never far from water during other visits to Canada, I enjoyed a windy ride with my family down the Detroit River to Bois Blanc Island on a Bob-Lo boat, felt the mist rising out of the Niagara Gorge, and at a family picnic poked at the chilling watermelons bobbing about in a park's frigid mineral water.

When I was nine years old, we rented a small lakefront house for the month of July in the Ontario town of Belle River. Located on the southern shores of Lake St. Clair, Belle River, as far as I was concerned, consisted of no more than a fishing pier and an ocean-sized lake. On many mornings my father and I made the short drive to the pier, which was located a mile or two from our vacation house. The pier was made of two parts: a narrow metal I-beam section and a wider concrete part farther out. Maybe it was a lack of funds or some fault with the lake bottom that necessitated the pier to be of two parts, but whatever the case, I was fearless when traversing the I-beam. My father and I could always find a vacant spot to sit on the concrete walkway, and it was there, above Lake St. Clair's murky waters, that I first experienced the boyhood joys of fishing.

I learned how to secure a sinker, heartlessly thread a worm onto a hook, untangle a bird's nest of fishing line in my rod's reel, and to be patient and not strike on a fish's first bite. I lost and landed bass, catfish, and yellowish-orange black-striped perch. Between nibbles and bites, I viewed diesel-powered cabin cruisers motoring out of the channel with their trolling outriggers set skyward. "Muskies" (short for muskellunges), were the trophies my father said they were after. Should my luck run out, the other fishermen and their catches were always there for my amusement. On one windy morning, when no fish seemed interested in my line, I watched a boy my age and his father lose an epic battle to a bowfin, though they called it a dogfish.

Over the weeks, I never lost the thrill of seeing my rod tip take its first dip toward the water. Although as an adult I quit fishing some time ago, those times on the pier fishing with my father rank among my happiest. Should there have been a heaven on earth for such a young boy as I was, it was on that pier.

Unlike the fishing pier, the lake in front of our vacation house was a disappointment. Resembling more a marsh than a lake, the waters off our beach were filled with slimy algae balls. The bottom sloped so slowly that instead of swimming, my time in the lake was limited to tramping about in water no deeper than my shins. Sidestepping the algae, I would amuse myself by grasping at minnows or rousting an occasional catfish from its hiding place. Should I stray too far away from the beach, I would hear my mother call my name from our cabin porch. Our vacation lake house then had all the amenities: a sandy beach, a few whispering pines, and a beautiful lake view—everything save water that one could swim in.

No one seemed to know why the lake was filled with what my sisters and I called the "icky algae," nor did anyone have any ideas on how to remove it. I thought it would be a great idea to scrape the lake bottom in front of our cabin with a bulldozer that sat outside a nearby cabin, but the machine never moved during our stay. Perhaps acting out of the frustration at not being able swim, my sisters and a couple other children took turns dumping buckets of sand over each other after dinner one evening. Later, my mother voiced her displeasure while washing the endless grains from my sisters' hair.

Unable to swim during the hot afternoons, I would wander down the road outside our cabin and catch bright green frogs outside a spider-web-filled drainage pipe. Other times, I would throw stones at the passing freight trains that ran near our cabin. Most times, though, I was content to stand or walk along the beach and watch the freighters entering and leaving the Detroit River. The freighters and factory smokestacks visible on the horizon hinted at the Midwest's industrial might, and although it was distant, I knew I stood at the threshold of a great enterprise.

At the corner of our beach, close to the lake, lay a pink-hulled rowboat. Weathered and appearing much like driftwood, a pair of gray oars lay half-buried in the sand near the boat. The boat's serviceable days were long past, but unable to resist my cajoling, my father decided to resurrect the boat. After riding into town with him, I stood by while he purchased some brushes and a few gallons of black tar. Back on the beach, I helped him wire brush the hull and then watched as he coated the hull with the tar. Although we gave it more of a quick patch than a lasting repair, the old boat was again ready take to the water. I had found a way to breach the algae and venture out onto the lake.

It was Saturday when my mother's brother Jack arrived from Toronto. When I was growing up, my mother's brothers—Jack, Arnold, and Paul—were my athletic idols. Jack was the eldest of the three, and in the years after World War II, he boxed professionally, eventually winning the middleweight championship of Canada. Arnold, the middle son, was a standout hockey and lacrosse player, who my mother often said, "had a tryout with the Detroit Red Wings." Arnold moved out to British Columbia before I was born, and I knew him only through stories and photographs. Jack and Arnold—one perhaps too old and the other too distant—it was my mother's baby brother Paul with whom I felt the closest. Paul lived with us during his last year in high school, during which he captained his basketball team. With my father out of town, Paul was at the hospital when I was born. When younger, I loved to sneak up on him as he reclined in a chair and dare what he called his snake-fast reflexes. When we were outside, he was always a step too fast for me whenever we raced or played football.

The exact sequence of events are lost, but not long after Uncle Jack arrived, my father loaded my sister and me into the tarred boat. Walking alongside the boat, he and Jack led us out through the algae. The water deepening, my father climbed into the boat and began rowing. I still have a vivid image of him shirtless, pulling hard on the oars.

Like the first time a person views land from on high, I was both fascinated and frightened to see our cabin and the shoreline recede. Well clear of the algae, Uncle Jack swam a side-stroke to keep pace with the boat. "How deep do you think it is?" I asked him. "Oh, about twelve feet," he said. Without life preservers, we were off shore, afloat upon my grand lake.

I soon noticed water beginning to seep into the boat bottom. There was not too much, maybe an inch or two. My father and Uncle Jack did not seem worried, but I could not help feeling uneasy. Back on the beach, I could see my mother clad in a bright red blouse gazing out at us. I scampered about the boat looking over one side and then the other. I imagined the boat sinking and my father and uncle swimming us back to shore. Water was coaxing me, and although enticed, years would pass before I would ever swim so far offshore.

We probably were never no more than a half mile out, but for a nervous nine-year-old, it was a relief to turn around. I do not remember how our adventure ended, but I doubt if the pink-hulled boat was ever rowed again. After Uncle Paul arrived later that day, a reunion of the Dugans ensued about a fire lit on the beach that night. The next morning while walking the beach, I studied the charred remains of a wooden chair and the boat oars. Back at the cabin I wondered aloud about the fire. "Your Uncle Jack and Paul were acting crazy last night," said my mother.

We returned to our cabin the following summer, but like most attempts to recreate past pleasures that summer failed to match the joy of the first one. I was a year older, and the algae balls seemed more numerous, the frogs in the drainage ditch not as green, and the fish off the fishing pier, while a little easier to catch, never quite as large.

We never returned to Belle River, and my last two adolescent trips to Canada would begin and end beside a small, nameless lake a couple hundred miles north of Toronto.

After his boxing career ended, Uncle Jack worked as bouncer in Toronto and as a prison guard in northern Ontario. Later he became the director of a boys' club in Toronto. He was a natural with children. I heard the halls filled with the shouts of, "Mr. D, Mr. D" whenever I visited his club. Games, arts and crafts, and physical activity—particularly sports—were paramount at his club. Pick-up basketball games were a constant fixture in the club gym, and I was always happy to play. I recall playing game after game one afternoon until leg cramps ended my day. Until then, I had not thought so many muscles could cramp at once; neither could I imagine a worse pain. Wearing a plastic trash bag stretched over his sweatshirt, my uncle would occasionally join in. While watching him jog up and down the court on his aching knees, I imagined his days trying to make weight for his next fight.

Sometime near the end of my elementary school years, Uncle Jack bought a small camp just south of North Bay, Ontario, a four- or-more-hour drive from Toronto. My uncle's idea in buying the camp was to offer his boys a way to escape Toronto's summers and enjoy Ontario's backwoods. Outside of a main lodge, a couple small cabins, and a few playing fields, the camp's main attraction was a lake, a short walk down a slope from the lodge. Like my mother, my uncle also spent some of his summers at Birch Point Lodge, and no doubt his fondness for the lodge and Lake Kashagawigamog played a part in his purchasing the camp.

The lake at my uncle's camp surely had a name, but I never heard it spoken. Unlike Lake Kashagawigamog, the lake's banks were heavily forested except for the short stretch of sand down from the lodge. A quarter-mile wide and a mile or two long, the lake was puny compared to Lake Kashagawigamog, and unlike Kashagawigamog, its waters were darkish, if not opaque. When I waded off the beach, the lake water obscured its bottom after only a few steps. This, coupled with hungry leeches that swam out from the shallows, made the lake unappealing for swimming on all but the hottest afternoons. Not long after arriving with my family, I watched a boy catch a leech with his bare hands and toss it into some nearby woods. The leeches were tenacious, though, for there was one evening when I felt a bit queasy studying the dried remains of a leech hanging off a camper's ankle.

Life at the camp was not easy. Leeches were not the only creatures out for blood. Stinging green flies were a constant companion when we were walking in the woods, and at dusk the air filled with mosquitoes hungry to bite any exposed skin. After toasting marshmallows, performing skits, or telling stories, campers were sent off to bed as a gas-powered generator—run for only a short time after dinner—was the camp's only source of electricity. As I was fourteen years old and my uncle's nephew, I was allowed to stay up later. On most nights, after the campers were settled, my uncle would sit before a gas-fired lamp in the kitchen and enjoy a cigar. One night, curious after my mother forewarned me "your Uncle Jack is acting silly," I walked into to the kitchen to see him sitting on his favorite stool wearing a

LAKE KASHAGAWIGAMOG

stainless steel pot on his head for a hat. Puffing on his cigar, he sat motionless with a pellet rifle in hand, patiently waiting for a mouse to venture out from its lair in the wall.

Like most champion prize fighters, my uncle lived (as much as man with a wife and young daughter could) life boldly. If able, he never let propriety or others opinions deny him a laugh, joke, or prank. As a boy, I learned from my mother that he had picked up the basics of boxing from my grandfather, who had also been a boxer. My uncle's first fights were against neighborhood kids inside a makeshift ring set up in the backyard of the family's Peterborough home. Joining the Canadian Armed Forces in 1941 as a member of the Tank Corps, he continued boxing, eventually winning the Armed Forces middleweight championship. After the war, he turned professional, and fighting under the moniker "Irish Jackie Dugan," he won the Canadian middleweight title in early 1947. Said to be "a beautiful boxer, with a great left hand, and great movement," and "one you couldn't hit with a box of rice," my uncle held his title until he retired undefeated in 1951. When I was young, my mother told me about her brother's visits to Peterborough's pubs during his fighting days. There, with his identity concealed, he discussed and debated the boxing merits of the fighter the patrons disparagingly referred to as "that bum Dugan."

During my stay at the camp, no day passed without me wandering down to the lake. Although not wishing to swim, I nonetheless loved being near the lake and walking along its banks, hoping to spy a frog or fish. Still the fisherman, I tried my luck near the beach. Never able to catch anything more than small black fish the campers called chubs, I wondered if the lake's dark water had anything to do with the lack of larger fish. My uncle took me, along with a couple other boys, out on his pontoon boat to fish one afternoon. Despite a full tackle box of lures and live worms, none of us had even a nibble. Years later, my uncle recounted how some game wardens came to the lake, and after shocking the water, they netted numerous large fish. "The fish had too much natural food," was the reason given to my uncle for the poor fishing.

Occasionally a hot day would drive me into the lake to brave the leeches. There was an afternoon when, outfitted with large inner tubes, I ventured out with some other campers about my age. Floating atop the dark water, I again felt the thrill to see the shore recede. Leaving my tube I swam a few tentative strokes out into the lake before returning. I wondered what it would be to swim to the far shore or to the small island to my left. Like survivors of a shipwreck, our frothing kicks propelled us back to the beach at the afternoon's end.

Four years would pass before I again visited Canada, but those weeks I spent beside my uncle's nameless lake helped, even if only a little, to stir my torpid mind and impel me into adolescence.

Like a pair of bookends, my next visit to Canada and the last one described above bracketed my high school years and a universe of growth on my part.

A half a foot taller, I traveled north with my father and mother in a borrowed pick-up truck. My ten-speed bicycle and my motorcycle resting in the truck bed, we crossed the border north of the falls and then drove west along the Queen Elizabeth Way, past the towns of St. Davids and St. Catharines. The highway ran north, and I glimpsed the aqua color and enormity of Lake Ontario. Like so many of our visits to Canada, our destination was my mother's sister Dale and her husband Max's house outside the city of Hamilton.

Located on the western terminus of Lake Ontario, Hamilton sits in the middle of the Golden Horseshoe, an industrialized region extending from Niagara Falls to Toronto. The Niagara Escarpment (the geological formation responsible for Niagara Falls) separates Hamilton into upper and lower halves. Referred to as the mountain by its residents, the escarpment was located just a short way from my aunt and uncle's house and offered spectacular views of Hamilton.

I remained behind after my mother and father returned to the States. I spent August living with my aunt, uncle, and grandmother, Helen. With Dale and Max at work, I filled most days reading or chatting with my grandmother. When needing a change, I rode my bicycle to the nearby library and perused its stacks. On some evenings, I bicycled to a park where I played tennis with others my age. On those nights when hockey practice emptied the courts, I coasted down the mountain on my bike to explore Hamilton neighborhoods until nightfall. Having few wants and no plans for the fall, I cannot recall a more carefree month than at my aunt and uncle's house located on aptly named Upper Paradise Road.

Ultimately preferring the muted, physicality of riding my bicycle over my motorcycle, I did not ride over to visit Uncle Jack until the near the end of my stay. Leaving on a Friday, I wended my way down the mountain and blended in with the traffic on the Queen Elizabeth Way. My Honda twin zinging me along, I was soon walled in by Toronto skyscrapers. Riding northwest out of city, I arrived at my uncle's home in the mid-afternoon. With his modest ranch house left unlocked, I let myself in, and while waiting, thumbed through his trucking magazines.

Jack's daughter Patty was the first to arrive home. Patty—a few years younger than me and accompanied by a fellow with shoulder-length hair—surprised me with how much she had grown in the four years since I had last seen her at my uncle's camp. I sensed, but was not ready to accept, that my childhood view of Canada needed enlarging. Canada could no longer remain the narrow, happy little world defined by my mother and her siblings.

Not long after Jack and his wife Betty arrived, I was again on the road, this time a passenger in my uncle's van. Sitting on a flimsy plastic chair between Jack and Betty, I watched the sun extinguish itself in Ontario's rocky landscape. It was about midnight when we arrived at my uncle's camp. Using a flashlight, I found a sheetless bed on a lower bunk, and tired, I slept well into the next morning.

The next day I was busy helping secure the camp for the winter. Whether it was tossing the football around, rowing a boat out into Lake St. Clair, or as with that morning, stacking mattresses, I always felt most comfortable around my uncle when active. Looking back, I suppose we never really had much to say to each other. Perhaps it was because of the near thirty-year age difference, but more likely it was because of our vastly different upbringings. A product of soft suburbia Trix cereal, Wonder Bread, and Captain Kangaroo, I was surely a sad sight in his eyes.

I do not remember what we had for dinner that evening; neither do I remember sleeping upstairs in the lodge's empty dormitory. What I do remember was walking down to the lake after breakfast on Sunday morning. Standing on the small beach, I gazed about. To my eyes, four years had in no way changed the lake. The water level seemed the same, and the same darkness obscured its waters. For the first time, I sensed a lifelessness inhabiting the lake's waters. I had heard about acid rain and wondered if this could have something to do with the lake's deadness. Remembering, for a time, fishing for the black chubbs along the shore and finding the leeches that lurked off the beach, I walked off the beach to my right and into the woods.

Following the shore outline, I made my way over fallen limbs until I was out of sight of the beach and lodge. Seeing where the land came to a small point, I moved in that direction. Making my way forward, I walked out onto the point.

The lake narrowed there. Farther on to my right, I saw where the encroaching land had pinched the water into black ooze filled with skunk cabbage and rotting logs. I found a felled tree to sit on. A chill was in the air and the sky was gray, threatening rain. Summer was fast departing from these north woods. In a few weeks, the first

LAKE KASHAGAWIGAMOG

frosts would come, and soon after, snows would fall. I would be back in the States then. I was finished with high school, a n d life would be different for me. Decisions and choices would have to be made, but here, away from the noise of family and friends, I had perfect solitude. I reflected on my life, but there was more, as a strange exhilaration swelled in my chest. I felt uplifted. The past mattered nothing to me, as my future beckoned and opened before me. Deep in the woods, beside the dark lake, I sat transfixed, resonating with the stillness.

After a while, I felt raindrops. Accustomed to the summer's heat, I began to shiver. Goose bumps rose on my forearms and legs. "Aunt Betty and Uncle Jack must be wondering where I am," I thought. "I'd better get back."

After rising, I paused, and then turning, I retraced my path back to the beach. Knowing I would probably never return, I stood on the small beach and took one last look at the nameless lake.

~ ~ ~ ~

Saying goodbye to Janet, I step out of our motel room. Breaking into a jog I leave the motel parking lot and run west on Lansdowne Street. There is a bracing lightness to this Canadian night air that is a gratifying after our hot drive up from Connecticut. Eight hours was much too long to be in a car without any air conditioning. Although after nine o'clock, there is still a fair amount of traffic about. Perhaps people feel so cooped up during the winter that they cannot resist being outside on such a nice summer evening, or maybe it is simply because today is Friday, and tonight is just the start of another weekend here in Peterborough.

Reminded of a Canadian stereotype, I smile as I run past a convenience store displaying a brightly lit beer sign. A while later, I pass a young woman walking alone along the sidewalk. Seemingly unafraid, she underscores a difference between Canada and the States.

The road pitches upward, and a memory flashes before my eyes.

I am sitting in the back seat of our old Ford station wagon. My father steps on the accelerator, and the transmission drops into lower gear. The car climbing, I am pressed back into my seat. Near the hill crest, I look behind to see a rising sun, clouds, blue sky, and far-off Lake Ontario. "Yes. Now I remember. My father was driving us up this hill on our way to Haliburton," I think. Not wanting to leave the lit streets and shops by running out of town, I turn off where the hill plateaus. Here I alternate between fast bursts and slow jogs around a furniture store parking lot.

Other than some thunderstorms around Albany, our drive up here today was uneventful. Driving across Hill and Wellesley Islands, we crossed into Canada north of Watertown. My father, wanting to see New York's Thousand Islands region, once drove us west along Lake Ontario on a drive back to the States from Toronto. Curious to again see the sparkling water and forested land, I slowed our car and watched as the St. Lawrence River swirled past the green islands below.

Seeing it is getting on to ten o'clock, I run my last lap and head back down the hill, toward the motel.

When I let myself into the room, Janet asks, "How was your run?"

"Okay. I ran laps in a parking lot up the hill on Lansdowne Street," I say.

Looking at me, she says, "Coming here feels strange. It's like we picked some town at random, drove there, and checked into whatever motel had a vacancy sign out."

"I know. I feel disconnected too. Things will be better tomorrow; I'll call Mary in the morning," I say.

"Are you sure she knows we are coming to see her?"

"Yes, I'm sure. My mother called and wrote her that we would be visiting Peterborough. She is an old family friend; she will treat us well."

The next morning, Mary, happy to hear we're in town, gives me directions to her apartment. After turning the wrong way, I eventually find her apartment complex up the same hill on Lansdowne Street I ran last night. Mary is waiting outside as I park the car.

"What, did you get lost?" she asks curtly. "Yes, I did, Mary," I say.

"Well, come on in," she says. After I introduce Janet and myself, we follow her down a hallway and find her apartment on the right. Inside, Janet and I take seats in her living room.

Mary is not too tall, with thick brown hair. Now in her eighties, such as most women who have reached her age, she is thin, but not yet frail. Mary's discerning hazel eyes, prominent but well-formed nose, and deep voice all contribute to her rather stern demeanor.

Like us, Mary also does not know many people in her hometown of Peterborough. The all-too-frequent outcome of aging, Mary's friends and family have either moved away or died. A widow, she has little or no contact with her stepchildren, but speaks highly of her landlord and a neighbor who looks in on her.

In chatting with her, I learn Mary had worked in the legal field, and true to her appearance, she brooks no nonsense. Although annoyed by her diminished eyesight, she remains upbeat and readily offers her sharp-eyed observations on my mother's family.

"Yes, I've known you Dugans for a longtime. I just adored your mother's mother, Helen," she says. And then adds, "I can see you're a Dugan. You remind me of your Uncle Paul."

"That's what everyone says," I reply.

I mark her words when the conversation turns to Uncle Jack. "I had to tell him, 'Jack, listen. You are getting mixed up with the wrong people here in town.' But you know, he just had to learn."

Her eyes brightening, she says, "There was the time Jack knocked this guy out at the Brock Street Arena. After the fight, he came over to tell us to meet him downtown for dinner. Walking into the restaurant, he looked so handsome with his hair brushed back. His face was shining with that salve they smear on before a fight."

We take Mary to a Chinese buffet for lunch. Later, after trips to a mall and pharmacy so she can purchase a few items, we tour Peterborough with her.

Stopping in front of my mother's two-story childhood house on Westcott Street, Janet takes my picture. The house's beige brick is stained with black soot. Shrubs grow on a small front lawn, and the detached garage set a way behind the house appears new.

Surveying the neighborhood, I spy some nearby railroad tracks and recall the times my mother said that she was born on the wrong side of the tracks. Noticing a female neighbor appears concerned, I suggest to Janet that we walk back to the car and drive on.

Passing the gray-stone-walled Sacred Heart Church, I ask Mary where the ice rink where my mother skated was.

"Oh, that's all gone. I think it was over there where that playground is now," she says. "I guess your mother told you your great grandfather helped build this church."

"Yes, she did," I say.

After circling the block a few times, I drive down George Street, eying the shops and the red brick clock tower of the Market Hall Performing Arts Centre. Driving on past the old Quaker Oats building, I find parking near the lift lock.

Mary is not interested in seeing the lock, so stays in the car while Janet and I leave her to walk along the waterway. Built in the nineteenth century to bring timber from upper Ontario, the Trent-Severn Waterway was not long after displaced by the railroads. Nowadays the waterway is mostly used for pleasure boating.

Appearing like a concrete fortress with two drawbridges, the lift lock is set into the side of an immense grass mound. Canada's Maple Leaf waves atop the lift lock's center tower. Nearing the lock, I hear a tour boat's PA system announce its approach. Water pours down as the boat enters the seventy-foot-tall gate. Much like an elevator, in no more than a minute the lower gate rises and the boat is brought down.

After the boat passes by, I study the lock, recalling the time my father brought me here as a boy.

While I am walking back to the car, a boy holds up a small perch he has just caught. Further on, a couple is dismayed when I relate that a boat has just passed by.

On the way back to Mary's apartment, she points out a cemetery on Lansdowne Street where my mother's father is buried. Mary is not able to remember the grave's location, so we drive on.

Uncle Jack was inducted into the Peterborough and District Sports Hall of Fame back 1980s. I had seen a picture of his commemorative plaque, which has a caricature drawing of him smiling broadly below his full head of hair. His plaque hangs in the Memorial Centre, but when I inquire about the Centre, Mary says, "Oh, that's all closed up now."

Back at Mary's apartment, Janet and I help her in with her purchases. Hoping we will stay for dinner, she says, "I'm going to treat us all at the Carousel."

"I'm sorry, Mary, but we have to get going. I promised Jean we would get to Haliburton tonight." I say.

Clearly saddened, she insists we return next summer. After exchanging our addresses, Mary gives me a glove compartment map she cannot use anymore because of her eyesight. All three of us walk together down the hallway and step outside. Mary remains close to the building door and waves to us as we drive north toward a dark, threatening sky.

A heavy rain is falling when Janet and I reach Haliburton just before nightfall. We find Jean's home a few miles out of the village, and she welcomes us inside her red two-story farmhouse.

Jean is my mother's first cousin, the lone child of Aunt Marion and Uncle Bruce. Aunt Marion, my mother's father's only sister, and her husband Bruce ran Birch Point Lodge for years. I had not seen

Jean since driving up with my mother and father for Aunt Marion's funeral nearly twenty years ago. We stayed away from the lodge and Lake Kashagawigamog during that visit. Too self-absorbed during a particularly unhappy time for myself, I remember little more than April's drab grays and browns, Uncle Jack's eulogy, and seeing Aunt Marion in her coffin dressed in white, her gray hair pulled tightly back.

Sitting in Jean's quaint living room, Janet and I recount our trip. Jean is in her early eighties. Although her light gray hair has thinned noticeably, her pleasing, full face is smooth and full of color. I am struck by her distinct resemblance to my mother's sister, Aunt Dale, and Uncle Jack.

Jean has many family photographs displayed. These serve as her cues as she traces the Dugan family history for us. From her bookshelf, Jean passes us *Fragments of a Dream: Pioneering in Dysart Township and Haliburton Village.* Written by Leopolda z L. Dobrzensky, a friend of Jean's, the book details lives of the area's first settlers. Thumbing through the book's pages, I pause to study the photographs of the two brothers: John and William Dugan. After coming to Canada from Ireland about the time of the Civil War, William and John established a homestead in Haliburton. While William raised a large family and lived out his years in Haliburton, Dobrzensky writes that "after a few years spent helping his brother, John moved south to Peterborough."

Pointing at the photograph of John, Janet says, "Look, there's your great-great-grandfather; I can see the resemblance."

Jean takes time to relate news about her three children: Tim, Dennis, and Nadine. We learn that her husband, Earl, is a patient in a nearby nursing home and is suffering from Alzheimer's disease. Jean visits him daily. Harboring no illusions about his condition, she says matter-of-factly, "Oh, well. He's gone, you know."

We also hear that Birch Point Lodge has been sold, but the new owner, still undecided about the lodge's future, chose not to open the

LAKE KASHAGAWIGAMOG

lodge this summer. "This is the first time in more than eighty years that we've not had guests," says Jean.

Jean has a fair number of black bound scrapbooks containing hundreds of black-and-white snapshots, along with handwritten notes from guests. Browsing through these books, I learn guests returned summer after summer to fish, canoe, or just sit quietly beside the lake. I see pictures of my mother, Aunt Dale, and Uncle Paul. Clad in his swimsuit, a youthful Uncle Paul stands near Lake Kashagawigamog, ready for a swim.

The night growing late, Jean shows us to our room upstairs. She is surprised when I say, "You know, Jean, we will be happy just to spend tomorrow down at the lodge."

The next morning, I am up before breakfast and out the door. Running down to the village, I pass an old steam locomotive I remember seeing from my visit here as a boy. Haliburton is small town with one main intersection and a few side streets. I run along, looking into shops and businesses. Feeling fit, I am enticed by the long hill we drove down into town last evening, but seeing it is getting late, I turn around. I run along Head Lake, make a left turn at the locomotive, and head back toward Jean's.

After breakfast, we say goodbye to Jean and promise to be back in time for dinner. After picking up some fruit at a grocery store in the village, Janet and I drive over to the Haliburton Highlands Museum. Here I buy a copy of Dobrzensky's *Fragments of Dream*. Admission is pricey, and as the museum appears to house the usual artifacts—old photographs, farm implements, Ontario taxidermy, and a birch bark canoe—we leave and drive over to the lodge.

Finding the lodge's entrance, I park outside a lodge's locked gate. Walking down the slope, I wrestle with my inflatable kayak in its sack. The grass here is overgrown and is reclaiming a faded shuffleboard court. Up ahead, I see a woman probably in her thirties and a young girl standing down by the lake. Seeing us, they disappear behind a line of trees. Reaching a picnic table, I plop the kayak down. Not seeing the pair, I wonder how they could have slipped away so quickly.

Janet and I spend some time exploring the grounds. Walking along a gravel drive, I point to the long line of small single room brown cabins and say, "Aunt Marion's husband Bruce built all of these."

"When did he pass away?" asks Janet. "Sometimes in the sixties," I say.

Behind the lodge, we come upon a couple of bed sheets lying in the grass. "Laundry was done back here," I say.

We walk over to the lodge and peer inside the kitchen. "My mother told me of baking pies and how hot it got in there," I say. "They made three meals a day in there, all pretty much from scratch."

Around to the front of the lodge, I stop and gaze at a weathered tennis court. A memory resurfaces from a visit here when I was twelve or thirteen. The image of Aunt Dale's husband, Uncle Max, passes before eyes. Shirtless, he stands with a wooden tennis racquet in hand waiting for a ball to be served.

Back at the picnic table, Janet says, "Well, let's get the kayak blown up. That's why you're here, to swim, right?"

I inflate the kayak with its foot pump, and after walking the boat out into the lake, Janet hops in. Pausing, I look out over the water. Jet skis and throaty power boats with wakeboarders and skiers in tow are speeding up and down, reminding me more of a highway than a lake. I watch as three or four teenage girls riding atop a long yellow tube are pulled behind a speeding motorboat. They soon vanish in a splash of spray beyond a point of land. "Lake Kashagawigamog has changed," I think.

I dive under and surface to fit my googles and swim cap. The northern water is bracing and raises goose bumps on my arms and legs. The point of land that gives the lodge its name extends out into the lake, forming a sandbar. A yellow-hulled power boat rests there, its occupants enjoying the afternoon sun. Janet has paddled to the point's other side and holds water, waiting for me to swim over. I swim in her direction, but my hands touching bottom, I stand and walk across the point.

I recall my father rowing us around this point one gray evening. My mother's father, who rode up with us from Peterborough, kept pace with us along the shore. "Daddy, why won't you come out with us?" my mother kept asking him. Wearing a red plaid shirt and already ill with Parkinson's disease, he said no more than the occasional, "Nah."

I swim to where Janet floats in front of the lodge. The old dock and dive platform are gone. Over on the grass bank in front of the lodge stands a large brown deck. The deck has steps that lead down to the water. Having lost a support, the steps sag toward the lake. On the deck frame, close to the water, is affixed a neon sign that reads Open. Having noticed piled sections of dock during our walk around the lodge, I say to Janet, "See the sign? People came here in their boats to eat and drink."

"I think you are right. Look at that lodge over there," she says while pointing.

Looking to my right, I catch sight of white umbrellas emblazoned with the word Cinzano shading the neighboring lodge's deck tables.

"It's convenient. Drive your boat in, dock, and relax with a drink or something to eat," I say.

From the kayak, Janet takes a few pictures of me in the lake and passes me the camera. I snap one of her in the kayak.

"Are you ready?" she asks.

"Yes, but you have to keep an eye out for the boats," I say.

"Where should I aim?" she asks.

Pointing to short stretch of sand to the left of the Wigamog Inn, I say, "See that little beach and opening behind? Let's head there."

CROSSINGS: A SWIMMER'S MEMOIR

Janet clear on our landing, I swim off. While breathing to my left, I see her pull alongside. Vigorously stroking and kicking, I waste little time getting up to speed. With the power boats and jet skis, my swim across this lake will little resemble my mother's night swims years earlier. The lake water is turbid, much different from the glassy water I remember as a boy. Its brownish-green color reminds me of many other ponds and lakes I have swum in.

The water deepening, I am surprised to see the light brown weeds extending up from the lake. Entering the lake's central channel, I alternately rise and fall in a passing boat's wake. Pausing, Janet assures me the way is clear. The water takes on a hint of blue color here. I would like to stop and gaze about, but afraid of the powerboats, I swim on. The channel is no more than a couple hundred yards wide and the water soon changes back to its brownish-green color. Thicker and taller now, the weeds reappear. I grab some with my hands and feel them scrape along my body. Janet, falling back to take my picture, I swim on toward the beach. Finding bottom, I walk up onto the sand.

Janet lands the kayak and joins me up on the grass. The land here has been cleared and leveled. From the wooden stakes in the ground, I suppose some sort of development is planned. Off to our right sits the Wigamog Inn. The inn has undergone a couple expansions since its founding in the 1920s. Green roofed, the inn's white three-story main building is set back from an expansive beach. An orange trampoline floats off shore, and the thought of swimming over to it passes through my mind, but knowing that we are not guests there, I say nothing to Janet.

No more than a third of a mile back across the lake sits Birch Point Lodge. Empty and silent, the brown lodge could pass for no more than a single-family house nowadays.

Preparing for the swim back, I see a portly man emerge out of the woods. Not too tall, he wears a beige sun hat above his clean-shaven face. Dressed in khaki pants and a blue-collared dress shirt, he walks over and greets us. I detect a British accent when he speaks. His name is Michael, and he is a new resident to Haliburton, having moved south from Kirkland Lake. Appearing to be in his fifties, he displays little interest in our trip across the lake, but is piqued to hear of my relation to Jean. "I hope Birch Point does not become another one of those time shares you see sprouting up along the lake," he says. He asks Janet if she swims too.

Janet relates that while she swims some, she mostly practices tai chi.

Exclaiming, "Tee chee!" in his high-toned accent, Michael alludes to the political repression in China and hopes Janet keeps safe.

Michael presents me his card advertising himself as a wordsmith. Relating he has authored books on northern Ontario, he also notes he has written a book on Haliburton.

Assuring him that I will keep an eye out for his books, I move toward the lake. Seeing I am eager to get going, Michael wishes us well and walks off.

While talking to Michael, I noticed the lake remained busy with powerboats and jet skis. Janet now in the kayak, I ready myself for the swim back, but before wading in, I stop to watch a single-engine pontoon plane tear down the lake and take to air where I plan to swim.

"Look at that," I say to Janet.

"That could have been us out there," she says.

"Crazy Canadians. What are the rules of the road on this damn lake?" I grumble.

"Who knows? It's scary. I'll watch out for us."

My swim back across goes by quickly. Walking up to the picnic table, I supposed—albeit long delayed—to have joined the line of Dugans who have swum across Lake Kashagawigamog. Now half a century old, I look back across the lake feeling satisfaction in my accomplishment, but before becoming too prideful, I remember Uncle

Paul's phone conversation with Janet before our trip. "Make sure you tell the old man that I swam across that lake when I was twelve years old," he said.

After I changed in a cabin I found unlocked, Janet and I take our seats at the picnic table and snack on grapes. Both of us facing the lake, she says, "It's a shame what has happened to this lake—all those power boats and jet skis out there, so much machinery."

"It's like everyone brought the city up here with them," I say.

"Why can't people be still and just enjoy themselves by the water?" she says.

"I don't know. Everyone needs to be entertained these days, especially the kids. Like Bruce, your tai-chi instructor says, 'Our nervous systems are all screwed up.' People just can't relax anymore," I say.

After finishing our grapes, we climb into the kayak and paddle out to explore the lakefront. Lake Kashagawigamog is seventeen miles long, so I do not expect to see very much of the lake. I sit in the stern and Janet sits in the bow. We soon find our rhythm and paddle over to the lodge with the Cinzano umbrellas. A modern-looking gray lodge sits at the back of a well-manicured lawn. Like the Wigamog Inn, there are no cabins, only a main building. "People don't want to stay in cabins anymore; they want a hotel," I say.

Turning about, we paddle past Birch Point and survey some of the spacious private homes along the lake exuding wealth. I say, "Uncle Paul mentioned a couple of Toronto Maple Leaf hockey players own homes along the lake."

We come to a rest. Feeling the kayak bend and flex with some boat's wake, I say, "You know, Uncle Jack's ashes are scattered somewhere along here."

"Do you know where?" asks Janet.

"No, not really. Last June, after his memorial service, my mother spoke of bringing his ashes over to Aunt Marion's summer home, a place she called Sunny Slope. I'm not sure if the house is even on this side of the lake."

Back at the picnic table, Janet gathers things up as I deflate and stow the kayak. After walking up the slope, we pack the car and return for one last walk around the grounds. I try to imagine which tree might have been alive when I first came here and waded into the lake. There are numerous birch trees growing, particularly near the water. Most are saplings, but finding a more mature birch tree, I peel off a strip of its soft bark for a souvenir.

I recall that there was another Jack Dugan who once roamed these shores. A descendant of William, this Jack Dugan stood six feet six inches, worked as a lumberjack, and, according to Uncle Paul, "could singlehandedly clean out a bar." When I was boy, my mother used to speak of these "giant backwoods Dugans." Like Don Quixote, I too believed in giants, but not wanting to slay them, I instead wanted nothing more than to meet these big-shoed seven-footers that I imagined tramping about the Haliburton backwoods.

On our way back to Jean's, I turn off into a golf course a short way from the lake. "There is a hole here where the tee is set up on a high cliff. It's a real novelty," I say. Stopping near the green and pointing up to the cliff, I add, "My mom always loved relating the time a golf ball just missed her here."

Turning around near the clubhouse, we pass some middle-aged women neatly dressed in their golfing plaids. Wheeling their golf bags, they stare at us with bemused and perturbed looks. "I guess we look too scruffy to be here," I mutter.

Jean is preparing dinner for us when we arrive. Interested to hear how we spent the afternoon, she listens impassively as we describe the lodge, its grounds, and our trip across the lake. Hearing of our meeting with the author Michael, she is chagrined and laments,

"A friend of mine and I counted fifty-three mistakes in his book on Haliburton."

After dinner, Janet and I step outside into the evening air. Jean's black tomcat tags along as we walk across the lawn toward a small barn. Stepping inside, we spend time looking at old magazines, typewriters, telephones, and other items collected by Jean's husband Earl. Earl worked many years for Canadian Bell Telephone.

Down a slope is a small gazebo set before a small ornamental pond. Behind the pond, at the edge of the Canadian bush, grows a pair of thick-trunked willow trees, a living connection to the past. Jean later tells me the willows go back to the original homestead in the 1860s.

The next morning is clear and warm as we load the car. After taking pictures, Janet and I thank Jean for our stay and promise to write when we get back to Connecticut. Waving goodbye, I drive down her gravel drive, past a line of tall blue pines. Looking back, I cling to my last view of the grounds, the red farmhouse, and Jean.

After passing through Haliburton Village, I turn right at the main intersection. While I am driving up the long hill out of the village, Janet says, "Let's go see Uncle Jack's house."

Although it is not far, I had assumed our adventure was over, and wanting to return home, I say, "That's down is Apsley; it's sort of out of our way. Besides, I don't even know where his house is there."

"Let's go anyway. We're here now and probably will never be this close again," she insists.

After more debate, I concede. After pulling over, we map a route.

While I drive us over the hilly, rocky landscape, Janet, who is reading Dobrzensky's *Fragments of Dream*, says, "Did you know the Dugan brothers, William and John, walked all the way from Peterborough to Haliburton to look for land?"

"Tough fellows; it's hard to imagine anyone doing that now," I say.

"And later, William used to walk the sixty-five miles to and from Peterborough on unpaved roads just for jury duty."

"Now listen; this reminds me of you," she says and reads aloud, "'William Dugan and his friend Stothart were at odds with their church's congregation. The two men felt that the purchase of a parlor organ, which the Presbyterians were contemplating, was unnecessary. "What do we need an organ for? A tuning fork will do just fine," was Dugan's comment.'"

"That's funny," I say.

Nearing Apsley, the land levels and we pass flat, glassy lakes named Monk, Paudash, Eels, and Silent Lake. Wishing I could stop and swim across every one of them, I say, "So many lakes, you could train to swim the English Channel up here."

After descending a winding hill, we stop at a small grocery store in the village. Janet asks a couple clerks if they knew where Jack Dugan lived. No one is able to help, but I then remember the last time I spoke with him on the phone. Hinting we might one day visit, he said in his terse, clipped way, "Yep, bud. We're in Apsley, just up the hill on the right."

Back in the car, I now see a different hill leading out of town. "Let's drive up there," I say.

Cresting the hill, I spot a modest two-story white house set close to the road. A For Sale sign is set out front close to the road. "This place looks like the picture my mother showed us," I say hopefully.

I slow, pull over, and park. The front gate is chained shut, but we are able to squeeze through.

"This must be his house. There's the barn, and that building over there is probably where Gail ran her daycare business," I say.

We spend the next half hour or so looking into the barn, the daycare, and the house. A pickup truck, a camper on its bed, rests in the high grass. Aunt Dale's red sedan is parked in an open bay in the barn. In another section of the barn, numerous shovels and rakes and buckets stand ready. Peering into the house, I see a picture of Jack's daughter Patty on the wall. On the right hangs a framed certificate honoring my uncle's work at his boy's club.

Surveying the grounds, Janet says, "There is a lot of cleaning up to do around here."

"It's long way for Uncle Paul to drive over here from Detroit to empty this place out," I say sadly.

"I wish we could help him, but we live so far away," says Janet.

"It's strange. I keep expecting Uncle Jack to walk out of the house. It all came to an end for him so fast. Gail left him, and only a few months later, he's gone."

"It must seem unreal to you," says Janet.

Uncle Jack passed away a few weeks after collapsing inside this house with a stroke the previous January. Busy finishing up my classes at school, I could not get away for his memorial service in June.

Janet sets off to inspect the daycare, and I walk to the rear of the barn. After stepping over a dirt mound, I walk out a short way into a small tract of land that must have once served as horse pasture. No longer in use, the tract is now overgrown with hip-high thistle. A peculiar hum fills the air. Looking down, I see countless yellow jackets buzzing in and about the purple thistle flowers. Looking up, I follow a gray wood fence to where it ends at a stand of trees. Off in the corner, a boulder spotted with pale green lichen peeks above the thistle. Although the summer is fast waning, there is no sense of hurry here. Far to the south, a hurricane is ravaging New Orleans and the nearby Gulf Coast this morning, but the land here, paying its heavy debt each winter, rests unperturbed.

Alone and warmed by the late morning sun, I recall the time I stood before the lake at Uncle Jack's camp. A turning point for both our lives, my uncle's marriage would soon end, and later he would lose his job at the boy's club when it was decided a master's degree was somehow required to work with children. After some years working as a tour bus driver, he moved here with his girlfriend, Gail. "Uncle Jack always wanted to move up north and back into the bush," said my mother.

In the decades after leaving my uncle's camp, I would count on one hand the number of times I saw him. Memories coming, I see him now—he's stealing the dance floor at my sister's wedding reception, and later he's imitating Muhammad Ali, his left jab firing out from his perfectly aligned six-foot frame. And there he is, the happy-go-lucky Irishman, kissing a handful of dirt before tossing it into Aunt Marion's grave. And last summer, the last time I saw him, his hair white and thin, he sits across from me, enjoying steak and eggs at a New Jersey diner.

Janet and I phoned him last fall, a few months before he fell ill. Making reference to the taped oral histories people often make, I suggested he record something about his life. "Well, I suppose I could; I walk around here all day talking to myself anyway," he said. But later, when talking with Janet, he pretty well nixed the idea, thinking his life might prove a little too rough and unsavory for my ears and others.

And now that he is gone, I have only a couple newspaper clippings highlighting his life, my recollections, and the part of him that lives on in me that likes to compete, contend, and even fight.

Dancing until the end, he was hard to hit. Rarely could anyone—or life for that matter—lay a glove on him.

"Did you ever get knocked out?" I once asked him as a boy. "Yes," he said.

"Didn't you see the punch coming?" I asked.

"Sure I did, but there was nothing I could do about it," he said.

I recall some lines from an Irish ditty my mother used to recite.

There was a wild colonial boy, Jack Duggan was his name.
He was born and raised in Ireland in a place called Castlemaine.

He was his father's only son, his mother's pride and joy,
And dearly did his parents love the wild colonial boy.

Stopping, I look behind me and see Janet waiting by the barn.

"Do you know that when I was growing up, I'd always test my grip against his, whenever I shook his hand? Even last summer, I was never a match for him," I say wistfully.

Turning to look over the field, I say, "Look at all the purple thistle and listen; the bees are everywhere."

"Come on, Peeps. Let's get going. You're chasing ghosts," she says.

CHAPTER 3

Sources

Where did we get our start? Where is our ultimate beginning? Can we apprehend and embrace our very first freshet, rivulet, or rill —our own Nile's source?

As a child, intuiting my swimming incompetence was at best an annoyance and at worst a menace. I was circumspect about pools, diving wells, ponds, lakes, and the ocean. When I was swimming with neighborhood friends, the popping in my ears and water constricting my chest and throat usually brought me to the surface first after an en masse dive underwater. Whenever the inevitable dunking and water wrestling broke out, the fear of being held under exempted me from the fray. Resting against the pool wall, I would excuse myself, saying, "I don't want to get my hair wet."

I recall summer afternoons away from home, lying on a poolside recliner with a parched mouth and sweaty palms while screaming kids cannonballed, dove, or ran off a high-dive platform. With eyes fixed on each diver, I suffered that same fearful desire of watching, but never riding, as a roller coaster took its first plunge. Some thirty years later, my nine-year old daughter Clare did what I could not do by running off a three-meter dive platform in Texas. She was nonplussed to hear that I had never jumped from such a height. Away from pools, when piloting a canoe or rowboat, I kept the boat close to land. During summer vacations with my family at New Jersey's beaches, I ignored any lifeguard's screeching whistle, for I never was the swimmer out of bounds.

Among the images my mother captured with our eight-millimeter video camera are some silent films of my father, two sisters, and me bobbing about in the back-bay salt water of Stone Harbor, New Jersey. Viewing this footage nearly forty years later, I see myself take a few reaching but ineffectual strokes. My head held high twists purposely from side to side, but I make little progress. No one had pointed out, and I was incapable of knowing, that my dropped elbow was cutting my power. My father floats on his back while my youngest sister, Roseanne, buoyed by a five-and-dime life preserver, bobs about nearby. Watching my other sister, Mary Helen, manage a quick wave to the camera, I realize our swimming skills were limited to doggy paddling, treading water, and a few crawl strokes. We entered the bay there from a short pier. The buoyant, calm water was a pleasant change from the Atlantic waves. It was my sisters' and my favored spot until an impossibly long silver eel was seen lurking about the barnacled pier pilings.

More film from the same vacation shows me on the beach appearing white and thin. The day is gray and overcast, and although I take a few steps toward the surf, I soon retreat. After rubbing suntan lotion on my arms and legs, I hover about our towels; never do I run off and dive into the surf. What physical strength I possess is concentrated in my legs. My chest, shoulders, and arms appear flaccid and underdeveloped. Snapshots from later years invariably show me standing or wading in pools and lakes, my face comfortably dry.

Despite being averse to swimming, I would be haunted by swimming and swimmers.

SOURCES

My father's pursuits did little to encourage my interest (now bordering on an obsession) in swimming. Although he claimed to be a fair golfer as an adolescent, he was neither very athletic nor much of a swimmer. Instead, his interests ran more along technical and scientific lines. Watching the power and accuracy with which he could drive a ball, I never doubted his golfing skills. But whatever aspirations my father might have had were squelched by the Second World War, along with being a southpaw forced to play on courses designed for right-handers. About swimming, he once related his attempt as a boy to swim across the Delaware River south of where the Pennypack Creek empties into the river. "I was almost halfway across, but when I looked back and saw how far I'd swum, I became frightened and turned back," he said. As a Depression kid, as he liked to call himself, growing up in the 1930s, he also spoke of seeing the Delaware River being turned blood red by the tomato skins the Campbell's Soup plant in Camden, New Jersey, discharged in making its famed tomato soup.

A member of Tom Brokow's *Greatest Generation,* my father enlisted in the Navy a month after we entered the war. When he was not on land, he served as a radar man on the USS *Roe*, DD 418. Here, DD designates destroyer and 418 was the *Roe's* hull number. The Department of Navy's Naval Historical Center in Washington notes that the USS *Roe* was the second destroyer to be named after Francis Asbury Roe. Born 1823 in Elmira, New York, Francis Roe was commended for gallantry twice during the Civil War. My father's *Roe* was built at the Charleston, South Carolina, Navy Yard. At nearly 350 feet in length, the *Roe* was manned by a crew of 200.

I found a few photographs of the *Roe* on the Internet. No location is given for one, which shows the *Roe* hull painted in large swatches of camouflage instead of the traditional haze gray. Seven sailors are seen standing at attention just ahead of the forward gun turret. Another photograph credited to a Robert Hall, on what must have been a glorious day, shows the *Roe's* prow resting high on dry dock just before her launching in 1939. Two construction cranes, their booms turned away, tower in the background. The Stars and Stripes hangs limply from a pole set in the *Roe's* bow. Below the flagpole hangs a red, white, and blue billowy banner. The *Roe's* anchor is pulled tight against her hull, and naval pennants adorn long stays extending down from the radar antenna atop the bridge. A solitary figure dressed in white stands on the ceremonial platform. On the dry dock, several seamen await the ceremonies. My father would often show me the wrinkled black-and-white snapshot of the *Roe* he kept in his wallet. I can recall now no more than the *Roe's* jutting bow and her white hull numbers.

John Steinbeck, whose 1943 war dispatches for the New York *Herald Tribune* were later collectively published as *Once There was a War*, perhaps characterized destroyers best when he wrote the following:

> A destroyer is a lovely ship, probably the nicest fighting ship of all. Battleships are a little like steel cities or great factories of destruction. Aircraft carriers are floating flying fields. Even cruisers are big pieces of machinery, but a destroyer is all boat. In the beautiful clean lines of her, in her speed and roughness, in her curious gallantry, she is completely a ship in the old sense.
>
> The battleships are held back for the killing blow and such a blow happens only once in a war. The cruisers go in second, but the destroyers work all the time. They are probably the busiest ships of a fleet. In a major engagement, they do the scouting and make the first contact. They convoy, they run to every fight. Wherever there is a mess, the destroyers run first. They are not lordly like the battleships, nor episcopal like the cruisers. Most

of all, they are ships and the men who work them are seamen. In rough weather they are rough, honestly and violently rough.

A destroyer man is never bored in wartime, for a destroyer is a seaman's ship. She can get under way at the drop of a hat. The water under fantail boils like a Niagara. She will go ripping along at 35 knots with the spray sheeting over her and she will turn and fight and run, drop depth charges, bombard and ram. She is expendable and dangerous. And because she is all these things, a destroyer's crew is passionately possessive. Every man knows his ship, every inch of it, not just his own station.

My father's *Roe* had a short life. Just over six years after her launching she was undergoing overhaul in the San Francisco Bay when the war ended. Soon after, she was decommissioned and sold for scrap in 1947.

According to the Naval Historical Center, the *Roe's* early years included escorting merchant convoys to Panama and the United Kingdom and between Newfoundland and Iceland. In October of 1942, the *Roe* is said to have operated between Trinidad and ports in Brazil. Later in the fall of 1942, the *Roe* assisted in Operation Torch, the landings in North Africa. Part of the Northern Attack Group, the *Roe* screened transports to Mehedia, Tunisia, and "provided gunfire support for the troops as they pushed to take Port Lyautey, the Sebou River, and the Sal airfield" in Morocco. The *Roe* also "assisted the light cruiser *Savannah* in temporarily silencing hostile fire from the Kasba, an old citadel situated on a cliff commanding the mouth of the Sebou."

As a young boy, I could have corroborated the *Roe's* voyages to Brazil. On a ledge in our basement laundry room sat a cracked glass frame enclosing a faded beige-and-aqua certificate. Resembling a diploma and possessing detail to rival most nations' currencies, the certificate had upper corners that depicted a pair of long-haired mermaids caught in spinning whirlpools. The bottom corners showed another mermaid pair, each riding fish with oversized bovine-like heads. In the watery aqua border swam jellyfish, eels, shrimp, and fish. Filling the certificate's upper third, an aged, bearded monarch was pictured emerging from the sea beneath an arching banner bearing the Latin script "IMPERIVM NEPTVNI REGIS." Flanked by two pairs of stallions, Neptunus Rex's naked torso was shown surfacing before a rising sun. A trident in his left hand and his fully extended right arm and open palm called attention to the following text:

TO ALL SAILORS WHEREVER YE MAY BE *and to all Mermaids, Sea Serpents, Whales, Sharks, Dolphins, Skates, Suckers, Lobsters, Crabs, and other Living Things of the Sea* GREETINGS: *Know Ye: That on this 28th day of August 1943 in Latitude 000o 00', there appeared within Our Royal Domain USS Roe bound from Port of Spain, Trinidad to Belem, Brazil.*

BE IT REMEMBERED

That said Vessel, Officers and Crew thereof having been inspected and passed on by Yourself and Our Royal Staff

AND BE IT KNOWN: *By all ye Sailors, Mariners and Land Lubbers, who may be honored by his presence, that*

Charles Edward Joscelyne

having been found worthy to be numbered as one of our Trusty Shellbacks, has been gathered to our fold and duly initiated into the

SOLEMN MYSTERIES OF THE ANCIENT ORDER OF THE DEEP

Be It Further Understood: That by virtue of the power invested in me I hereby command my subjects to show due honor and respect to him whenever he may be

DISOBEY THIS ORDER UNDER PENALTY OF OUR ROYAL DISPLEASURE

Given under our hand and seal this 28th August 1943

Davey Jones	Neptunus Rex
His Majesty's Scribe	Ruler of the Raging Main

Stealing into our laundry room, I would often pore over the certificate's wild cursive writing and sea creatures. A tradition dating back to the eighteenth century, my father's Shellback Certificate commemorated a sailor's crossing the equator, or in seamen's terms, when a pollywog became a shellback. With its bawdy mermaids and associations to a sailor's misdeeds in exotic ports of call, a laundry room display—even if obscured most times behind the door—was maybe all a family man could have hoped for in those days.

In 1943, The Naval Historical Center has the *Roe* performing escort duty to "Gulf and Caribbean oil ports and resupply and reinforcement convoys to Casablanca." Involved in operation "Husky, the invasion of Sicily," the *Roe's* time in the Mediterranean was marked by a collision with the USS *Swanson*, a larger Gleaves-class destroyer. Despite both ships' limited mobility, the *Roe* and *Swanson* were able to fend off an attack of German aircraft the following day.

One of Steinbeck's "busy ships," the *Roe* performed patrol, picket, and escort duties in Pacific. She made strikes against Iwo Jima and the Volcano and Bonin Islands (islands 500 miles south of Tokyo.) The *Roe* made numerous sea rescues in the Atlantic and Pacific throughout the war. Most notable was the rescue of ten survivors from a downed B29 off of Iwo Jima a few days before Christmas in 1944.

In 1944, the last full year of the war, the Roe "transited the Panama Canal and traversed the Pacific to report at Cape Sudest, New Guinea." The *Roe* would remain in the Pacific theater "until the war ended for her when she was ordered to West Coast in June 1945." The *Roe* earned six battle stars during the war.

My father was reticent about his time on the *Roe*. "He doesn't like to talk much about the war," said my mother. Over the years, she would come to blame my father's hearing loss on the *Roe's* guns. Steinbeck, in his newspaper dispatch titled *Symptoms,* perhaps had an explanation for my father's and other veterans' reticence when he wrote, "During the years between the last war and this one, I was always puzzled by the reticence of ex-soldiers about their experiences in battles. They would discuss their experiences right up to the time of battle and suddenly they wouldn't talk anymore." After empathetically describing combat's searing effects on a soldier, Steinbeck concluded that "Only recently have I found what seems to be a reasonable explanation, and the answer is simple. They do not remember—and the worse the battle was, the less they remember. Men in prolonged

SOURCES

battle are not normal men. And when afterwards they seem to be reticent—perhaps they don't remember very well."

Sometimes certain events would release some memory from my father, and I would rivet onto his every word. My chest resonated with the deep, guttural "ka-booms" he sounded in our garage while imitating the *Roe's* five-inch guns.

A white-green streak, a blue sky, and a thin seaman crouched forward staring into a dim green glow appeared before me as he related, "I was manning the radar screen and happened to look out to see a white streak headed right at us. I braced for the explosion, but nothing happened. The Japanese torpedo passed right underneath us."

Stoic faces buoyed by khaki lifejackets, sea-green water, yellow flashes, and deafening cracks were my sights and sounds when he related, "It was near sunset, and we came upon some wreckage with some Japanese sailors floating around. We offered them a rescue, but they wouldn't come aboard. One guy took out his forty-five and started shooting at them, but before he could get off many shots, the old man (the *Roe's* captain) said, 'Let's get out of here.'"

Hearing of the pot shots taken by the sailor made me cringe, and in every mental replay the shooter would always miss.

The wreckage in my father's last story was most likely the remnants of what the Naval Historical Center described as a "destroyer converted for fast transport service" that the *Roe* and destroyer *Case* sank on Christmas Eve 1944. The Bushido ethos of death-before-disgrace displayed by the Japanese survivors in my father's tale is corroborated by the destroyer *Case's* naval record.

> *Case* joined in a smashing bombardment of Iwo Jima once more on December 24, 1944, during which she and *Roe* were dispatched to attack a fleeing Japan transport. A two-hour chase at full speed followed, both destroyers firing as the range closed. At

1559, the effect of accurate gunfire told as the transport sank, her survivors refusing any assistance from the American destroyers.

Some years back, I toured the World War I vintage battleship *Texas*, which had been anchored in the Gulf waters south of Houston. Wrought from cold and indifferent steel, chromium, and brass, the *Texas* was a study in metallurgy. Surely, like on the *Roe*, there was nothing soft on the *Texas* except the bunks in sickbay. As hard as life must have been on the *Roe*, my father did disclose some lighter, cheerier times, such as sleeping on the deck during hot nights in the Pacific, taking shore leave after pulling into the Brooklyn Navy Yard for repairs, and sailing into Brisbane on Australia's western coast to pick up supplies such as mutton—a meat in later life he could never stomach.

Along with his shellback, my father also had a few war souvenirs tucked away in our laundry room. There was some Japanese currency he deemed worthless, a German infantryman's helmet he sold many years later without much regret in a garage sale, and a couple of bayonets that I used to unsheathe for friends. Pointing to the protective layer of reddish grease on the blades, I would say, "Look...blood!" Despite his war trophies, my father was never given to any flag-waving patriotism. Too much the realist, he would say about the *Roe's* captain, "Yeah, the old man knew how to stay out of trouble."

My father did enjoy sitting in our basement on nights to watch the black-and-white documentary *Victory at Sea*, though. Seeing him before the television, I would walk over and perfunctorily ask, "What's on?"

"*Victory at Sea*," he would say.

Listening to Richard Rodgers's surging score, I would join him in watching the opening sequence, a rolling high sea reflecting a setting sun, but not long after a wide-swathed white V appeared on the screen, I would soon lose track of the storyline. Becoming bored, I would wander off, leaving my father to his reverie.

Perhaps from his years on the *Roe*, my father possessed a deep love for the sea. "You shouldn't fear the ocean, but you should respect it," he often counseled. His was not a swimmer's love for a sea—water with a limitless expanse. Instead, his was a love acquired from a ship deck where water is at once at hand and yet kept comfortably at a distance, where one could escape the crowded, irksome land forever to enjoy clear skies arched over empty, sparkling seas.

There was a night during one of our summer week's stays in Stone Harbor when my father left our car and strolled out onto an ocean pier. A chilly sea wind was kicking up the surf. Left alone with my mother and sisters, I sat there trying to keep warm. Growing impatient, my mother said, "Go see what your father's up to."

Stepping out of the car, I walked halfway out onto the pier and halted. I did not dare disturb him as he stood staring out over the white-topped breakers into the black void, journeying back over the years to again feel the *Roe's* roll and sway, taste the salt spray, and see her bow awash as she plowed the waves. Shivering, I stood impassively waiting for him to finish his communion with the sea. My father soon joined me, and we walked silently together back to our car.

As I write this, I wonder what was his war, compared to those days of grinding sameness with his wife, children, and work?

꩜

I am finishing up my morning run along the sidewalks and roads near my childhood home. Looking at my watch, I suppose Janet is up and about. We did not arrive until after eight o'clock last evening. We were making good time on our drive down from Connecticut, until stalled traffic on the New Jersey Turnpike caused me to lose even more time meandering the back roads of Mercer and Bucks counties. Despite vowing not to, we always to end up staying at the same dreary motel, whenever we visit my sister and her family here in Pennsylvania.

South of New England, it is good to again feel the hot August sun, hear the cicadas' racket and trace the familiar slope of the land. The trees here were no more than saplings when I was growing up, but the thick trunks of some oaks and maples I run by impress time's passage on me. On what was the land of the old Hunsberger Farm, I stop running and approach a blond-haired landscaper busy cutting back a line of vegetation. He looks to be about my age, and his shirt is already wet with sweat. He pauses from his work, and we exchange greetings and shake hands. "Did you know cows used to graze here and drink water out of a concrete cistern right over there?" I say.

"No, I didn't," he says.

"I was raised in a house up that hill. Over there, where those apartments are, was a pasture. Cows used to graze over there too; later there were a couple horses that used to roam about. Everything is so built up now."

"Yes, there have been a lot of changes around here, but you can't fault people for selling their land and retiring. Still, there ought to be some way to preserve the open space," he says.

"It all started with the baby boom after the war," I add.

We chat some more, comparing more mental notes on the new developments. Sensing he wishes to return to his work, I break off our talk, shake his hand again, and say, "Good talking to you."

"Me too. It's always good to hear from an old-timer who remembers things back then," he says.

Turning away, I run up the slope toward Newtown Road. I am a little stung about being referred to as an old-timer. Funny, it seems not that long ago when older men referred to me as young fella. When did things change? True, I turned fifty in June, but a stranger like him would not have known my age. Have I slipped that much? Has something changed in my demeanor? Was it some wrinkle, a dullness in the eye, or a slight stoop that led him to use such a term? I console myself when I realize the events we were talking about were in fact some time ago. I suppose it follows: olden times—old-timer.

Back at the motel Janet is almost finished packing. After I shower and change, we leave the motel and I drive along the roads in my old neighborhood. After reading aloud the names Allen, Barbara, Florence, Marilyn, and Paul, I say, "I was told these roads here were named after the builder's children."

We come upon my old house on Ann Lane and pull to a stop out front. A teenage boy who is walking toward the front door pauses and looks back at us with concern. "Suspicion and fear are our first emotions these days," I say. Feeling uncomfortable too, I drive off.

The land here is part of Warminster Township, a rectangular tract twenty miles north of Philadelphia. An 1876 township map I came across on the township website shows that long before the roads were cut, my neighborhood was parceled into farms belonging to individuals named Walton, Shoemaker, Kline, Hallowell, and Bennett. Besides the farms, the map also traces the paths of several streams. As a boy, I discovered those streams in the few woods left untouched by the builders. The newts, crayfish, and yellow salamanders that I bucketed home were proof of my tramps. I was happy to see one of these old streams still flowing beneath the line of growth that the landscaper was cutting earlier this morning

Tracing these streams on the old township map, it appeared to me that a couple of them have their source near my old house. Each of these streams, as in the 1800s, eventually finds its way to the Pennypack Creek. As a boy, I did not need maps or dowsers to learn about the watery underground near my home, for near my home stands a brick municipal pump house that continues to draw water for the township.

I have often amused myself with road maps by carefully retracing a river or its tributary's crooked path back along roads and through towns in search of its source. My searches are seldom conclusive though, for roads and places are the main interests of such maps. These maps can direct, but they cannot fix a river's source.

Leaving my old neighborhood, we drive southeast along familiar roads—County Line, Heaton, Byberry, Paper Mill, and Huntingdon Pike—and past old landmarks—the United Methodist Church, Bryn Athyn Cathedral, and Raymond Pitcairn's castle *Glencairn*. I follow the water's downward rush. Later today we will visit my sister and her family back up in Warminster, but for now, we follow the land's tilt downwards.

Completing the steep drive up the hill on Red Lion Road, I expect to see the Budd Company plant with its sprawling aircraft-hangar-like building. Instead, what I remembered is gone and a golf driving range lies where the plant once stood.

"There used to be a huge factory called the Budd Company here. They made railroad cars," I say. "It looked like a huge airplane hangar. Coming home at night, after visiting my aunts and uncles, I loved looking at plant and its silver water tower. The tower had the word Budd spelled out in blue neon light. It's gone now."

"My father told me about getting a job there right after the war. The place was so big that some guy found a place up in the rafters where you could go and sleep. He and my dad would sneak up there for a nap after lunch."

"That's funny," Janet says.

Seeing the sign for Verree Road, I turn right. "The roads here are smoother and wider than what I remember," I say. "There is even a bike lane. Growing up, we all assumed Warminster was a better place to be than down here, but Northeast Philly seems like a pretty nice place now. I haven't been back here in a long time, and I guess a lot has changed. I wouldn't mind living here now."

Coming upon the Pennypack Environmental Center, I turn into

its parking lot. Janet and I get out, and after scouting the grounds, we find the center closed. Behind the main building, we find a zigzag path that leads down to the Pennypack Creek. Grand old oak, tulip, and sycamore trees that rise up from the creek bed shade and cool us.

All morning Tinker, our miniature Schnauzer, has endured the heat with us in our Honda Civic. Spying the creek now, she surges ahead and wades out into a clear pool up to her ears. She cools herself by casually lapping the water, all the while keeping a tenuous foothold on the gravel creek bottom. Following her lead, I take off my shoes and socks and wade in.

A father and his two boys with fishing rods in hand appear on the other bank. They venture out on what looks to be an old concrete dam. The word Pennypack comes from an Indian word meaning "deep, dead water." The creek here is shallow, though, with many exposed rocks.

After returning to the car, I drive along roads that follow the creek's meandering path. The wooded land on each side of the creek makes up Pennypack Park, one of Philadelphia's city parks. Without a map to guide me, I occasionally lose the creek's way and must backtrack. We end up in a cul-de-sac lined with two-story brick row homes. "Philadelphia is famous for its row homes," I say. "In Philly, they're called row homes, not row houses. Whenever I came down here as a boy, it seemed to me like the whole city was nothing but row homes. It used to be—maybe still is—a dream of a lot people to own a row home. My father told me that he wanted to buy one of these homes somewhere around here, but my mother wouldn't let him. 'None of my children are going to be raised in a row home,' she said.

"When I was growing up, the TV news always seemed to have a story about some row home fire. I used to think living in one would be horrible. They don't seem so bad, though—low cost, easy maintenance—sort of cozy, all packed together. It's true; buying a house out in farmland Warminster was not what my father wanted; he'd as soon lived here."

"You would have been a Philly kid," says Janet.

"Funny, isn't? I would have turned out different. My father never ventured far, when I think about it. He only moved upstream a ways up on the Pennypack Creek."

Back on the road, winding with the creek, I have the sense of the land running downhill. We reach Frankford Avenue, and turning left, I drive north. Unable, even if asked, to retrace my route, I am glad to see the slender blue-green steeple of Saint Dominic Church up ahead. Frankford Avenue takes a sharp dip under a railroad bridge, and crossing over the Pennypack Creek, I say, "This is Holmesburg, at least what I remember of it."

Turning onto Ashburner Street, I make my way down to Hegerman Street. My father's boyhood home is the first steep-roofed brick house on the left. Climbing out of the car, I take Tinker with me on her leash.

"I don't know if it still is, but the house was a duplex when my grandparents lived there," I say. "They lived on the left side. I was always told 'the Beans' were the source of the odd sounds I heard through the walls. I had to be quiet whenever we visited. It looks as if someone painted the house. I don't remember the bricks being that dark red."

"I'm going to take some pictures," says Janet.

"Okay," I say.

Gazing down the street, I recall the open field where a number of small buildings now stand. The field might have been where my father and friends dug and roasted potatoes on fall nights. Afterwards, each took turns running across the field while the others, as if an unexploded land mine, lay waiting to bash you.

I then recall the time when an uncle recruited my cousins

and me for a foot race down Hegerman Street. I was proud to have finished second, losing only to a boy four years older. Directly across the street, I see there still stands a dingy industrial building with its opaque windows. A line of trees to the left of the house still stands. I picture my grandfather sitting at a picnic table under these trees shelling peanuts. "You're full of soup," he was always saying. There was hubbub one afternoon, when a neighbor burning leaves and brush uncovered a nest of snakes. The snakes, too elusive, slipped off before I could catch sight of them.

Janet, having finished taking pictures, walks over to me and asks, "Have you seen enough?"

"Yeah, let's get going. It's too hot to stand here any longer."

Back in the car I relate, "For years, my grandfather drove thirty miles each way to his job at a Ford factory down in Chester. It's sad, though; he didn't live long after retiring. I was about six or seven when he died in that house. My grandmother found him lying on the bathroom floor. Afterwards, my grandmother sold their house and bought a house on the same block where Uncle Ed and Aunt Helen lived. It's only a few miles from here. I'll drive by on the way back. Like my father, my aunt and uncle never strayed too far from the Holmesburg."

I drive out to Torresdale Avenue and pull over across the road from the stone-walled Holmesburg Prison. "Crazy looking place, isn't?" I say. "Looks like a medieval fortress. It seems out of place with the park and houses so close by. My mother told me that when I was a baby, she used to push me in my stroller on that sidewalk over there."

Crossing Torresdale Avenue, I park in a small lot outside the prison's south wall. "For years, whenever we drove south along I-95, the prison was the landmark my sisters and I used to find my father's house. I've always associated Holmesburg with this prison, but I've never been this close," I say.

Getting out of the car, I walk over and touch one of the wall's large blackish-brown stones. It and the adjoining stones are pockmarked, reminding me of volcanic rock. A fellow unloading a truck on the other side of a razor-wire fence tells us that we are not allowed to park here.

"He probably thinks we're trying to break someone out," I say.

While Janet walks over to talk to him, I study a patinated guardhouse that sits atop a cylindrical stone protuberance where the two walls meet. Taken together, the guard house and bulge in the wall look very much like a small lighthouse. It soon dawns on me that like in a lighthouse, there must be a spiral staircase hidden inside the stone.

Holmesburg Prison has had both a flamboyant and dark past. Bank robber Willie Sutton detailed his brazen 1947 escape from here in his *Where the Money Was: The Memoirs of a Bank Robber*. Disguised in stolen prison-guard uniforms, Sutton and his associates used a couple of ladders to scale the east wall on a snowy winter night. "It's all right," was all Sutton needed to say to a curious guard to effect his escape. A sadder story is told in *Acres of Skin: Human Experiments at Holmesburg Prison; A True Story of Abuse and Exploitation in the Name of Medical Science*. In his book, author Allen Hornblum chronicled dermatological and other medical tests performed on Holmesburg inmates during the decades after the Second World War.

I see Janet walking toward me. "That guy says half the prison is in use. Women are imprisoned here now."

"Really? I thought this place was shut down," I say. "Let's get out of here."

Ashburner Street arches over the Washington-Boston Amtrak rail line, and an old memory of the trains and tracks flashes before my eyes.

"My mother used to take me for a walk up on this bridge. With a dungeon-like prison and speeding trains, old Holmesburg had more than enough wonders for a little boy," I say. Driving south on State Road, we cross the Pennypack Creek again. I see a sign for the recently opened park, Pennypack on the Delaware. Turning left onto an access road, I peer at a brick complex set behind a high fence topped with coils of razor wire. "My god! There are prisons everywhere around here," I say.

The road sweeps broadly to the left, and the Delaware River, at last visible, lazes on our right. "There is the Delaware River, the end of the road for us," I say.

The park is an expanse of open grassy fields interrupted here and there by baseball fields. Most of the baseball diamonds are being used. "There seems to be some sort softball tournament going on," I say. We look for a place to park, and I eventually find a spot amid the many sedans and SUVs.

After getting out of the car, I feel the hot noonday sun sear my back. The hot air rising off the asphalt reminds me of an open oven. With Tinker in tow, we walk across a grass field toward the river's edge. On our right, some softball players and their families recline under canopies with drinks in hand. A couple of charcoal grills smolder nearby.

Janet and I reach the water's edge and gaze out over the river. A hazy mix of smog and humidity hangs in the air over the river. Shrouded by trees and brush, the far-off shore appears blue-green. Down the river to our right a grassy, earthen pier extends a short way into the river. The pier appears to be off limits. "That's New Jersey over there. Center city Philadelphia is farther downriver," I say.

"How far do you think it is across?" Janet asks.

"Not far, maybe a thousand yards," I say. "It would be an easy swim. Do you see that small sandy beach over there?"

"Yes." says Janet.

"That's what I always remembered about New Jersey when I was a boy. Cross any bridge along the river here, and the first thing you notice on the Jersey side is sand. See, there are rocks along the river here, but over there, only sand. I always wondered why. The river is not that wide. Why should there be such a difference? I thought maybe there wouldn't be any sandy beaches left, with all the development going on, but the shore looks pretty much untouched over there. Maybe it's too wet and swampy to do anything with. My father told me when he was a boy his mother used to say, 'New Jersey was once part of the Atlantic Ocean, and someday the ocean will take it back.'"

Janet smiles as we walk off toward a couple fishermen.

I ask about the fishing, and the nearest fellow sitting in a beach chair relates in a raspy voice that he catches catfish here, but he would never eat anything out this water. The other fisherman is a husky guy with shoulder-length hair and numerous tattoos on his arms. He sits on a cooler smoking a cigarette, oblivious to our presence. Following one of their fishing lines to where it meets the river, I try to discern its flow. The river is tidal up to Trenton and appears to be ebbing now. The chance, lazy swirls I see on the surface might be tell-tales of stronger currents underneath. Out in river's middle, several white-hulled daysailers with jib and mainsail unfurled tack to and fro. I puzzle aloud about a yellow power boat floating near the sailboats, and the nearest fellow tells me that it is a sail tow and adds that it is "out there to help any sailboat in trouble."

After leaving them, I say, "They sure were tough, no-nonsense guys. You often hear Philadelphia referred to as gritty, working class, a city of sharp elbows, and looking at those guys you know why."

Back at the car, Janet and I take some time to talk about my half-baked plan of swimming across the river.

"You really aren't going to try to swim across, are you? You don't even know what currents are out there or how dirty the water is," she says.

SOURCES

Upon hearing her words, I open our car trunk and stare at our inflatable kayak, stowed away in its duffle bag. "It wouldn't be that hard. Just think of all the swims I've made this summer. You could just paddle alongside, as we do back in Connecticut. I'll ask that fisherman back there to watch Tinker until we get back," I say.

"But there is a no-swimming sign right over there," says Janet.

"Yeah, I know. I saw it."

"So, that means you can't swim here, right? Listen, times have changed. What was it? Some seventy years ago when your dad swam here? That was a different time. Things are different now. Anyway, if you really want to swim across, if it's that important to you, you can always come back later, after you learn more about the river and get some sort of clearance."

"Maybe you're right. The tide looks like it is going out. It would probably be better to try just before or at high tide. I didn't plan this part of our trip very well," I say.

"Well, you didn't know. We drove down here today to explore your father's old neighborhood, and this is part of what we learned," says Janet.

"I had wanted to end the trip with a swim across the river here. I'm sure I would have been all right, but with that no-swimming sign there, I might have been picked up out there and ended up on the evening news as some nut who tried to swim across the Delaware," I say.

After I close the trunk, we walk back toward the river. A few days later, I will read a news story about a seventeen-year old New York City boy who, about the time Janet and I were having our discussion, drowned while trying to swim across the Delaware River up near Easton. On a kayaking trip with some friends and their father, they had stopped for lunch when Elizer, apparently lured by the New Jersey shore, attempted to swim across. The river was only 120 yards wide at the spot, and Elizer was said to have gone under three-quarters of the way across.

Janet and I are back together now beside the river, and she takes some pictures while I step out and balance on a couple of the flat reddish-brown rocks that line the riverbank. Reaching down I wet my hands. Close up, the river is colored a murky greenish-brown, not at all like its far-off pewter color. Upriver, my sight is blocked by a dense line of trees. The Pennypack, carrying Warminster's waters, meets the Delaware and ends its life just beyond the line of trees. The no-trespassing sign and a high chain-link fence that mark this park boundary banish any thoughts I might have had of exploring the Pennyback's mouth.

Philadelphia is a city of two rivers, the Delaware and the Schuylkill, each much different from the other. Without a single dam along its entire length, the Delaware is wild and unruly, often overrunning its banks. Sustaining steel and chemical plants, docks, piers, and old wharfs, the Delaware in places brings to mind coal and oil as much as it does water. For so much of its length, the Delaware is a working river. The much narrower Schuylkill, at least where it enters the city, brings to mind Fairmount Park, Boat House Row, and the Greek-temple-like art museum. Philadelphia painter Thomas Eakins's sensuous rowing paintings are set on the Schuylkill, while his *Shad Fishing at Gloucester on the Delaware River* depicts weary fisherman toiling with a seine net on the river south of here. Oil refinery and gasworks lining its banks, the aristocratic Schuylkill is remade though where it empties into the Delaware. I suppose that swimming across the river here at my age calls for some sort of aquatic comparison. Today being the day, I would have completed life's cycle by following the Pennypack to the Delaware, the river itself on its own way to the sea. The Delaware River here in Holmesburg is my river; it is my source. I might as well swim China's Yellow River as to swim a river as foreign as the Schuylkill.

By chance, our trip here this weekend coincides with the end of my father's war sixty years ago. Maybe because we have been traveling or people are forgetting, I have not heard the anniversary mentioned in the news. Like other children of veterans, I requested my father's military record a while back. His record—marking the dates when he was on and off the *Roe*, his radar training, and the notable operations for when he was on board—although unremarkable, provides facts, where before there was only conjecture on my part. Occasionally I remove the photocopied sheets from their manila envelope and study his fingerprints, his youthful signature, the record of his honorable discharge, his qualification as a shellback, and that he passed a fifty-yard swim test.

About the time that I requested my father's records, I also contacted ten or so surviving veterans from the *Roe*, inquiring if any of them remembered my father. One fellow responded, writing that he shared night watches in the Atlantic with my father. Another took the time to find my phone number and called me one evening. He remembered my father, but in love with his ship, he wanted to talk only about the *Roe*. We chatted about Christmas Eve 1944, the night the *Roe* and *Case* sank the Japanese destroyer. He impressed on me it was the *Roe* that "finished her off," the destroyer *Case* "falling back because of bearing trouble." He was a crusty old fellow. My ear rang when he yelled in the receiver, "This is history, damn it!" Upon my bringing up the story about the fellow shooting at the shipwrecked Japanese, he said, "There were a lot guys like that" and "that guy is still alive." Before hanging up, he invited me to attend the upcoming reunion that *Roe* veterans and their families hold each year.

Not long ago, I borrowed from the local library and viewed all twenty-six episodes of my father's favored *Victory at Sea*, a visual history of the naval war. One segment ironically contained footage of a shipwrecked Japanese sailor attempting to flee by swimming away from a U.S. ship. Swimming only a few strokes, the sailor is machine gunned down and quickly disappears below the water's surface. The codes of war were apparently different in my father's day.

My father haunted these shores when he was a boy. Somewhere along here he slipped into the Delaware waters and swam off for the other side before turning back. Maybe it is best I leave his river undisturbed. He lies at rest not far from here in a small family plot at Saint Dominic Church. We will visit his grave on our way back. We are all equal in death, and his granite headstone is identical to the others in that part of the cemetery. Just above the well-cared-for lawn, a small American flag sits atop a bronze metal marker identifying him as veteran and his dates of service: 1941-1945.

Life on land was often too much for my father. When land's problems became overwhelming for him, he sought the usual escapes. In his last decade, he found some solace beside the sea on Florida's east coast. The population there was sparse and the coastline long. I can see him now in the distance, trudging the beach alone. "You can breathe out there," he would say after returning from his walks. But I was never fooled. Although he would talk about his walks on the beach, I knew he was elsewhere. He was where he loved most to be, on the deck of the *Roe*.

I can see Janet; she is waiting for me. It is time to leave. I have no doubt; the tide is ebbing.

CHAPTER **4**

The Swimmer

"I'm swimming across the county."—Ned Merrill

When I was growing up in the 1960s, weeks would pass during the summer without a thought of television; such was the draw of friends and the outdoors. The three major networks, now indistinguishable from the hundreds of other cable and satellite stations, showed reruns until school and colder temperatures forced children and their parents back indoors.

Of the little television I did watch during the summer, one repeated instance stands out. Free from school, I awoke early, and slipping down to our basement, I switched on our black-and-white TV set. My father, wishing our set to run cooler or perhaps tired of fiddling with the screws when replacing a tube, had removed the set's back cover. While waiting for the set to warm up, I maneuvered to the back and squeezed in against the wall. Warned of television's dangers when my father told me a capacitor discharge had knocked him out, I did no more than peer at the miniature city of dust-covered aluminum boxes, glass tubes, and the rainbow of wires spewing from the picture tube.

Like watching a campfire's first flames, I sat fixated, listening to the crinkles and cracks of the warming metal and glass. Rising hot air, with its peculiar hot, dry smell filled my head and the tubes' orange glow warmed my face and chest. Moving around to the set front, I waited for the moment when our television sprang to life. Pulling our cranberry- colored rocker closer to the screen, I marveled at the circles, numerals, and spray of lines of the Indian Head test pattern. The Indian's feathered headdress set above his chiseled profile was in stark contrast with the numbers and grids. Positioned at twelve o'clock on the screen, his face promised me adventure and assured me that dull numbers and dreary science would never vanquish a wild, free spirit.

A witness to history, I turned up the volume to hear the test pattern give way to the national anthem. Heralding the start of another broadcast day, I watched Old Glory flap in a gentle breeze. I never stopped hoping stampeding horses or flying saucers might appear, but after a few minutes of watching the U. S. farm report, I grew bored and trudged back upstairs to sleep.

I cannot imagine today's children being entertained in such a way. Television, wrought from cold silicon, no longer needs test patterns to fill nonexistent dead time. The workings of television were integral with its viewing back then, though. "They're nothing but a type of valve," was how my father described our TV set's cheery, glowing tubes.

Fourteen or fifteen years old and having no conscious interest in swimming, I was nonetheless intrigued one Saturday afternoon to read in the newspaper that a film titled *The Swimmer* was to be aired that evening. Having long since moved beyond test patterns, I was becoming more introspective, if not moody, and solitary evenings were not uncommon.

Living rooms being sovereign back then, our new color television was relegated to our basement's far wall. A dark brown tile, mottled with beige, covered the floor, and wood sheets stained a deep cherry paneled the basement walls. A row of chest-high, jalousie windows looked out onto our backyard.

Come nightfall, I switched off the lights and stepped down the stairs leading from our kitchen. After switching on the set, I reclined on our couch's foam cushions. While waiting for the set to warm up, I watched fireflies flit by the windows. A gentle breeze rustled the trees in our backyard, and the cool night air pouring through the screens filled the room with the scents of honeysuckle and rose. I breathed easily, and a pleasant slackness came over me. Only by my heart's faint pulsing stirred me.

Alone in the dark, I watched as a middle-age Burt Lancaster, clad only in a black swimsuit, emerged from a rabbit- and deer-filled woods to dive into a light blue pool. Swimming the pool's length, Lancaster is seen rising through a lens of glass containing a wedge of lemon. A reunion of sorts with the pool's owners, Don and Helen Westerhazy, and their guests Stu and Peggy Forsburgh ensues.

"Neddy! Ned Merrill, how are you? Where've you been?"

Lancaster, distant and hazy on his recent whereabouts and his family says to his old camp bunkmate Stu, "Look at that water, look at that sky. How about a swim? Remember how we would take off our suits and swim up that river? We just never got tired."

"Yeah, we had nice, new pink lungs in those days," says Stu.

Undeterred, Lancaster goes on, "And the water up there. Remember that transparent light green water? It felt different. God, what a feeling! We could have swum around the world in those days."

Lancaster soon learns that the neighboring Grahams had put in a pool the prior June. He then is possessed by a vision: with the addition of the Grahams's new pool, he can now "swim" home.

"Pool by pool, they form a river all the way to our house. Call it the Lucinda River after my wife. This is the day that Ned Merrill swam across the county," he announces.

Amid laughs and bemused looks, Lancaster dives into the

CROSSINGS: A SWIMMER'S MEMOIR

Westerhazy's pool, swims across, and after hoisting himself out of the water, disappears into the trees and bushes. Over the next hour or so, I watched as Ned Merrill swam pool after pool on his hike back to his house. Filmed in New York's Westchester County, "I'm swimming home," is Merrill's answer to one pool tenant's query of what brought him to their pool.

Despite the film's auspicious beginning, with each pool that Lancaster swims, leavings of the disaster that is now Ned Merrill's life are revealed.

Merrill has lost his job, his house, and his family, but because of some alcohol-induced amnesia, mental breakdown, or other malady, he is oblivious to the reminders his former neighbors cast his way.

Merrill injures his leg leaping over a jump in a horse ring, is shoved to a pool deck disputing the ownership of a hot-dog wagon, ducks a beer can tossed at him by a passing car, has his eyes stung by the heavy chlorine in his town's crowded pool, and at the last pool, he is rebuffed by his bitter ex-mistress, Shirley Abbot.

Alongside Abbott's pool, whose waters appear a somber lead color, Merrill laments, "The sun has no heat. I'm cold. And I used to believe in things."

"That is before you got thrown out of your golden playpen," says Abbott.

The film ends in a rainstorm, with Merrill hurling himself against the locked door of an unkempt white house. The camera pans across the house's picture window, and the inside is seen to be empty except for a few boxes of odds and ends set in the middle of a bare wood floor.

The Swimmer script was based on John Cheever's short story of the same title. The above retelling is based on my recent viewing of the movie. When I first saw the movie back in the 1960s, I recall being

THE SWIMMER

disappointed that the film was less about swimming than the anger Merrill evoked in his neighbors.

Cheever's original story is a sun-drenched, airy, but desperate tale. A brilliant chronicler of angst and unhappiness in well-off, leafy suburbs, Cheever writes of "light-green, sapphire, and lighted cerulean water," Merrill's "contempt for men who did not hurl themselves into pools," Ned's "choppy crawl," and Merrill's sense that "to be embraced and sustained by the light green water was less a pleasure. . .than the resumption of a natural condition."

Cheever's short story was the inspiration for Englishman Roger Deakin's *WaterLog: A swimmer's journey through Britain,* a sharp-eyed, go-as-you-please account of his year traveling and swimming in Great Britain.

Another Brit, Charles Sprawson, in his *Haunts of the Black Masseur: The Swimmer as Hero,* devotes several pages to Cheever's story and subsequent film. "*The Swimmer* traces a swimmer's decline from self-delusion to delusion," writes Sprawson. He also notes that making the film "required Burt Lancaster to undergo three months of swimming lessons to help him overcome mild hydrophobia."

More than a decade after playing Ned Merrill, aquaphobe Lancaster swam again when he played Lou Pasco in Louis Malle's bittersweet film *Atlantic City*. The white-haired Lancaster cast as Lou is a two-bit gangster, "a dinosaur," lost in the memory of his post-war past while legalized gambling remakes his Atlantic City. In the film's most affecting scene, Lou is seen strolling along the Boardwalk with a twenty-something bearded hood named Dave. Behind them, a purple-gold sunset reflects off Atlantic City's Steel Pier. The day is cold and the Boardwalk is mostly empty. Lou, reminiscing about a past that never really was says, "Yes, things were beautiful then, what with the rackets, whoring, guns. Sometime things would happen, and I'd have to kill a few people. I'd feel bad for a while, but I'd jump in the ocean and swim way out, come back in feeling nice and clean, and start all over again."

"I've never seen the Atlantic Ocean till just now," Dave says.

Stopping to gaze longingly back at the ocean, Lou says, "The Atlantic Ocean was something then. Yeah, you should've seen the Atlantic Ocean in those days."

At the start of my senior year in high school, I befriended a classmate named John. John's house was located in a small borough of Victorian houses not far from my own home. I never knew exactly (or if told, I have forgotten) when John's two-story white house was built, but from its quaint look, I assumed it was one of those eighteen- or nineteenth-century Pennsylvania farmhouses that dotted the Bucks County landscape back then. John's home was equally rustic in its setting. To the north and west stretched pastures and cornfields, which developments have since claimed.

A curiosity for me back then was the mature grove of English holly trees that grew on the large tract of land to the rear of John's house. John and his parents cut bundles of this green holly with its red berries in November and December for mail order and local nursery sales. Although his parents were busy for a time, I understood they took no more than a gentleman farmer's interest in the holly. True to the popular carol, John's father cut a large bough of holly, which he set in a corner of their house's main room and festooned with strings of white lights at Christmas.

John's father stood six feet tall and was solidly built. Below his not-too-thick white hair, brown horn-rimmed glasses framed his dark brown eyes, which stared impassively whenever he spoke. Having studied classics at the University of Chicago, he was acquainted with Paul Goodman and was said to have had the endurance to have read Dostoevsky's *The Brothers Karamazov* in a single night.

At a time in adolescence when one forms friendships and opinions much like trying on hats, I spent many afternoons and evenings around John's kitchen table, conversing and reading with John, his parents, and friends. Those hours sitting before their rather unremarkable wood table served as my introduction to the intellectual life. There, issues of the *New Yorker* served as drink coasters; a small black-and-white television lay entombed under stacks of books in a window nook, and names such as Turgenev, Nabokov, and Mishima filled the air. Often I would excuse myself and stroll into the main room to gaze up at book shelves like mountains to be climbed and housing Mortimer J. Adler's *Great Books of the Western World*. I would pull down a volume of Boswell, Freud, or Montesquieu and say to myself, "one day." On a nearby coffee table stood two dark-blue slipcases. One slipcase was usually empty, its *OED* splayed open, a magnifying glass resting over the last word query.

Back in kitchen, John's father's at-times-aphoristic opinions and views usually held sway at the table.

"I don't take Michener seriously." "Actors, hah! What is acting anyway?"

"Boston was originally the nation's cultural center and New York its financial center, but New York now fills both roles."

And "So and so is a fifth-rate writer."

Often John's father would quote Aristotle or relate a Greek myth to resolve some disputed issue. He had a penchant for giving extended monologues on cultural and artistic issues, and my mind raced through what seemed a maze of meanings as he spoke. Picking a promising path here or there, I was often led to a sense unrelated to what I was then hearing. His intellectual discourses were formative mysteries for me though, for they spoke more of possibilities than actualities.

Like Ned Merrill, pools with their limpid waters bewitched John's father. Whenever talk strayed to sports, he readily extolled swimming, its high rank in athletics and his times swimming when he lived in Chicago. Perhaps envisioning his already completed pool, he

CROSSINGS: A SWIMMER'S MEMOIR

often said with conviction, "I am going to have a lap pool built out by the holly trees."

I recall a Saturday morning when I sat across from him at the table. Looking stout and ready, he sat with his back to the kitchen windows. Bathed in the late morning light, I listened as he related with what I thought was a tinge a pride (perhaps because the danger was not great) of rescuing John's younger sister, after she had slipped below the surface of Lake Michigan. Upon questioning her later, she described her time underwater matter-of-factly as a "peaceful waiting."

Perhaps preoccupied or just too averse to pools and swimming, I was oblivious to the lap pool's construction. Having no recollection now of the month when the pool was completed, it was not until sometime nearing the end of spring when friend Rick said to me, "You need to check it out; John's pool is done." It was true. When I did drop by and walked out toward the holly grove, there at the forefront of the grove lay John's father's new lap pool. Designed purely for swimming, the pool embodied a new concept for me. Narrow and uniformly shallow, it lacked the slides, diving boards, and odd shapes I had come to associate with other backyard pools. From the cement walkway, one had a clear view of the holly rows. A hint of light azure from the neighboring Miller's pool was visible across a well-kept lawn. A pair of chrome handrails visible from inside a green chain link fence around the Miller pool seemed to beckon a swim, but that pool was always vacant.

John's house, with its expansive front lawn, holly grove, oaks, dogwoods, willows, and a spreading magnolia tree, made the pool and grounds the sort Ned Merrill would have liked to drop in on for a chat and swim.

With the weather warming as summer approached, our kitchen forums were moved outdoors to chairs set on the pool deck. The night after our high school graduation, while waiting for John to

THE SWIMMER

return, I watched candle lights flicker in the lap pool's dark waters while talking of my plans and aspirations with John's parents.

Although, none of my friends from the kitchen table were particularly skillful swimmers, we regularly jumped into the pool to cool off on hot days. Rick, who might have passed for the blond Olympic swimming champion Don Schollander, had the strongest front crawl. I have a noisy, hazy blue memory—a memory now bordering on dream—of attending a high school swim meet with him. "Swimming is the best exercise there is," he said up in the stands. Casting an impressive bow wake and trailing a white churn, Rick's back, down to his trunks, rode high up in the water whenever he overhanded the pool length. "He has a nice stroke," John's mother observed. My thrashing, although able to propel me a lap, garnered no praise.

Swimming in the lap pool was a fatiguing, if not a painful chore for me. My best efforts to swim smoothly notwithstanding, I tired quickly. After only a few laps, I usually retreated to a vacant wall, where, as many non-swimmers are likely to do, I reclined with outspread arms. Basking in the sun, I would watch the others splash by.

I suppose it was the following summer or the subsequent one when on a hot afternoon, friend Doug and I decided to drop by John's home. It was an awkward and somewhat lonely time as many high school friendships were falling apart. Old ties probably needed to be broken, but how to do it or when it should happen were still questions to be resolved.

We did not expect to find John home, as he was a promising cyclist and was often away racing. Years before Greg Lemond's Tour de France victories, John would be among the first Americans to travel overseas to race as a professional in Europe.

Leaving the car, we walked up the tree-canopied, cut-stone path toward the house's rear porch and kitchen door. When we approached the house, the family's Rhodesian ridgeback, Sheba, lumbered out to greet us. Reaching the porch, I knocked on the summer screen door and waited. Greeted by silence, Doug intoned a loud, "Hello." The large trees about the house cooled the breeze flowing through the kitchen's far windows. Standing there, I imbibed the air's grassy scent as it mixed with the kitchen's woods, books, and spices. So pleasurable was the moment for me that the dimly lit kitchen interior appeared to phosphoresce for a time.

With no one answering, we turned away from the house and walked across a shaded patch of lawn toward the lap pool. After winding our way through a blind of shrubs and bushes, we stepped out into brilliant sunshine. Through the wire fence, as if emerging from the ground, a pair of arms moved in alternate overhand sweeps before the holly grove. Opening the pool gate, we found some deck chairs and sat down.

Facing west, I squinted through the sun's waving reflection as John's father swam laps. Not wearing goggles, he kept his eyes closed except when making an open-air turn at the pool ends. Committed to his swim, he took no notice of us. With his swimming sounding a rhythmic "ker-plop, ker-plop, ker-plop," I withdrew into myself, away from the flashing sun.

Imagining John's father's years of swimming in and around Chicago, I envisioned aged, cavernous indoor pools with chipped, faded aqua paint; pools that gagged and nauseated with their humid, chlorine-filled air. I heard swimmers shout and felt the splash of a slapping dive. I saw silhouetted ore freighters pasted on a whitish-blue horizon, straining white jibs and main sails, banks of looming buildings, and expansive lakefronts where husky, barrel-chested men and broad-shouldered women plied their way through Lake Michigan's blue waters.

Sitting there I soon felt overwhelmed, powerless, for my dreaming

THE SWIMMER

made swimming and water all too taxing and vast for me. Swimming was reserved only for the gods.

Overheating sitting in the sun, I left my dreams and returned to an impatient wait while John's father finished his swim. When done, he stood up and rested against a sidewall.

"Hello, Doug, Buddy. Have you been here long?" he asked.

"No, not too long," I said.

"Johnny's not at home, you know. He's in Italy. But anyway, how have you two been?"

"Pretty good, I guess." said Doug. "We haven't been by for a while. We just thought we would stop by."

After catching up on news about John and chatting about what we have been reading, John's father invited us in for a swim. Not having swim trunks, we cast off shoes, socks, and shirts and dove in with only our shorts on. Glad to cool off, I joined Doug in the pool, where I slogged through a couple laps with a beginner's breaststroke, simultaneously pulling and kicking. Concerned with what he saw, John's father insisted that I stop and learn the proper stroke. Like my first swim lesson years before, he buoyed me while I tried to coordinate my movements to his instructions.

"So strange; the kick and pull are separate," and "Why didn't I know this?" were my thoughts.

My feet slapped at the water and my neck and back weakened as I tried not to gulp water. I felt naked and helpless, trapped in what seemed like a hellish blue well. John's father continued with his lesson, but discouraged by my flaying, he soon stopped and moved away.

Older and more sensitive, I suffered my failure and hid for a time by diving underwater. Learning requires an interest and a resolve, and I possessed neither for mastering the breaststroke that afternoon, but I took heart, for I was a tennis player, a player who could smack a forehand, hit a dipping topspin backhand, and put a volley away for a winner all in a single point. Surely my athletic inclinations and talents were not of the aquatic sort. Could not I then guiltlessly sidestep and forget the breaststroke, along with this whole awful sport of swimming?

Along with the water, my towel wiped away any taint of shame I might have felt. My swimming no more improved, I said goodbye to John's father, dodging for a time Ned Merrill's entreaties to swim in every pool's waiting waters.

༄ ༄ ༄

The stiff wind off Lake Michigan feels cold, and I shiver, taking my first steps into the water. The clean sand is hard packed, and nearby a chunk of dark green seaweed bobs about in the surf. The lake has an aqua color this morning, much different from the bright blue I recall from a visit some years ago.

The Chicago skyline rises behind me and stretches north along Lake Shore Drive. Ash-gray clouds obscure the upper floors of the Sears Tower and the John Hancock Center. No more than a couple hundred yards wide, the beach here is bracketed by concrete seawall to my left and stone block seawall to my right.

I wade farther out and turning sideways. I stand on my toes and jump in the air to avoid the sharp, peaked waves. I am no different now from when I was young; I still detest the first shocks of cold water. When I was young there always seemed to be two types of swimmers: those who would dive in and the ones that lurked on the steps or the shallows, taking their time getting used to the water. I continue to be the latter type.

A wave slaps my thighs and splashes up onto my chest. Shivering uncontrollably, I hold on tightly to my swim cap and goggles. Wading out some more, I wait for the next wave and porpoise under it. Surfacing, I stand in waist-high water and struggle to keep my balance. Scooping up a cap of water, I stretch my swim cap over my head and fit my goggles. Leaning forward, I leave my feet and swim off into the chop.

Having flown west yesterday with my wife, Janet, I am here to swim in the annual Chicago Master's Big Shoulders Open Water Swim Classic. From our plane last night, Lake Michigan looked like a dark peninsula set in a sea of white and yellow lights. With the Chicago skyline looming ahead, I stared down from the plane, wishing I could touch the lake and assure myself that its waters were warm and calm.

But overnight, a northeasterly gale blew in and kicked up large surf all along the Chicago lakefront. Riding south this morning with Janet and my mother's brother Paul, I cringed at the sight of the angry, ocean-sized waves breaking on the beaches. Even though this beach is protected by a stone wall breakwater a mile or so off, the wind racing down Lake Shore Drive continues to fetch sizable waves.

This yearly swim takes its name from Carl Sandburg's poem "Chicago," whose first few lines are as follows:

HOG Butcher for the World,
Tool Maker, Stacker of Wheat,
Player with Railroads and the Nation's Freight Handler;
Stormy, husky, brawling,
City of the Big Shoulders:

According to the event website, despite Chicago's reputation as The Windy City, over the last few years the swimmers here have enjoyed warm and "relatively calm water." Today, though, is different, but no matter, I think. What would Sandburg's "Stormy, husky, brawling" city be without days like this?

I have been swimming on three different tacks, each one paralleling a leg of the triangular buoyed course that I will soon have to navigate. Stroking into the wind, my torso slams into waves and falls into troughs. This buffeting reminds me of the thumping felt when an outboard skiff skips across rough chop. When swimming downwind, I feel the water ebb and flow. Occasionally a few quick strokes will allow me to catch a short ride on a wave, much like when bodysurfing. Breathing to the leeward, I roll and pitch in the crosswind, the longest leg of the three. I swim on this tack for some time. I find open water swimming much like sailing in conditions like this.

Stopping, I tread water and reconnoiter the two far orange buoys. Having seen flags, balls, and buoys plainly visible from the shore disappear when swimming in open water, I follow their highs and lows in preparation for the race start.

Swimming again, I warm up my breaststroke with some quick in sweeps, dives, and kicks. The breaststroke—my old nemesis from John's father's lap pool—is a fairly comfortable stroke for me now. Although I swim more slowly, the breaststroke allows me a respite from the crawl. While swimming in open water, the breaststroke offers a better alternative than just treading water: I can both catch my breath and assess my progress, all the while still moving forward.

Feeling ready for the race to start, I pause and gaze about before swimming back to the beach. The lake and skyline are on such a grand scale that I cannot imagine a more spectacular urban setting for a swim race.

Back on the beach, I wander about the gathering swimmers and spectators looking for Janet. Catching sight of her, I wave and walk over.

"How is it out there?" she asks.

"It's pretty rough, but I'll be okay," I say. "Where is Uncle Paul?"

"He is parking his car. What wave are you in?"

"I'm an old guy. I'm in wave number four. The waves are sent off every five minutes, so I have some time before my start."

Swimmers and spectators begin to crowd the beach. I watch as the

THE SWIMMER

first wave of swimmers enters the water. The swimmers assemble in a loose pack a distance from the beach. Engulfed by the enormous lake, the swimmers are reduced to little more than blue-capped heads bobbing about in the waves. The horn soon sounds, and they swim off.

"Look at them. They're getting after it," I say, and it is true. Except for a few stragglers, the swimmers in this wave are whipping the water with quick overhand strokes. The conditions apparently matter little for this group.

Janet waves and shouts to Uncle Paul.

He joins us and asks, "Hey, Bud. Ready for this?"

"I hope so. Want to join me?" I ask jokingly.

"Oh no, not me. My rotator cuff in this shoulder couldn't take it. How far are you swimming?" he asks.

"I'm signed up for the max: two laps—a little over three miles," I say.

"Whew! What's a good time for this race?"

"World-class guys can go under an hour. I'm hoping for an hour and a half, but in these conditions, who knows?"

Having made this prediction, I feel uneasy. My training has not been what it should have been this summer. Janet and I moved from Connecticut to Delaware in June. The move has left me feeling flat. My weight is up, and I seemed to have lost the edge.

Another two waves head off, and I am up next.

"Look for me," I say. Hearing Janet's and Paul's good luck wishes, I walk forward with the other white-capped swimmers.

Since registering for this race last month, I have tracked the water conditions here in Chicago. A news report I came across citing city beach closures because of bacterial contamination led me to contact the race organizers. Their terse reply was that "there were no reports of closures here at this Ohio Street Beach this summer."

At check-in this morning, the water temperature hovered at a balmy

72 degrees Fahrenheit. The water is probably too warm for most serious open-water swimmers, but it is fine for me, after spending the last few months in a hot and muggy Delaware.

The cold wind raises goose bumps on me again. I dive under and join the fifty or so other swimmers bobbing about before the start buoy. After adjusting my goggles, I look back and wave at Paul and Janet, who is filming the start. The horn sounds, and I am off.

I am nearing the end of the first lap. I have swallowed water, suffered kicks from other swimmers, been tossed about by the waves, and had my goggles knocked off my face a couple times by wayward waves. My lats and triceps muscles are tired and aching. Weary, I am not particularly motivated to swim the second lap. Passing the start buoy, I pause and stand up. The beach looks enticing. Thinking I might get out and rest or maybe even stop, I take a few halting steps toward the shore, but soon changing my mind, I turn around and in a sort of daze, stumble back into the lake.

Seeing a man and woman are resting near the buoy. I swim over and ask, "Are you going around again?"

"I don't know about him, but I am," says the woman. "Okay. Maybe I'll tag along," I mumble.

Without saying a word, the man swims off and the woman follows. Swimming alongside them, I brace myself for the waves' battering.

After the long solitude of the first long loop, it is a boost for me just to have the opportunity to talk with someone out here. Hacking away at the waves, I think about the time and cost it took to come out here to Chicago for this swim. I would surely have regretted not swimming this second loop.

I eventually round the first buoy, and I am glad to be done with windward swimming. Feeling myself roll in the crosswind, I point myself toward the next buoy. The progress is slow, though. Most of the strength has left my arms and back. My lack of training this summer is showing.

Nearing the next buoy, I move up alongside a fellow swimming the butterfly. Wearing a black wetsuit with a white stripe down its side, he reminds me of a porpoise or small killer whale emerging from the waves. At water level, it is great fun to watch him swim. There are several swimmers swimming the butterfly today. Studying the order of finish after the race, I would learn this fellow is the legendary Thomas Boettcher. According to the event website, Boettcher is "Big Shoulders original butterfly solo 5K ground breaker." Now in his eighth straight year of swimming the butterfly—like me—Boettcher is struggling to round the second buoy.

I sense the wind has picked up. The buoy ahead has been placed outside the stone breakwater's shadow, and large waves are rolling in from the open lake. Swimming in bursts, I creep on. Pausing, I joke with a lifeguard on his kayak about having swallowed half the lake. "Better you than me, man," he says.

Determined to make the turn and be done with this buoy, I bury my head and whip the water. My muscles burning, I watch as Boettcher drops back and wonder if he will be able to round the buoy. Feeling as if I am swimming against a white-gray torrent, I finally reach the large orange tetrahedron float and peer out into the lake.

A mile to the north juts the North Avenue Pier. According to a state geological report, in the summer of 1954, a seiche (pronounced "saysh"), a standing wave brought on by an atmospheric disturbance, reflected off the Indiana shoreline, and eighty minutes later drowned eight fishermen when a ten-foot wave slammed into the pier. The report notes, "Unlike a tsunami, which can travel across the open ocean at hundreds of miles per hour, a seiche moves much more slowly." Nowadays the National Oceanic and Atmospheric Association regularly issues warnings to Lake Michigan mariners and lakeshore residents whenever weather conditions favor seiche development. Although I am no doubt safe from seiches, because of the stone breakwater a half mile or so off to my right, such is the scale of the marine phenomenon that can be encountered on this lake.

Interestingly, Romanian-born Johnny Weissmuller (black-and-white movies' Tarzan) got his start somewhere along the lake shores here. "I started out as a scrawny kid in Chicago, and even that was lucky. It got me to swimming. Then all the good breaks in the world happened and kept on happening," he was quoted as saying.

I would have hoped for a stronger swim on the downwind leg, but stomach pains have nearly sunk me. Swimming a tired breaststroke—the stroke I resisted learning thirty years earlier—now propels me home. I watch Boettcher butterfly by and suppose he was somehow able to round that last buoy.

My cramps abate some, and regaining my crawl stroke, I progress toward the beach. I see Beottcher scramble up onto the sand, and I soon follow. Not thrilled with my performance, I am nonetheless relieved, though, to hear the timing chip on my ankle beep. One hour and fifty-nine minutes was much too long to be swimming in Lake Michigan this morning.

༺༻

Feeling my ears pop and the engines throttle back, I know we have begun our descent into Philadelphia. It is nearly two o'clock in the morning; Janet and I will not arrive home until sometime after three o'clock. I will catch a few hours of sleep before getting up to go to school and teach my classes. My students will ask how the swim went, and I will say no more than, "It was rough, but I finished." Indeed, in a few days the Big Shoulders website will note, "The simple fact remains that everyone who dared set foot into Saturday morning's choppy soup performed some measure of self-testing that they'd never dare on an ordinary day."

THE SWIMMER

On our ascent out of O'Hare Airport, I again gazed down on Lake Michigan, a black expanse unbroken except for an odd boat light. I wondered when, if ever, I would swim there again.

Now on our final approach, I think about my boyhood home and the old lap pool lying out there in the night.

Last summer, when visiting my sister, I stopped by for another look at the pool. I had heard that the house and grounds were on the market, John's father having remarried sometime after John's mother passed away. He was spending most of his time in Washington, D. C.

Feeling the plane's gentle jostling under me; I drowsily recall my visit.

Stepping out of my car I stand for a time looking around. Not seeing or hearing anyone, I walk toward the house. I suppose the decaying doghouse set on top of a small woodpile belongs to the ridgeback Sheba, who is long gone.

Approaching the house, I see its white grout face needs painting. The trees and shrubs appear as I remember them, though. I knock on the kitchen door, but when no one answers, I turn about and walk toward the holly grove.

Nearing the pool, I stop and stand outside the short wire fence. I entertain the idea of hopping over and diving in for a swim, but thinking this too rash, I do no more than stand and gaze about.

The holly trees in the grove appear stouter, but oddly no taller. Somehow time has dulled their green color for me. Like so many old sites when revisited, the lap pool appears much smaller than I remember. The concrete walkway seems to have held up well, and the bordering lawn looks as if it was recently cut. Off to my left stands a tree where we were all amused to spy four or five owlets perched in a row on a branch. Never moving, they did no more than stare knowingly down on us all afternoon.

More memories flood my mind, *but then I hear a door open and slam shut. Turning about, I can make out through the trees and bushes John's father emerging from the house. Clad only in a dark blue bathing* suit, he has a white beach towel slung over his left shoulder. Above his brown, horn-rimmed glasses his white hair shines in the afternoon light. Walking purposely across the lawn, he stares straight ahead, intent on his swim.

My gaze is then drawn to the splashing I hear in the neighboring Miller pool. "Someone is swimming there," I think. I see a muscular fellow climb up the pool steps and vault himself over its green link fence. Wearing only black swim trunks, he starts to jog my way. ...

I am walking back toward my car. The lap pool behind me is empty except for a lone Styrofoam float lazing near where water pours out of a chrome pipe.

CHAPTER 5

Water's Weight

"One woe doth tread upon another's heel, So fast they follow."
—Gertrude in Hamlet

Officially known as the Constitution State, postage-stamp-shaped Connecticut also goes by the name of the Nutmeg State; Connecticut: We're Full of Surprises, when promoting tourism; and the Land of Steady Habits, in reference to its Puritan heritage. Of the state nicknames and slogans, the idea of steady habits is the most intriguing to me. Having now lived a number of years in the Farmington (an old town west of Hartford) historic district, I can vouch for if not the state's moral uprightness, its constancy. Days, months, and even years can pass without the slightest hiccup.

In March, melting snows give way to violet and white crocuses, yellow daffodils, and red tulips. The venerable old oak, maple, and tulip trees along Farmington's Main Street turn green just in time for the Garden Club's June home tour. Summer day lilies, daisies, and lavender clover wilt not long after the October frost, it being what the drab green mums had waited all September for, before initiating their varicolored show. Yellow, orange, and crimson leaves faithfully cover the ground in November, the leaves falling early enough to allow a few weekends of raking before December and January snows blanket the ground. And although the seasons might change, not much else ever does here in Farmington.

Driving north along Farmington's Main Street, one passes an old cemetery. The town's earliest settlers are buried here, and should anyone need a reminder, there is inscribed in black on the graveyard's masonry gate the somber *Memento Mori*. Set in the town center stands the eighteenth-century Puritan meeting house of the First Church of Christ, Congregational, 1652. The church is reminiscent of a multilayer wedding cake, its plain white spire rising above an open, columned belfry, which from certain vantages appears uncannily to hover in mid-air. A town constant, the church bell calls the faithful to service every Sunday morning.

Occupying the land on all sides of the intersection of Main Street and Mountain Road is Miss Porter's School. The plain white sign with black lettering, "Founded in 1843," attests to the fact that Sarah Porter's school for girls has been a Farmington fixture for some time.

Timeless red brick or white-and-black shuttered mansions front most of Main Street. A few of these stand behind high stone or brick walls, while others are set so far back from the road as to be indiscernible. Although a rare tag or estate sale might afford an outsider a glimpse of the life lived inside these manors, from the street, most of these dwellings stand as cold, unapproachable testimonies to the town resoluteness. Generations may come and go and the world may change, but the mansions' message is clear: the town's charming character will forever be preserved.

Habitual, routine, languid, slumberous, or perhaps even in stasis might be apt words when describing Farmington and other parts of Connecticut, but even here in Farmington, no matter of how habitual day-to-day life is, life can change and be irrevocably altered.

This summer is slipping away. Preoccupied with my swimming, I have yet to give my legs the sort of workout they need to be ready for the rigors of an Olympic distance triathlon. I plan to change that today.

The day is hot and dry, and the sky is empty except for a few isolated white puffs as I pedal away from our house on Garden Street. Happy to be shaded by the old silver, Norway, and sugar maples that line both sides of the street, I am also feeling a bit overwhelmed. Trying not to weigh the whole bout of exercise I have set before myself, I say to myself, "One piece at a time." I both love and hate this workout: three repeats of an eleven-mile cycle ride followed by a three-mile run—six pieces altogether. My front porch, soon to be littered with empty sports drink bottles and energy bar wrappers, will serve as my base camp for the next few hours. There is a strong sense of accomplishment at this workout's end, but starting off is disheartening.

The human body is wonderful in its ability to adapt to new demands and stresses. Increase the training workload, and if given enough rest, the body acclimatizes and improved fitness results. Progress soon plateaus, though, if the same training regime is followed. To improve, an endurance athlete needs always to be breaking old habits, to shock one's body to new levels of fitness. This is what I aim to do today. Probably not having athletics in mind, Walter Pater, a Victorian English essayist, nonetheless keenly observed, "To burn always with this hard, gemlike flame, to maintain this ecstasy, is success in life. In a sense it might even be said that our failure is to form habits." Every endurance athlete—even here in steady Connecticut—innately grasps Pater's words.

Turning right onto Meadow Street, I ride out onto the Farmington River flood plain, known colloquially as the Meadows. The town of Farmington leases much of the open land here to tomato, pumpkin, and corn farmers. The sun feels hot on my back and shoulders. Unimpeded by hills or trees, a strong wind out of the west slows my progress.

Before setting off, I stood with Janet in our backyard and watched as a helicopter hovered nearby, partially obscured by some tall trees. We wondered aloud about the noisy craft's mission. Now out in the meadows, I again catch sight of the blue-and-white helicopter. Near its rear rotor, written in blue lettering, I read the words Life Star, but because the road has little or no shoulder, my attention is drawn to the fast-moving asphalt, and I lose track of the helicopter.

I am on the downward slope back to the meadows. The following wind makes the ride a rush. I have been trying out different scenarios on what might have brought the Life Star helicopter here, and then it dawns on me. Since leaving my house, my route has followed the river, and the helicopter has followed me. Of course, there has been some sort of accident on the river.

Back at my front porch, I dismount, gulp some sport drink, and lace on my running flats. Starting off, I shuffle along, my muscles slow in making the transition from cycling to running. I soon envision a different three-mile loop—one that will take me down to the river. Initially hesitant, I vow to return to my usual route after the next cycle piece.

I run west along busy Farmington Avenue. The lack of wind, along with the heat coming off the blacktop, makes breathing difficult. Turning into an access road after a mile or so, I see a fire truck parked a way up ahead. Soon passing a lone fireman sitting in the driver's seat, I follow a dirt road out to the river.

At an overlook, a police officer and several men are busy loading a small boat onto a pick-up truck. They ignore me as I approach. After some maneuvering, I spot a couple of red boats down from where the river bends to the right. The rope swings on the opposite shore are a favorite hangout for the town young. I am surprised, though, to see them hanging still on such a hot day. Farther downriver from the swings, I see a large group of people gathered in a clearing near the river's edge. Having swum in the river there, I have experienced how the water abruptly deepens. A yellow rope with red flags tied along its length runs between the two banks down from the clearing. The rope apparently marking some sort of boundary, I walk over to the police officer and ask, "Has someone been lost in river?"

"Yes," he answers curtly.

Back on Farmington Avenue, I run west and cross the river by way of a rails-to-trails bridge. Running along a wooded trail, I feel somewhat ashamed of my let's-go-see-the-fire interest in this mishap. Rationalizing my decision with plans to get back on my bike soon, I run on, following the river's flow.

Passing a clearing, I watch as a man and a woman stand by while their golden Labrador paddles back to shore with a stick cradled in its mouth. At another clearing, teenagers splash about not far from the riverbank. Near the bend in the river, I stop and listen as a couple drifting downstream on inner tubes are told by an official that they "will be able to go no farther."

Thinking it odd that those so near should be unaware of the mishap, I run a short way before stepping out of the woods and into the clearing.

Clad in whites and blues, I survey the thirty or so rescue personnel gathered here. While a few stand back, most sit on the earthen ground just up from the river. All stare intently out at the flat water. Having driven here from all parts of the state, their jeeps, SUVs, and emergency vehicles have gouged the earth and trampled stalks in a nearby cornfield. Strangely, no one is conversing. As in a library or church, a reverent silence pervades.

Out of uniform, I feel like a voyeur. I expect to be asked to leave, but no one seems to notice me. The run has me feeling thirsty, and I am tempted by the many coolers filled with water and sports drink. One fellow with a blond crew-cut stands out. He looks to be in his thirties, and so fervent is his focus on the river that he seems to be in a trance. I watch as a rescue boat lands and a chestnut-colored

◄ CROSSINGS: A SWIMMER'S MEMOIR

Newfoundland dog is put on board wearing a red rescue blanket. His floppy-eared face makes him so lovable that if we were anywhere else, everyone here would be hugging and ogling him. He takes a seat in the boat bow, and his massive muzzle points the way as the boat motors off. I wonder what role he will play. The Newfoundland breed is renowned for its swimming, but the search has clearly moved far beneath the river's surface.

Upriver, several boats float a short way out from the rope swing. I suppose divers are down there. Although I dare not ask, I can guess that someone went under after jumping off the rope swing. The number of youths using the rope swing made it inevitable that there would be an accident here one day.

I have been standing too long. Not only is my workout finished for the day, but it will also be a chore to loosen up for the run home. Before setting off, I follow a path through a short tract of woods that leads to a water fountain in the nearby town park.

Emerging out of the woods, I am surprised by the number of fire trucks, ambulances, and television station vans I see parked about. Walking through the parking lot, I recognize a female television reporter familiar to me for her on-site TV reports. I soon notice several Hispanic women and young girls huddled near one of the ambulances. Close by, a teenage boy with an Afro haircut sits passively on a concrete car stop, clearly out of place among all the rescue personnel and reporters. I imagine these people are either the family or friends of the victim. "What a lousy place to wait," I think.

Turning away, I jog off to the fountain and then on to home.

Running along Garden Street, I hear Janet call my name. Looking to my left, I see her sitting with a few of our friends on a second-floor open-air porch. Entering the building, I walk up a set of stairs and find them. I ask, "Have you heard about the accident down on the river?" Concerned looks tell me the news of mishap has yet to reach here. Questions follow, and I answer, "Someone was lost near the rope swings. I don't know anything else, but I'm sure we'll hear more about it on the news tonight."

Ending her visit, Janet and I walk across an asphalt parking lot toward Garden Street. A well-kept lawn slopes off to our right to form a wide, shallow depression, once the Pitkin Basin, a turnaround for canal boats on the Farmington Canal. Before the advent of railroads, the canal ran from New Haven on the Long Island Sound north through Farmington before reaching the town of Northampton in the Massachusetts Pioneer Valley. Built largely by immigrant Irish labor in the early eighteenth century, the canal was never financially solvent before soon falling into disuse with the arrival of the railroads. It was here where water claimed yet another soul when Foone, a freed slave from the famed slave ship *Amistad*, drowned in the basin waters. Foone is buried in the cemetery adjacent to the basin. His weathered headstone notes his connection with the *Amistad* and that Foone, a native African, "drowned while bathing in the basin August 1841."

Janet and I learn no more of the afternoon's accident until the late evening, when the TV news reports that a twenty-nine-year old man drowned in the Farmington River. "Carlos, a father of three," says the reporter, had traveled from a neighboring town with two younger boys. Swinging off a rope, he slipped under while trying to swim to the opposite bank. He struggled for a time, but the two boys along with some others were said to have been unable to get to him before he disappeared below the surface. More than four hours later, his body was found by a diver in twenty-six feet of water not far from where he was last seen.

The cameras were rolling when news of the recovery reached one of the Hispanic women I saw in the park. She was no doubt holding on to hope until the end. When told the news, she became inconsolable. A few days later, another afternoon run took me again down along the Farmington River, where I saw life had returned to normal. Boys and girls in their bathing suits were back on the rope swings, laughing and screaming as they flew off into the river. Most did not know, or if they were told, would probably have shown only passing interest in Sunday's mishap. I supposed, even if erected, no memorial commemorating Carlos would last long in face of vandalism or long Farmington winters. Other than Carlos's family, friends, coworkers, and would-be rescuers, few will remember the events of that hot summer afternoon or the soul that was lost.

Not much ever changes here in Farmington, a timeless town set on an ancient river flowing through the Land of Steady Habits.

Like so many Florida coastal towns, Vero Beach is a town of two parts. There are those— typically native Floridians—who live and work on the mainland, and then there are those winter residents or well-off retirees, who reside on the barrier island. Although no distinction is made in Vero Beach, either geography or development can warrant two names for the two halves. Here, Cocoa and Cocoa Beach or Miami and Miami Beach come readily to mind.

North Hutchinson Island—Vero Beach's barrier island—is a twenty-five-mile long strip of plush lawns, royal palms, private country clubs, sprawling live oaks, stucco walls, high hedges, and guarded gates. Not long after moving to Vero Beach, a mainland native related to me, "That island out there runs this town." Dappled with waterfront developments such as John's Island, Orchid Island, The Moorings, and a Disney Resort, Vero Beach, at least for island's residents, is faithful to its Italian namesake; it is a true beach.

Mainland Vero Beach is for the most part a patchwork of modest houses, mobile home parks, and newly built condominiums. Inside the mobile home parks, miniature white picket fences, plastic flamingos, spinning pinwheels, and American flags adorn tidy yards. The narrow asphalt park roads look as if they were paved yesterday, and almost every carport shades a shiny American sedan. Looking like geysers and serving as beacons for those searching for everlasting youth, runoff water rockets up from drainage-pond fountains set outside the many condos and shopping malls.

America's ethnic and racial divisions are readily apparent in coastal Florida towns. The two communities of Gifford and Oslo—one to the north and the other to the south of Vero Beach's business district—are home to Vero Beach's poor blacks. Chain link fences, sandy yards, full clotheslines, and squat cinderblock homes are the sights along Gifford's or Oslo's dusty roads. Migrant Mexican workers arrive sometime in the fall to labor in the orange and grapefruit groves west of town. These workers live in scattered housing, and other than in supermarkets, Laundromats, or walking along the roadside, they are invisible to the casual eye.

For the years my daughter Clare and I lived in Vero Beach, we called a two-bedroom house in a development named Dixie Heights home. Dixie Heights was an apt name, for we were south of town and looking east from my porch, I could watch the masts of slow-moving sailboats in the nearby lagoon. The numerous parked vans, pick-ups, and trailers loaded with shovels, rakes, and lawn mowers spoke of the many Dixie Heights residents who earned their living laboring under the hot Florida sun.

Each morning, while the school where I taught was in session, my daughter Clare and I would leave Dixie Heights and drive north along Route 1. Crossing the Indian River Lagoon by way of the 17th Street Bridge, we would enter the paradise that is North Hutchinson Island.

The bridge's concrete roadbed, like other Florida causeways, climbs gradually atop concrete pilings set into the lagoon below. From the bridge apex, one glimpses the Atlantic Ocean meeting the horizon ahead, and on clear days it is sky blue on aqua. Off to the right, the lagoon stretches south, narrowing with perspective until melding into Fort Pierce. To the north, the Barber Bridge, and beyond it the causeway at Wabasso, both shallowly flex above the murky green lagoon waters. Because of zoning, North Hutchinson Island, snaking low and green along the oceanfront, is free of the many high-rise hotels and condominiums that clutter other barrier islands. After you descend the bridge ramp, one- and two-story houses with sport boats moored beside short docks fill the panorama.

At the end of the bridge, there is no reason to notice a gray stucco one-floor house off to the right. The roar of traffic on the bridge makes the location far from ideal, and although ample, the house is unremarkable by island standards. Inside the rear porch screen mesh, plastic white beach chairs sit empty around a matching table. Outside, two tarp-covered jet skis rest undisturbed on their trailer. The house and its grounds have an unused, if not forlorn, appearance. The small backyard ends abruptly at a concrete seawall. Floating a few yards offshore, tethered to the bottom by cord, is a Styrofoam ring. A wreath fashioned out of plastic green leaves and yellow-white daisies is set atop the Styrofoam. On most days the wreath does no more than bob and roll in the lagoon's gentle waves.

My classes are finished for the day. Having copied quizzes and tests for tomorrow, and with Clare at basketball practice, I can slip out for a run.

Thursdays at school are rife with anticipation. Though not quite the week's end, it might as well be, for tomorrow my students will be preoccupied with planning their weekends. Tests and quizzes are best given on Fridays, as not much else can be accomplished. Should high school students learn any lesson, it is that success in life demands consistent application, and this begins with the five-day workweek.

I know now I was somehow meant to be a teacher, but this was not always the case. While far from being a creator of ideas, I can readily grasp the abstract and recast it concretely. Moreover, I like learning and bouncing ideas off others. Not much of anything else has ever felt as edifying for me as teaching. When employed in other fields, I often felt trapped and suffocated. I used to detest my predilection for teaching, loathing the observation, "you are a born teacher," said once by a person who knew me better than I knew myself. Although I have often felt a little bitter that I was not made for something "better," aging, paying bills, and having a child to raise have softened me. Nowadays, fortunate to have my health and a job I like to do, I sometimes feel embarrassed to have become so misguided years after praying for a vocation in Sister Mary O'Connell's sixth grade catechism class.

Although the day broke cool and clear, the late afternoon February sun has enough strength to make me comfortable running in only a T-shirt and shorts. Off on my usual route through a large housing development and then back along the beach, I exit the school and run south. Normally it is a solitary run through empty streets and over a vacant beach, but today there is a commotion in the air. A police car whooshes north and another soon follows. I then hear the wail from a fire truck pulling out of its nearby station. Not long after, a police helicopter roars north over the lagoon in the direction of the 17th Street Bridge. All then falls quiet. Seeing the crisis is elsewhere, I run on, the ado fading from my consciousness.

Later, on the drive home, Clare and I come upon the emergency vehicles' destination. While approaching 17th Street Bridge, I spot a fire truck parked outside a one-story, gray stucco house. Several firemen, clad in orange jackets, and police, dressed in their official blue, loiter behind the house. A police rescue boat floats in the lagoon not far from home's seawall. There seems to be little sense of urgency among those gathered there. Whatever brought them appears to have passed. Dismissing the gathering to a false alarm, I drive west up the bridge ramp, on toward our home in Dixie Heights

At school the next day, I read in Vero Beach's local paper, *The Press Journal,* a story with the headline, Boy Drowns in River. Backyard Fishing Turns Into Tragedy For Vero Family. The article relates, "A four-and-a-half-year-old boy fishing with his grandmother Thursday afternoon drowned after he fell into the Indian River when she left the boy alone for a few minutes. Garrett's lifeless body was found in nine feet of water, forty minutes after he fell off a dock behind his Point Lane house, next to the east foot of the 17th Street Bridge. Garrett was rushed to Indian River Memorial Hospital, where he briefly regained a pulse before being pronounced dead."

Later that day, I overhear my colleagues discussing Garrett's drowning in the teacher's lounge. Jerry, a fellow in administration, claims to have been in the vicinity at the approximate time of the accident. He expresses his regret, if not guilt, for not being close enough to have saved the boy. Others in attendance undoubtedly harbor similar sentiments.

Fantasizing themselves as rescuers, or silently playing what-if games, they play out (as I do) alternative scenarios: If only I had been there; if only Jerry had noticed something; if only a neighbor had been there; or the most painful, if only Garrett's grandmother had not left him alone.

I also hear my students in between classes speak of the drowning. Unlike my colleagues, the students speak in a distant, detached manner. As teenagers, they have not lived long enough to have suffered firsthand such a loss. Feeling and thinking themselves immortal, they lack empathy and regard the tragedy as just another piece of curious news.

The Press Journal carried Garrett's obituary a few days later, but by then everyone, as is often the case, had moved on to other stories.

Sometime later the newspaper published an article detailing the daily stresses paramedic and rescue workers face in Indian River County. The article cited Garrett's drowning as an exceptionally painful case for the responders, as there was apparently hope of saving him until the end.

I do not remember exactly when Garrett's daisy wreath memorial first appeared in the waters off his home's seawall, but it must not have been long after his death. Of course, I never had any contact with Garrett or his family. I had no mental image of him or knew any more details concerning the accident other than what was reported in the paper. I supposed his grandmother was taking care of him while his parents were at work or running errands. She was most likely entertaining him by allowing him to fish off the seawall until his parents returned.

In the months after the wreath's appearance, I found myself trying to catch a glimpse of it on our morning drives over the bridge. After a storm, I was pleased to see the wreath still tethered to its anchor, floating intact. On some mornings, I could fix the prevailing wind or current by the wreath's direction. Occasionally a bottlenose dolphin or two could be seen surfacing near the wreath. On one Saturday morning, I paddled by the wreath during a kayak race up the lagoon with my school swim team. Nearing the concrete bridge pilings, I paddled past the wreath on my right. Its greens, whites, and yellows appeared strangely alive and vibrant. The high school swimmers, so focused on their paddling, took no notice of the wreath as we spun our kayaks about.

On some mornings when I was descending the bridge, my thoughts naturally turned to Garrett's family. I thought how difficult it must be for them to continue living in that gray stucco house. While moving might offer some release or easing from that awful afternoon, remaining there seemed to necessitate finding some way to create new memories. I do not know if Garret's family ever did move away, but the wreath remained anchored off the house's seawall until the end of our stay in Vero Beach.

༄༄༄

I remember the time. It is well after sunset on a Saturday in June, and I am standing atop a short set of stairs up from our living room. I do not know if it was some sound or a flash of light that brought me out of my bedroom, but somehow I know that a car has just pulled into our driveway outside. Peering through the living room window's translucent white curtains, I see the car's lights go out and then hear car doors close. The front porch light is on, but the curtains obscure the two figures walking toward our house. The front door opens, and I see my father walk into our foyer. His head is downcast. The peeved, disgusted look on his face chills me. He says nothing and does not look at me as he walks into our kitchen. I know the look on my father's face well; it is the look I have come to associate with the worst of times. That he did not greet me adds even more gravity to what must already be a dire situation.

I see my father pick up our black kitchen phone. While I listen to the ratcheting of the rotary dial, my father's mother—Nana Joscelyne, as my sisters and I call her—enters through the front door. She is a not-too-tall woman in her early seventies. Her white hair, which is always curled, set, and sprayed, has thinned with age. Matronly overweight but not obese, she joins my father in the kitchen. Noticing the redness in her eyes, I surmise that she has been crying. I do not recall what exactly is said, but I somehow learn that she is here to babysit my sisters and me while my mother finishes her nursing shift. It seems my father has been unexpectedly called away.

My father left our house sometime that night. I was asleep when my mother arrived home.

A thousand miles or so north of North Hutchinson Island lies another barrier island. Normally not thought of as a barrier island, Ocean City, New Jersey, is an eight-mile long spit of sand no more than a mile wide. Directly south and a counterbalance to Atlantic City, Ocean City proclaims itself as "America's greatest family resort" and prides itself on being a family town. Ocean City was founded as a Methodist seaside vacation town in the 1800s and has been dry ever since. Originally called Peck's Beach, the barrier island had its ecosystem disrupted in the early 1900s when a more than two-mile-long boardwalk was erected atop its grassy dunes. Unpretentious and South Jersey kitsch, during the summer, attractions such as a Mediterranean style white-and-pink music pier, a century-old baby parade, a freckle contest, and a boat parade called A Night in Venice can all be enjoyed while chewing salt water taffy, slurping a gelato, or crunching Johnson's famous caramel-covered popcorn.

First generation Italian American writer Gay Talese, who was born and raised in Ocean City during the 1930s and 1940s depicted a side of the beachfront rarely seen by warm-weather tourists in his prodigious multigenerational saga *Unto the Sons*. "The beach in winter was dank and desolate," and the sea gulls, "when not resting strutted outside locked doors of vacated shops," he writes in the book's opening pages.

While I was growing up in a suburb of Philadelphia, nearly every family I knew had a favorite South Jersey seaside vacation town. Imagining nothing but sun, sand, and surf, none of us gave a thought to Talese's snow-covered beaches or winter gales. Returning faithfully each season to towns named Avalon, Cape May, or Wildwood, all children had a week at the shore as part of their summer plans. Our family—because my mother liked its quaintness—favored Stone Harbor. My father's younger brother, Uncle Ed, vacationed with his wife, Marie, and their three boys each summer in Ocean City.

The next morning is clear and warm when I bring my bicycle to a stop outside a home's open garage. The house is located one block down from my own, and although it has a different color scheme, it has an identical design. After dismounting my bike, I find a pair of wire cutters and snip the wire bindings on some large bundles of *The Philadelphia Bulletin* that lay strewn on the asphalt driveway. After counting out some eighty of the thick newspapers, I find a spot to sit and begin folding the papers in half before cinching each tight with a blue-green nylon stocking top. This folding and tying is an unquestioned ritual I perform every day before loading the papers into my bike baskets and bag. As a paperboy, the ink from front-page headlines such as the Tet Offensive, Nixon's defeat of Humphrey, Robert Kennedy's and Martin Luther King's assassinations, and the Apollo moon missions will all eventually meet my gaze and blacken my hands. Reading is a daily temptation for me, but customers always await.

Today, though, I am oddly drawn to article that is printed in a narrow strip along the front page left margin. The article headline states that a Philadelphia boy drowned at the Jersey Shore. Reading the first few lines of the article, I cringe when my last name jumps out at me from the print. Seeing "Joscelyne" in the text causes me to feel a little like those times in school when a teacher would call upon me and I was unprepared or just daydreaming. Reading farther, I gather the eldest son of Uncle Ed disappeared in the surf off Ocean City late yesterday afternoon. My cousin Edward and I were born within a couple months of each other. It seems impossible to me that he could now be gone. In disbelief, I reread the article, double-checking names and the home address. "My brother is out there," a quote attributed to one of my cousins, screams out at me. Needing to unburden myself, I say, "Hey, my cousin drowned at the shore." The other boys who sit on the asphalt folding their papers show little reaction and say nothing.

Returning home after delivering my newspapers, I walk into our kitchen, and my grandmother greets me saying, "I have some awful news to tell you."

Before she is able to speak, I say, "I know. I read about it in the paper." In talking with her, I learn it is not my oldest cousin who is missing, but the youngest—six-and-a-half-year-old Joseph. "That's not what was in the paper," I say.

"No, it is Joseph," she says. "Your father is staying with your Uncle Ed in Ocean City; Aunt Marie has come home with Edward and John."

Nearly forty years later, I find it curious that my initial sense was correct—it was not my oldest cousin who was lost. *The Philadelphia Bulletin* had somehow confused the names. It seems likely the error occurred when the story was hurriedly pieced together Saturday night, in time for the Sunday deadline. Although the subsequent days' memories are now lost, I do remember coming across a small item in the next Saturday's edition noting that Joseph's body had been recovered off the north end of Ocean City, in the Great Egg Inlet.

Over the years not much was ever discussed at home about the accident that took Joseph's life. My mother sketched a scene where Uncle Ed and Aunt Marie, after arriving at their weekly rental cottage late Saturday afternoon, were unpacking when my three cousins, Edward, John, and Joseph, eager to go to the beach, somehow slipped away. "I never saw the water like it was that day," was a quote she attributed to a lifeguard or perhaps some bystander. In hindsight, a rip current seems to me to be the likely culprit. As it was late in the afternoon when the boys set off for the beach, I have never been clear on what role the lifeguards played that afternoon, or even if they were still on duty. A search was surely begun before nightfall, but the changing currents and tides lessened the likelihood of a recovery with each ensuing day. No doubt the same, "If only..." type of rehashing and second guessing was ceaselessly played out among my parents and relatives, but being young back then, I was, of course, shielded from their remorseful talk.

Joseph's funeral was held on a hot summer morning at a northeast Philadelphia Catholic church named Saint Jerome's. After arriving in our un-air-conditioned Ford Fairlane, I remember walking with my father, mother, and two sisters across the hot asphalt toward the church's plain beige brick facade. Even before we entered the church, perspiration had already matted my polyester shirt to my chest and back. The service was brief and the image of Aunt Ruth shedding tears onto her lap is still vivid. "Joseph was called home for God had a need for him in heaven," was the reason offered by the priest for Joseph's passing.

After the church service, my father drove in line with the funeral procession as it wended its way along the Pennypack Creek toward the family burial plot at the Saint Dominic Church in Holmesburg. Uncle Ed and Aunt Marie hosted a luncheon at their modest red brick home after Joseph's burial. Not long after eating, I was caught up with laughing and playing with my cousins as we reaffirmed our right to life.

Joseph was, what I can remember of him, an extremely likeable and cute boy. Blond haired and freckled, he was doted on by all his aunts, uncles, and his two older brothers—his brothers having endearingly nicknamed him the "little onion head." In time, an oil portrait of Joseph appeared on the wall in my aunt and uncle's master bedroom. As my father and his brother were very close, our family often visited on weekends and holidays. Feeling the weight of their loss, I could never do more than surreptitiously glance at Joseph's image whenever I walked by the open bedroom door.

This tragedy, as might be expected, changed most everyone's summer vacation destinations. Uncle Ed and Aunt Marie never returned to the New Jersey shore, but in place had a vacation home built in the wilds of north central Pennsylvania. Those on my father's side who still had a preference for the ocean journeyed south to the beaches of Delaware and Maryland. My family also quit the South Jersey shore, choosing instead to spend vacations with my mother's family in Canada.

Since Joseph's death I have been to Ocean City twice. One trip was as a newly minted high school graduate riding my Honda Twin motorcycle with some other motorcyclist friends on a mad dash to the sea. After our breakneck rush through Jersey's Pine Barrens, we did no more than stroll aimlessly along the boardwalk, so bored we were with the empty shops and slack ocean on that day.

More than a decade later, on the invitation of a friend, I spent a weekend in Ocean City at the time of the Los Angeles Olympics. Foregoing a Saturday night drive up the coast to the casinos in Atlantic City, I chose instead to remain behind and watch England's Steve Ovett's and Sebastian Coe's changing fortunes on the Memorial Coliseum track.

Early Sunday morning, with the other house guests still asleep, I awoke, and after donning a T-shirt and shorts and tying on my Adidas flats, I ran east into a yellow-white sun. Slogging through the sand, I would run more than five miles that morning and be puzzled by what resembled a dented black stovepipe rising out of the sea. Only later did I learn that it was the sternpost of the *Sindia*, a sailing barque that ran aground during a winter storm years before. Nearing my run's end, the black rock jetties extending out into the ocean jogged my memory. "Jetties are put in to break up the waves," my father told me when I was young. I then recalled overhearing him talking quietly with my mother one evening about the week he spent there helping his brother search for Joseph. "Those rocks were slippery; I could barely keep up with Ed. You know Ed; he's relentless when he gets going," he said. "Those damn rocks, I slipped on them and got cut up."

Coming to a stop, I gazed out over the ocean. I thought back over the years and imagined my father trying to keep pace with his brother as they scoured the jetties for Joseph. I pictured children playing in the sand, oblivious sunbathers, and the horizon's salty-white haze from that time. The thoughts and images made me feel weak and sad. Hearing the gulls' cries and the surf's crash, I could not imagine a more sorrowful and mocking sight than my father and his brother—two solitary figures making their way over the black rocks—ceaselessly looking, but never finding their lost nephew and son.

A beach is the most timeless yet ephemeral of locales. Although seemingly eternal, the quartz grains trod upon today are replaced tomorrow. Like a living being, only when a beach is regarded as an abstract whole does it take on any permanence. The barrier islands along the New Jersey coast have long sandy beaches on their southern ends, thus betraying the prevailing north-to-south sweep of the tides. These tides have long since borne away the shell and sand from those desperate times. Indeed, all have passed on. My grandmother and father; his brother, wife, and Joseph all lie still in close comfort. Only the black rocks off Peck's Beach remain.

Like many other dailies, *The Philadelphia Bulletin*, once the largest afternoon newspaper in the country, folded in 1982 after nearly 135 years in print. A morning paper, *The Press Journal*, continues as the Vero Beach newspaper. The mordant role that these newspapers and an evening newscast played in the above telling is not lost on me. Surely any frequent and singular reading of newsprint or watching of news shows can warp our sense of what in truth are scant mishaps. Mishaps that are, as Joseph Conrad says in his short story, "A Smile of Fortune," "lost in the mass of orderly life like a few drops of blood in the ocean," yet any reflections on water must touch on its lethalness, for the statistics are telling.

Nearly one-half-million people worldwide drown in a given year. Drowning not involving a boat, such as those described above, account for more than 3,000 deaths, or an average of nine people a day in the United States each year. Almost everyone knows someone who has been lost to water or who has been affected by such a loss. Many schools and colleges require a swim test as part of their graduation requirement. These tests are often given at the behest of an alumnus who lost a son, daughter, or some other close relation to water. Despite such measures, none of us can ever be completely made drown proof. No matter how innocuous the setting, we imperil our lives whenever we enter the water. Compounding this d a n g e r is water's pervasive and unrelenting draw. In the weeks after Carlos' death, I would hear of three others who lost their lives while attempting to swim to the "other side" of various lakes and ponds in Connecticut. After each loss, the broadcast images showed the familiar rescue boats, a diver surfacing, and a crowded shore of onlookers. Only a cold front moving across the state could break the spate of deaths. So this raises the question, what can be done? Not too long ago while touring the antique shops along Maine's southern coast with my wife, Janet, I came across and purchased an old book titled *The Swimming and Diving Book*. First published in 1924 and replete with photographs, the book does a good job in depicting aquatic sports at the turn of the century. The book author, George H. Corsan Sr., dedicates his book "to the nine hundred and ninety-nine persons out of every thousand who are incompletely educated in the art of swimming," and in his book foreword, he optimistically hopes "that swimming will be made compulsory in every public school in the world within the next ten years, so that in another quarter century we will hear of no more absurd drowning accidents." Corsan, of course, was not the first to have suggested improved swim education might help solve the drowning problem, but despite his plea and many exemplary grassroots initiatives that have yielded new programs, drowning remains a longstanding problem seemingly without a cure-all.

Of all the vexing characteristics one can attribute to accidental drowning, it is their penchant for striking when we are at our weakest and most vulnerable. These mishaps, by their very nature, seem to conspire with chance occurrences, waiting for that rare, opportune moment to crash in, wreak havoc, and steal lives, and in doing so, they make our rueful second-guessing a moot exercise. Of course our imagining does allow us the opportunity—no matter how brief—to reverse the order of events in our minds and deny their terrible reality. In our own way, we grant ourselves a respite, a cushion so to speak, until the time when we are more ready and able to cope.

It is cruelly ironic that water, the giver and essence of life, should be so deadly. Although we cannot do without water, we can all be sadly undone by it. Every drowning—accidental or intentional—is poignantly sad, and such tragedies are rife in life, literature, and myth. "It is this madness. Nothing anyone says can persuade me," wrote Virginia Woolf only hours before wandering off to drown herself in Sussex's River Ouse.

"Too much of water hast thou, poor Ophelia," says Hamlet's distraught Laertes of his "drown'd" sister. Guided by Hero's lamp, if Leander's nightly swims across the Hellespont to Sestos would rank him among the first to swim, his swims would also ultimately place him among the first also to drown.

Having been knocked over by wave or having slipped beneath the surface of a pool or lake, many of us still harbor memories of burning sinuses and panicky gasps for air from being held under by the suffocating weight of water. It is in this remembering that we mark ourselves among the fortunate saved, and by continuing to venture into the water, we affirm the lives of those countless souls who have shared Carlos's, Garrett's, and Joseph's sad end.

CHAPTER 6

Naiant*

*Of a fish, etc.: represented in fess or horizontally, as if swimming.
—OED

Should one be seriously committed to improving in a sport, nothing does more to instruct and inspire than the study and emulation of that sport's best athletes.

When I was enamored with tennis in the early 1970s, it was a revelation for me to see Rod Laver, admittedly in the twilight of his career, play Czechoslovakian Jan Kodes at Philadelphia's U.S. Pro Indoor Tennis Championships. Using his trademark Dunlop Maxply racquet, Laver was consistently able to topspin and slice his shots into the netherworld of Kodes's court. The Maxply—a whippy and beautifully laminated wood racquet, although sapless compared to today's graphite composites— became a cannon when placed in Laver's Popeye-like left arm. The velocity of the redheaded Laver's shots was astonishing when he hit the then novel fluorescent yellow balls a mere inch or two above the tape of the net. Never hesitating, reaching every ball at the perfect moment, Laver would crouch so low for backhand slices that it seemed he might mash his face into the court carpet. The Czech, continually on the defensive and often out of position, in the end could not even count on his massive calves to save him that evening.

On a warm summer evening a few years later, I sit in the bleachers with a hundred or so other spectators. The sun is fast sinking behind a distant mountain ridge to the west. I have a clear view of the black rubberized track and grassy infield. At first glance, there is little reason to expect the track meet just getting under way should afford any remarkable performances.

In fact, an all-comer's mile race is winding down. Runners of varying ages and abilities straggle across the finish line. A time around four minutes forty-five seconds wins the race and leaves me feeling sorry that I had not entered, but not long after, the crowd stirs when a fellow built more like a NFL linebacker than a runner powers his way once around the track in forty-eight seconds.

My attention is then drawn to the right, outside the track, when I hear a loud grunt. I watch as a discus arcs across the sky. Al Oerter—a four-time Olympic gold medalist in the discus—has come out of retirement and is in the hunt for yet another Olympic medal. Oerter's throws will sail to more than 200 feet this evening

As the light fades, several sprint races are contested along with a mile race for high school boys. With the meet nearing its end, anticipation builds for the evening's marquee event: The Centre County Mile. Still enlivened by the afterglow of England's Roger Bannister's first sub-four-minute mile run in 1954 and Kansas's Jim Ryun's record-breaking mile runs back 1960s, a mile race is the highlight of every track meet.

This evening an exceptional local runner named Greg Fredericks will attempt to break the four-minute barrier. A twenty-one-year old South African runner named Sydney Maree is also entered; he hopes to spur on the browned-haired, slightly built Fredericks. Recently immigrated to United States and now enrolled at Villanova University, Maree waves to the stands when introduced. Other runners are announced, but everyone knows this race is between Fredericks and Maree.

Runners are called to the starting lines, and at the gun's crack, I am amazed at the speed, yet ease, of Fredericks's and Maree's running. With his bulging quadriceps, Maree appears more to shuffle than run along the track. Both runners seem to hover above the ground between their impossibly quick strides.

The crowd roars when a muscled runner, the race's rabbit, leads the field through the first lap in less than sixty seconds. The second lap slips by, and the PA announces the first half-mile was run in under two minutes. His job done, the rabbit jogs off the track, leaving Maree and Fredericks to suffer the third lap alone. The crowd's thunder drowns out the third lap's time as all sense a sub-four-minute mile is within reach. Fredericks surges to the lead along the backstretch, but Maree pounces and bolts by him around the far turn. The crowd is on its feet and yelling wildly. Everyone is transfixed by the pair's struggle, and time seems to come to a standstill. Maree leads around the final turn and fights off Fredericks's final rush to the tape. The roar is deafening when the PA announces that both runners ran in under four minutes.

The race was the first recorded sub-four-minute mile in central Pennsylvania and the first I had witnessed. Ethereal and transcendent, visions of this long-forgotten contest still stir me. As a footnote, both Fredericks and Maree were denied opportunities to compete at the 1980 Moscow Olympics. Fredericks was kept home because of the United States boycott over Russia's invasion of Afghanistan. Maree, a black South African, was cruelly barred from competing because of his country's policy of apartheid. Maree, naturalized in 1984, did represent the United States at the 1988 Seoul Olympics, where he finished fifth in the 5,000 meters.

Occasionally slacking, but most times flowing onward, my desire to improve my swimming has yet to ebb since the first time I took to the water.

From the beginning, the twenty-five-meter pool at the school in Vero Beach where I taught was my swimming classroom. Steve, the pool aquatics director, explained the purpose and use of pool toys such as kickboards, pull buoys, fins, and rotation metronomes. I watched his swimmers struggle against long lengths of rubber surgical tubing tied to their waists. Other times, I saw Steve tether his backstrokers to what look liked short fiberglass fishing poles. "Fish on," he would quip while walking by his thrashing swimmers.

When not swimming myself, I scrutinized age group, high school, and master swimmers as they traversed the pool lanes. A myriad of swim styles swam pass me, but after a year of trying to find my own way into swimming, I was still seeking swimming's Lavers, Oerters, and Marees. I would not have to wait long or look far.

A few weeks into the new school year, I was walking by the pool during one of our mid- morning breaks. Although well into September, the Florida sun still felt overpowering as it illumined the light blue pool bottom. At the far end of the deck, Steve was busy gathering up some fins and kickboards. I was about to shout out a hello when some movement caught my eye.

Beyond the starting blocks, protected by a building shade, stood a tall blond-haired fellow. Wearing a black swimsuit, he was shaking his arms as swimmers do before a race. Straightaway, I noticed his telltale swimmer's torso. Not overly developed, but rippled with taut muscles, his tapered torso stood atop sinewy quadriceps and calves. Plainly, he appeared to be the caliber of swimmer I had never seen.

Having some time before my next class, I unlatched the pool gate and walked over to introduce myself. Although I stand six foot three, I felt small and insignificant as I approached him. Shaking his hand, I learned his name was Mitja and detected a foreign, possibly German accent. By then Steve had joined us.

"So you've met Mitja?" asked Steve. "Yes, I have," I said.

"Mitja will be training with us for the next few weeks," said Steve.

"Oh. What strokes do you swim, Mitja?" I asked.

"Freestyle and backstroke," Mitja said.

Steve then smiled at me, causing me to think he knows more than what he was letting on. Before walking into his office, Steve said, "Mitja is a sprinter."

Chatting more with Mitja, I learned that he is indeed German. I also have my initial impressions about him confirmed when he related that he is training for next year's Sydney Olympics.

Having read Terry Laughlin, in his book *Total Immersion: The Revolutionary Way To Swim Better, Faster, and Easier*, tout Russia's Olympic gold medalist Alexander Popov as the world's supreme swimming stylist, I ventured to ask, "Have you ever swum against Popov?"

"Yes, I have," Mitja answered matter-of-factly.

Over the next weeks, I regularly stopped by to watch Mitja's afternoon practices. Accompanied by his coach Torsten, these practices were models of discipline and purpose. When he was swimming a front crawl, Mitja's hands would creep far ahead before catching the water and quickly vanishing beneath his chest. The manner in which his hands alternately extended on each stroke I came to see as uniquely Mitja's. This trait set his front crawl apart from all the others I had watched; it was his trademark, his own unmistakable signature when swimming freestyle.

Occasionally Mitja would sprint a lap off the starting blocks. Piercing the water with a narrow diver's splash, his dolphin kick propelled him quickly ahead, and just when he seemed to threaten to shoot the pool's length, he would emerge amid white water and stroke so violently that he appeared almost to plane across the water. Standing six foot eight, Mitja needed only a scant twelve or thirteen strokes to swim a lap. I watched as he swam 1,000-meter pieces with clock-like precision, covering each hundred-meter segment in little more than a minute.

Mitja's backstroke was swum with a smooth side-to-side roll while maintaining a narrow, arrow-like profile. Sometimes he would attach a monofin to his feet. Taking a few quick dolphin kicks, he would streak the pool length underwater. Watching from the pool deck, I thought he looked more like a porpoise than a man.

Other than barking German such as *"Schnell, stromlinie,* or *arbeit,"* Torsten was a silent presence during Mitja's workouts.

Steve invited the local newspaper, The Press Journal, to interview both of them. In the article, Torsten noted he was from the former East Germany. Previously a competitive swimmer too, he divulged that a shoulder muscle biopsy was performed on him when he was young to determine his best swimming event. The piece included a color picture of Mitja hoisting a weighted barbell overhead. I thought this an odd photograph to include of a swimmer, but I supposed the reporter wanted to add interest to the story. One of Steve's frequent laments was, "Most people just don't get it," the "it" being swimming. Being, most of my life, one of those singled out by Steve, I was now in the water, frantically swimming to make up for lost time. To watch Mitja swim was a revelation.

On the pool deck one morning, Steve remarked that a check Mitja and Torsten had been expecting from Germany had been delayed and the pair's rent was due. Having had some recent expenses himself, Steve asked if I would be willing to lend them the money. Feeling somewhat foolhardy, I nonetheless wrote them a check for more than a thousand dollars, viewing it as an investment in my swimming education. Although I had the capital to invest and was repaid in full, my weak swimming skills limited my returns to mostly afternoon amusement, rather than any real improvements that fall.

Mitja and Torsten left for Germany in October, but returned to train the following May. While swimming in an adjacent lane, I often caught glimpses of Mitja's strokes as he zoomed by. Steve made an underwater video of Mitja, which revealed to me the drag a swimmer's legs could create. I also studied and was surprised the quick wavy path Mitja's hands followed when he swam backstroke. As with icebergs, I grasped most of swimming's secrets lay hidden below the surface.

All was not unflagging training, though. On one sunny morning I rode my motorcycle south to a fifty-meter outdoor pool in Fort Pierce to watch Mitja swim a time trial. Steve was on the deck when I arrived. While Mitja warmed up, Torsten retrieved some precise hand-drawn graphs from a boxy aluminum case. Charting weekly distances, the graphs detailed Mitja's training during the winter months back in Germany. Chatting with Torsten, I gathered that he thought high-altitude training was not beneficial for a swim sprinter, as the lack of oxygen degraded muscle tissue.

When Mitja indicated that he was ready, Torsten recruited me to film Mitja's swim with their video camera. After taking his mark against the pool wall, at Torsten's command, Mitja threw himself backwards in an arcing dive reminiscent of a bullfrog leaping into a pond. Dolphin kicking far out into the pool, Mitja surfaced and cut the water with a frothy, windmill-like backstroke. Walking along the pool deck, I kept pace with him through the camera's viewfinder. Nearing the far end, Mitja drifted close to a lane line, but held his stroke until somersaulting off the wall. Torsten's husky shouts stinging my ears, I kept the camera steady as Mitja passed by my feet on the pool deck. Mitja extended his arm back over his head, and I watched as Mitja touched the wall, stopping Torsten's watch well under sixty seconds.

Torsten seemed happy with Mitja's time and the thirty-seven strokes he counted while reviewing the tape. Steve, a longtime swim coach, seemed content to sit and quietly reflect. Mitja, meanwhile, had hauled himself out of the pool and lay prone on some nearby aluminum bleachers. His heaving chest and quivering muscles reminded me of a spent billfish lying on boat deck after a battle lost to a rod and reel. While I gazed at his long, extended body, he emanated a new aura; he was naiant.

I more or less forgot about Mitja and Torsten after they returned to Germany sometime that summer. Too preoccupied with my own struggles in the pool, I was also busy planning and packing for my daughter Clare's and my move to New England.

Shortly before moving north, I asked Steve how Mitja fared in the German Olympic trials. "He missed making the team by one hundredth of a second in the backstroke," said Steve. I expressed my surprise, and Steve then remarked, "You know, he trains alone, by himself."

I paused upon hearing this, for as a runner I saw nothing wrong with solitary training. I could not yet appreciate Steve's perspective as swim coach, for I was just beginning to feel water's smothering isolation, its terrible heaviness, and the Sisyphean laps swimmers must endure. Steve had long understood the doubt leading to defeat that water could evoke in a lone swimmer; he knew that when swimming, there is not only safety in numbers, but also inspiration.

Leading up to the 2004 Athens Olympics, meteoric male swimmers with names such as Thorpe, Phelps, and van den Hoogenband received most of the press coverage. When the games were over, American Michael Phelps had won his expected share of medals, but failed to break Mark Spitz's record of seven gold medals from the Munich games. Australian Ian Thorpe again proved himself unbeatable in the 200- and 400-meter freestyle, while fellow countrywoman Jodie Henry took up the mantle as the world's fastest female swimmer with a world record in the hundred-meter freestyle. Although failing to break his own world record, Holland's Pieter van den Hoogenband was able to retain the title of the world's fastest swimmer by winning gold in the men's hundred-meter freestyle, but not even Alexander Popov, with his impeccable front crawl, could resist aging, as he failed to medal in his fourth consecutive Olympic Games.

Not willing to be held hostage by hours of ads, I watched few of the Olympic swimming broadcasts. Four years removed from Florida, I had not heard from Steve and had lost track of Mitja. I assumed that he might have been injured or had again not qualified for the German team.

Having been asked to help coach my school swim team, I was attending preseason swim coach clinic in New Jersey when I was surprised to run into Steve.

After getting over his initial shock of seeing me at swim coach clinic, he said, "You remember Mitja, don't you?"

"Sure."

"Well, he sent me a postcard. He won a silver medal in the 400-meter freestyle relay with van den Hoogenband and those guys."

Initially at a loss for words, I blurted, "But he's German!"

"Yeah. The Germans were not helping him out, so he moved to Holland a year ago." "Unbelievable," I said.

After the clinic was over, I looked up the results on the FINA (the governing body for swimming) website. Showcasing eight lanes of the world's thirty-two fastest swimmers, including Americans Crocker, Phelps, Walker, and Lezak; Australians Klim and Thorpe; and Russians Pimankov and Popov, the Dutch team with Mitja swimming the second leg and Pieter van den Hoogenband the anchor leg did in fact win the silver medal.

I was happy for Mitja after hearing Steve's news. Snooping around the web some more, I learned Mitja finished first at the 2001 German Nationals in the hundred-meter freestyle, but a hand injury prevented him from competing in that year's World Championships. A back injury also kept him from competing in World Championships two years later in Barcelona, Spain. I came to see Mitja as the prototypical modern athlete: committed, highly conditioned, scientific, and apparently willing to pursue athletic success across international borders. I supposed it did not rest lightly on the German swim officials that Germany finished last in the Athens 400-meter freestyle relay final, and Mitja swam a faster leg than two of the four German swimmers.

English runner Roger Bannister, in his book, *The Four-Minute Mile*, espoused the view that an athlete must be more than just a body in training. Believing sport to be preparation for life—a man or woman being called to do something more meaningful—Bannister saw sport as an avocation, albeit possibly an intense one. His was a noble ideal, but it is a naive view to hold nowadays. As long as my competitors are willing the train in lieu of other pursuits, I will be forced to do likewise, if I too wish to remain competitive. With a supreme prize such as an Olympic medal everyone's goal, athletic training will always escalate much like a nuclear arms race. No one reaches the Olympic podium these days without making their sport their life.

There is the sound of heavy rain falling when my alarm awakes me. Turning on a desk lamp, I crawl across the mattress and peer out the screened window. The cold rain spattering on my face and the black sky make me feel discouraged.

After shaving and getting dressed, I pack up and walk downstairs to the kitchen. Over cereal and juice, I study the map my daughter Clare lent me last evening. Although still not clear on my route once I enter Quebec, I fold the map and stow it in my backpack. Double checking that my wallet contains my tickets, I walk down a flight of stairs and brave the rain with a flimsy umbrella.

While I am driving north out of the downtown, the rain continues to pour down. In the predawn darkness, I can do little to keep the wheels on my Honda Civic from finding every pothole. I drove up here to Burlington, Vermont, yesterday and spent the night in a house Clare shares with other college students this summer. Off to an early start, I am driving to Montreal to attend the World Swimming Championships. Founded in 1908, the Swiss-based Federation Internationale de Natation (FINA) has staged the World Swimming Championships on a regular basis since 1973. The first ten world championships—beginning with the inaugural competition in Belgrade, Yugoslavia—have all been contested outside North America. Not since the 1996 Olympics in Atlanta has there been such a high level swimming competition so close to home. But even more importantly, I will see Mitja swim today.

Daylight has returned as I near the Canadian border. The overcast sky is breaking up and the rain has abated some. From a rise on the interstate, I catch sight of Lake Champlain. Hemmed in by the low green hills of Vermont and New York, the distant lake reminds me of the silvery-gray puddles that used to form in my childhood home's lawn after a summer thunderstorm.

When I drive up to a Customs checkpoint, an attractive young woman greets me. I state my purpose while showing her my tickets to today's swim events. "Oh yes. I know where you are going. Take the Jacques-Cartier Bridge," she says with a French accent.

"Thanks. I'll look for the signs," I say. Upon entering Quebec, I find the roads dry, and the sky up ahead reveals patches of blue.

Driving across the flat farmland, I reflect on these hardy French Canadians and the land they inhabit. They have carved out a life up here that many of us back in the States frankly consider uninhabitable. True, New York has its cold North Country, Vermont its quaint Northeast Kingdom, and Maine its wild Aroostook County, but for most of us who live well south of the Canadian border, locales such as these are our frontier; they are our outposts—the end of the road, so to speak. These locales are where our energies and perhaps our wills fail. More than mere geographical terminuses, places such as these stand as psychological blocks. Viewed by many Americans as cold, rugged, and foreboding, these are usually thought best left to eccentrics, outdoor types, or just wildlife.

I once heard a Vermont poet of some renown speak of life in that state. As he spoke, I sensed what was for me a timid and insular Vermont. "Should you wish to speak to a neighbor in Vermont," he said, "you drive your car and park it outside his house and wait. Should he too wish to see you, he will come out when he is ready."

How provincial, I thought. Could it really be that Vermont had adopted such a silly custom, when only a few hours' drive to the north stands Montreal, a vibrant, international city of more than a million people speaking a language other than English?

We cringe and shrink before those fellow Americans who brave our northern climes in small cabins, while just north of our borders, these Canadians have been raising glass-and-steel towers to the sky. Geography and climate—often no more than mental barriers—are of course in the end all relevant. For Quebec too has its overawing northland tersely named Du Nord.

I follow the signs to Montreal and soon cross over the Saint Lawrence River. I see my destination—Ile Sainte-Helene—marked by the steel geodesic dome erected on the island. The distant silver dome is a remnant from Montreal's Expo 67. As a boy, I received commemorative keepsakes from my Canadian relatives bearing the dome's image.

Realizing I have missed a turn, I continue across the bridge and ask directions from a young fellow at a bus stop. Driving north now, Habitat 67 (a Lego-block-like apartment complex from the Expo days) jogs my memory as I pass it on my right.

Parc Jean-Drapeau consists of a pair of islands—Ile Sainte-Helene and manmade Ile Notre-Dame—both set in the middle of the Saint Lawrence River. Previously named Parc des Iles, the two islands were renamed a few years ago in honor of longtime Montreal mayor Jean Drapeau. Drapeau was responsible for bringing Expo 67 and the 1976 Summer Olympics to the city.

Turning into the park, I find parking near the dome. The Pavillon des Baigneurs—House of Bathers—is a short walk away. Waiting outside, I look for Mitja among the throngs of arriving swimmers. There is no sight of him, but I do see Australia's Michael Klim and Japan's gold-medal breastroker, Kosuke Kitajima, pass by.

The gates eventually open, and I find a seat in the bleachers. Sporting events such as this are incomparable when viewed live, as television fails to capture the event's color or scale. I first realized this fact when my father took me to a twilight doubleheader at Philadelphia's old Connie Mack Stadium. Remembering the green infield, the whack of the ball in the catcher's mitt, and the smell of popcorn in the night air, I am no less impressed by the splashes of red, yellow, and blue I see in the pool below.

The pool begins filling with swimmers, and officials dressed in white are everywhere. I study strokes, starts, turns, and finishes, looking for both the familiar and new, anything that might help my swimming. I see a fellow swimming with a Finis snorkel and another performing a kicking drill on his side. Right beneath me, a Brazilian woman is practicing backstroke starts.

I strike up a conversation with a fellow named Rob from western New York. About my age, he has purchased tickets for the entire week. More a fan than a swimmer, he has traveled here with his family.

Rob relates the pool, the warm-up pool, and the diving pool were all reconstructed for these championships a few years ago. He agrees with me that we are fortunate to be here, as cash shortfall by the Canadian organizers caused FINA to pull the championships out of Montreal last January. FINA reversed its decision a month later.

After the Canadian National Anthem is played, the morning competition gets under way with heats of the women's fifty-meter backstroke. There are many open seats in the stands, as finals are contested only in the evening. I enjoy watching these races though. The fastest swimming may not take place this morning, but the myriad of competitors makes the heats interesting.

From Rob's heat sheets, I see Michael Phelps will swim the hundred-meter freestyle and the 200-meter individual medley this morning.

The backstroke heats conclude with Germany's world-record-holder Janine Pietsch easily qualifying for the semifinals.

As the hundred-meter freestyle heats get under way, I am surprised by the large numbers of swimmers of color. Since only swim finals are usually televised, it is not hard to view competitive swimming as largely a white sport, but from up here in the stands, it is obvious that swimming is now a global sport. Swimmers from Cuba, Columbia, Kuwait, Angola, Mozambique, Thailand, the Republic of the Congo, and Suriname all climb the starting blocks, dive in, and swim their fastest. While they will not qualify for the semifinals, by swimming, they set a standard for their countrymen to improve upon.

Mitja is slated to swim in the fourteenth heat. As the heats progress, not only do the times become faster, but also the swimmers grow taller. Others have commented on this trend. Terry Laughlin writes as follows:

> If you watched the finals of the hundred-meter freestyle at the 2000 Olympics, you might have noticed something striking about the finalists: They look like they would make a pretty decent basketball team. In fact, the fastest men averaged about six feet five, while the fastest women were five feet ten or taller. All things being

equal, this gives a six-foot-six swimmer an advantage of approximately ten yards over a six-foot swimmer in a one-minute race. Thus, the price of admission to a final where everyone swims about two meters per second (forty-eight to forty-nine seconds for hundred-meters) is a body that's about two meters tall.

Cecil Colwin, writing in his book *Breakthrough Swimming*, concurs. "The tall, lean swimmer appears to have the advantage of being able to apply force against the resistance of water through a greater range of movement. Today's top male swimmers are rarely under six feet two, while most of the top female swimmers stand five feet eight or taller."

New theories on what constitutes the perfect body type for a sport are always being proposed. One often hears phrases such as this: he or she represents the sport's new prototype. And it is true, in the short term, the medal winners' physiques match the sporting pundits' models. The theory works fine until some outlier appears. By breaking all the records, he or she issues a new revolution, overthrowing all the accepted sporting wisdom.

As with the human heart, the hydrodynamics of swimming are not very well understood. Surely there are parameters that govern swimming speed, but the fascination of swimming—as with any sport—comes from its small surprises and its improbable outcomes. The day when science has the final say will be the end of sport.

The swimmers in Mitja's heat are on deck. I catch sight of him as he removes his warm-ups. He stands before the starting block wearing a full body swimsuit emblazoned with Holland's orange and blue colors. Walking up to the edge of the pool, he bends forward and splashes water onto his face before donning his goggles. The swimmers are called forward and take their places before the starting blocks. Trying to burn off the nervous energy, some shake their arms or kick their feet. Others merely stretch their arms behind their heads or twist their torsos. All look somewhat sinister in their close-fitting suits and dark goggles.

The starter commands the swimmers to step up. I focus on Mitja standing atop his starting block. At six feet eight, he is the tallest in his heat. Taking his mark, Mitja bends down and grasps the block. The horn sounds, and Mitja, along with the other seven swimmers, launches himself forward.

Whenever Mitja practiced his starts back in Vero Beach, I was always impressed with his initial glide underwater. Compared to Steve's high-school swimmers, Mitja's start shot him so far out into the pool that should he have swum against any of them, the race would have been decided before the first stroke. But the Olympic-sized pool here makes him appear minuscule. Surfacing, I can see he is already in trouble. The two swimmers on his left are ahead. Compounding this fact is that his stroke appears sluggish. His turnover is too slow. Because he is tall, his strokes carry him far forward, but any advantage gained is lost to his slow stroke rate. Watching him swim, I mark the familiar sight of his hands extending far forward before catching the water.

After the turn, Mitja is in third place, a half a body length behind the other two swimmers. I hope for a fast finish from him, but I know water's resistance makes a come-from-behind victory almost impossible.

Mitja touches the wall in third place. He is the last to climb out of the pool. Watching him stagger off the pool deck, I recall his exhausted state that morning in Fort Pierce years ago.

Mitja's time placed him out of the top sixteen needed to advance to the evening semifinals. In the ensuing heats, I marveled at the swimming of Michael Phelps, Roland Schoeman, Jason Lezak, and Michael Klim as they all qualified. The progress in swim training and technique has been such that the slowest qualifying time from this morning was faster than the time USA's gold-medal winner Jim

Montgomery swam nearly thirty years ago in the 1976 Montreal Olympics.

Italy's Filippo Magnini had the morning's fastest time and would go on to win the gold medal the next evening. Not as tall or as muscular as some of the other swimmers, he proved physicality was not necessarily a prerequisite for fast swimming.

The morning session concluded with the women's 200-meter butterfly and men's 200-meter individual medley heats. In the latter, with his chin just grazing the water's surface, Michael Phelps showed his complete dominance by taking control of the opening butterfly leg before cruising through the back, breast, and freestyle legs. While watching him swim, I discerned that Phelps's deep underwater turns played no small part in his success.

In P. H. Mullen's book *Gold in the Water*—a chronicle of U.S. swimmers preparing for the 2000 Sydney Games—Mullen refers to the world's best individual medley swimmer as the "king of swimming." Whereas the United States' Tom Dolan was the Mullen's king in the 1990s, today it is multi-world-record-holder Michael Phelps.

Near noon, the morning session ends. I leave the stadium and head back to my car. A light rain has begun to fall. After my early morning wake-up and long drive up here, I feel drowsy. Reaching my car, I recline in the front seat. Cracking open my driver's side window, I nod off, occasionally waking when the odd raindrop smacks my face.

Refreshed, I step out of my car and walk across a short bridge to Ile Notre-Dame. To my right stands the futuristic-looking French and Quebec Pavilions from Expo 67. Their original purposes mostly forgotten, these stark white, soaring structures now house the Casino de Montreal. Walking on, I come upon the Olympic rowing basin. The basin is deserted except for a solitary sculler stroking my way. The concrete stadium near the finish line appears weathered, and grass is pushing up through the cracks. The drizzly, chilly air and large vacant space here leave me feeling forlorn. Once the site of Montreal's grand debut, Ile Notre-Dame now seems very much abandoned.

Back on Ile Sainte-Helene again, I sit in an indoor café set underneath the geodesic dome. The café is an annex to a complex that was once the United States Pavilion. The complex now houses an exhibit dealing with water-related environmental issues. I think of buying a ticket to the exhibit, but instead settle down to read Knut Hamsun's novel, *Hunger.* An engrossing book, I find it especially poignant for anyone who has tried to write.

Before purchasing tickets for these championships, I e-mailed Mitja to confirm his participation. In his reply, he thought we might get together while I was here. Since he is out of the championships and I plan to return to Burlington tonight, I doubt if I will see him.

With several hours to go before tonight's session, I close Hamsun's book and compose some questions for him. ...

Hallo, Charles! Finally I found some time to answer all your questions as good as possible for me.
What were your favorite sports to play when growing up in Germany?

My favorite sports in Germany were basketball and American football. Next to these, I played handball a lot.

When did you begin to swim competitively?

I learned swimming when I was three years old and I liked it a lot. I started to swim in competitions when I was about twelve and thought it was great, but when I got about fourteen I was bored of it and started all the other sports. In 1992 I saw swimming at the

Olympics and decided to try it again to reach the level I saw the guys on TV had.

Are there any swimmers you have admired or modeled your stroke after?

I would say Alexander Popov was the one swimmer whose stroke I tried to copy, and who I really liked to look at.

Do you depend on your arms or legs more when swimming the freestyle? Do you have a favorite training aid, such as kickboard or pull buoy?

I like swimming arms better than legs when swimming the whole stroke. I guess my favorite item is the pullkick from ARENA.

How important is dry land training for you?

I train on land three times a week. The last six months I was injured and couldn't train there too much, but I did pretty good in all the competitions I swam. So I wouldn't say it has to be done. But I still find it's important. Maybe I would have swam faster if I would have done it. You can never tell.

Do you follow a special diet?

I do not follow a special diet except after my vacations, when I gained a few pounds and try to get back to my competition weight.

Your moving to Holland in 2003 earned you a silver medal at Athens. Could you comment on the circumstances that led to your decision to move?

CROSSINGS: A SWIMMER'S MEMOIR

I moved to Holland because of arguments with the German Federation about how far I could get with my swimming, and because of the small support they gave me.

How are you now regarded in the German swimming world? Are there any lingering hard feelings either way?

I still have contact with all the German swimmers and they all come and congratulate me when I swam good. The head coach still has problems with this. So there are no hard feelings for me as long as I can talk to all the swimmers.

Do you train often with Pieter van den Hoogenband? In your view, what makes him the world's fastest freestyler?

I train with Pieter once or twice a day. He's got a lot of talent and lives his sport. And of course he has to worry about nothing anymore.

Are you still coached by Torsten?

Since I moved to Holland I am coached by Jacco Verhaeren, who is also the coach for Pieter van den Hoogenband, the World record holder and two time Olympic champion. I still have contact with Thorsten and see him nearly every week.

In the United States, a great emphasis is put on the "medal count" at each Olympics. Athletes here are under pressure not only to win for themselves, but also for their country. Excessive nationalism and patriotic pride evidently also continues to exist abroad. Would you like to see a greater emphasis on the athlete and less on their country at future Olympics?

I always said, in every interview I gave over the last years, also regarding to have switched my nationality, I never swim for a country. Everything I do in swimming is only for me, or if I swim in a relay for the three other guys who are standing next to me before the start. After the victory ceremony in Athens it was really great to see how many Dutch people where in the stadium to cheer for us. Nearly everything was orange. There I changed my opinion a little bit. I would still say I do it for me, but it's also nice to win for a country. I think the Olympic Games is the goal for every athlete and for every athlete this is a time he or she will always remember. Just being together with all the others in one big valley is great. You eat next to people you just know from TV and you never expected them to be like you.

Do you see any big changes in swimming technique in the coming years?

I don't think there will be any big changes in techniques of swimming. The only thing that will change will be the suits. They will find better and better suits for making people swim faster.

Obviously you were not happy with your time in the preliminaries of the hundred-meter freestyle in Montreal. Looking back now, how might have you trained differently? Did you have a good taper?

My training in Montreal and the training camp in Ottawa was great. I swam times I have never swum before and I really thought on a good day I could make the finals. Actually, I and my coach also think after on we should have set in the taper about four or five days later. Maybe two or three might have been enough, too. But I only have trained with Jacco for two years and it is pretty difficult for a coach to find the right day to start the taper with his swimmer. But I think we are on a pretty good way right now.

What are your plans after you retire from swimming competition? Do you plan to coach?

After swimming I plan a break of about six months to travel around the world. After this I can imagine to start coaching and give the knowledge I've got to other swimmers who might have the same dream I had. (So if you have a swim team at your college let me know about it). :-)

What advice would you give to a young person who wants swim in the Olympics?

Try to get a good technic, know that there is also a life beside the pool, and never lose the fun in training.

I hope I could answer all your questions. If you have any others just write another mail and I will try to answer it a little bit faster next time.

Greetings, Mitja

Mitja took the time to answer my questions early in the New Year. In another e-mail, he expressed his disappointment in not advancing beyond the preliminaries and missing the opportunity to see me in Montreal. As I could have guessed, he stayed in his hotel room, away from the evening races. For me, though, it was enough to have seen him swim again, years after his stays in Vero Beach.

As the above narrative relates only the events surrounding the morning swim session, I should comment on the evening competition, how I marveled at Michael Phelps's swims, was awed by the sheer speed of the hundred-meter freestylers in their heats, rose to my feet with the crowd to cheer on Australian Grant Hackett's world record swim in the 800-meter freestyle, and—while turning away the odd panhandler or two—was distracted by Montreal's many columned buildings and pantinated statues and lost my way, while driving back to Vermont. But to say more than this would be anticlimactic, for when Mitja's world championships ended, so in a way did my interest in the whole adventure.

Although Mitja's swimming career is not yet over, it is unlikely he will achieve the fame of a Spitz, Thorpe, or Phelps, but to have swum in an Olympics, to have won an Olympic medal, and to be forever known as an Olympian is for me, a mere water thrasher, otherworldly.

.

CHAPTER 7

Now a Triathlete

Swim, bike, run—the summer play of children.

Northern transplants to Florida often lament the loss of seasons. For the years that I lived in Vero Beach, I came to know that there were seasonal changes, but these changes were subtle, not gross. March's fragrant light air, July's wilting sun, October's warm days, and January's chilly mornings supplanted the cold rains, muggy days, falling leaves, and drifting snows of the North. In coastal Florida, one senses the change of seasons more than seeing them. I remember there was one evening in March when the air, soft and effervescent, was infused with the odor of orange blossoms. It was then that I realized that Florida, at least in Vero Beach, did have a spring.

The initial euphoria I felt for the progress I was making after first taking to water one November vanished when I saw my swimming stall the following February. Steve, the swim coach at the school where I taught, was busy with his age group and school swimmers and had little time or patience for my wallowing and thrashing. It was not until the summer, when I purchased Terry Laughlin's book, *Total Immersion: The Revolutionary Way to Swim Better, Faster, and Easier*, that I again made progress.

Partly out of frustration over my lack of progress in the pool and

NOW A TRIATHLETE

partly because I had registered for my first triathlon in April, in March I abandoned my school pool for the ocean off Vero Beach's Humiston Park. Here, on a stretch of beach just south of the park, I sprinted into the surf, swam parallel to the shore, and ran back up onto the beach. With my chest heaving, I recovered by jogging slowly back up the beach.

My markers when swimming were a pair of wooden access stairs. Arching over the dunes, these stairs were set a couple hundred yards apart. Beneath the stairs, I would jump up, and grasping a step, do a few pull-ups before dashing off into the surf for another round. The beach there was unguarded, and despite discomfiting images of sharks, these workouts were great fun; I had every reason to expect a strong performance at the Great Clermont Triathlon.

The night air is heavy with humidity as I step out my front door. I awoke at three this morning, and now, half an hour later, I am relieved to be finally getting under way. Before leaving, I make one more mental check, making sure my road bike, helmet, racing flats, cycling shoes, towel, goggles, and swimsuit are all lashed and loaded. Driving north toward town, I reach Oslo Road, and turning left, drive west. The road is dark and deserted. With their firefly-like eyes, raccoons, possums, and prowling house cats mark my approach. Entering Route 60, I leave coastal Florida and drive through miles of sandy wet lowlands flush with pines and saw palmetto. Patchy dense fog slows me; I stick my head out my driver's side window to help find my way. I play with my car's high and low beams, bouncing them off the fog to see which works best. Passing the Desert Inn at Yeehaw Junction, I follow or lead lone cars through the flat cattle land—the land of the Florida cracker. Reaching Lake Wales, I turn right and head north. Streetlights, lit gasoline plazas, and a four-lane divided highway are a welcome relief after the desolation of the two-lane blacktop. Nearing Clermont, a car with a green Celeste Bianchi bike tied to its trunk speeds by. "Another triathlete," I think. The fog begins to dissipate some as I drive north into Florida's hilly, limestone spine. The gray dawn reveals a long hill, and I say aloud to myself, "The bike leg is going to be interesting."

Passing the Clermont Citrus Tower, I next follow a sign to Waterfront Park. Two lean women out on a warm-up run tell me where to park. After unlashing my bike, I walk over to pick up my race packet and have my limbs marked with my race number and age. A carnival atmosphere pervades here at this first triathlon of the season. Like the Daytona 500, the Masters Golf Tournament, the Kentucky Derby, and the Indianapolis 500, the Great Clermont Triathlon is—albeit on a much smaller scale—another celebration of winter's passing.

Amid the hundreds of aluminum, steel, titanium, and carbon-fiber-framed bicycles, I arrange my bike and gear in the transition area. Studying my outdated road bike—poorly suited for a triathlon because of its lack of aerobars—I reassure myself, imagining the fitness level of many of my competitors does not match their bikes' technology.

Little concerned with twenty-mile bike ride or the five-mile run, I walk over to a small white sand beach that fronts Lake Minneola. Feeling uneasy about the swim leg, I plan a warm-up in the lake before the race starts. Against the lake's distant opposite shore, the one-third-mile swim course appears minuscule. Swim out, turn left at a tetrahedral orange buoy, swim parallel to the shore until reaching the next orange float, turn left, and then swim back to the shore. It is simple. All I need to do is swim three sides of a rectangle—two widths and one length. Reduced to this abstract, the swim this morning will be easy, yet I am unsettled.

Wading out into the lake, I take solace in the warm, calm water and soft sand bottom. I am struck by the lake's reddish tea-colored water. I recall swimming years ago in a New Jersey lake of similar hue. The terms *tannin water* and *cedar water* came to my mind. Later

NOW A TRIATHLETE

I would learn the lake's dark tint is because of the bordering cypress trees, and although the water is clean enough for swimming, its lack of clarity can sometimes close the beach.

After fitting my goggles, I stroke out toward the first buoy. The opaque water makes me feel uncomfortable, and I frequently stop swimming to look about. I keep the shore in sight and mark the position of other triathletes out for their warm-up swim. A young woman alternating between breast, back, and front crawl strokes glides by; she reminds me what a novice I am. Lacking the nerve to swim so far off the beach, I turn back before the first buoy. Closer in, I make short swims parallel to the beach. Back on the sand, I trust the resolve and courage to round the first buoy will emerge come race time.

As the triathlon start nears, a swimsuit-clad throng gathers on the beach. Competitors are segregated into groups called waves, according to gender, age, and ability. My wave is scheduled next to last, the final wave being men's Clydesdale (men weighing more than 200 pounds). One's swim cap color identifies one's wave. With arms crossed across my chest, I feel somewhat naked standing on the beach watching the first wave of elite men swim off. Hunter Kemper, America's premier triathlete, is in this wave.

Drafting, unlike during the cycle leg, is legal, and the swimmers fall into a pace line behind the leader. I fix on the leader, who vaults his body out of the lake every few strokes to fix his direction. The swimming prowess of this wave causes a false confidence to rise in me. "This swim will be easy," I think.

A new wave is set off every five minutes. With the numbers on the beach dwindling, I repeatedly check the electronic timing chip wrapped about my ankle, readjust my goggles, and tug on my pink swim cap. Moving to the rear of my wave, I listen for the starting horn. Hearing the blast, I wade slowly into the lake, letting the stronger swimmers go ahead. This being my first open water swim, I am content to follow. I desire only flat water and unimpeded swimming.

I am relaxed as I near the first buoy, but a collision with a swimmer upsets my stroke. Regaining my rhythm, I round the buoy. I am moving well and swimming within myself when the same panic that seized me once on a snorkel outing in Sarasota, Florida, paralyzes me. Hoping to compose myself, I flip onto my back to swim a weak backstroke. This move is of little help, as swimmers, orange buoys, kayaks, and the dark water all swirl about me, adding to my panic. The beach looks distant. The thought of being so far off shore, in deep water, terrifies me. An odd drop or two of water finds its way down my windpipe. My coughs, wheezes, and the sense of constriction in my throat and chest add to my misery. The previously foreign thought of drowning flashes across my mind.

Somehow I manage to suffer my way around the second buoy, but as I swim on toward the finish banner on the beach, my panic returns. I notice a rescue kayaker has taken an interest in me. My eyes meet his, and I want nothing more than for him to come over and paddle me in. Not in any way enjoying myself, I want to be out of this damn lake and back on dry land. Seeing through my mind's charade, I persevere toward the beach. A few bulky Clydesdales that started five minutes behind me underscore the ignominy of my swim by lumbering past me as I scramble onto the sand.

Several miles on my bike would pass before the tense hollowness in my chest lifted. Despite a pedestrian time of nearly twelve minutes for the swim, I would finish ahead of a couple other competitors. During the cycle and run portions, I made up some time, finishing in the middle of the 400 men who completed the triathlon.

The late morning sun made the last few miles of the run uncomfortable. Afterwards I was happy to sip from a water bottle while basking in Lake Minneola's shallows. I felt proud to have completed my first triathlon. Later, though, while I was driving north out of

NOW A TRIATHLETE

Clermont en route to Jacksonville to serve on a school evaluation committee, my mood changed; I could and must do much better.

The Great Triathlon Clermont released a torrent of physical activity in me. In the ensuing months, I suffered dry heaves to earn a medal in a run-bike-run event on a hot morning in Fort Pierce, traveled north to Melbourne with my cross-country team to run a road race benefiting sea turtles, joined my school swim team for kayak workouts in the Indian River, won my division in an ocean swim-beach-run biathlon, ran a cross-country race at the L.A. Dodgers' Dodgertown, and finished my second triathlon again up north in Melbourne. In this last race, I was hampered by leaking and fogging goggles. Near the swim's end, I felt helpless when a seeming horde of women from the trailing wave swam over me. The blood running down my shin after I walked into a submerged concrete block while exiting the water made me vow never to enter this event again.

Despite my growing collection of baubles and trinkets, when it came to swimming, I was profligate. No rounds of cycling or running, no matter how intense or large in number, could improve my swimming; for this I needed time in the water.

In preparing for triathlons, I naturally developed an interest in open-water swimming. Given salt water's buoyancy and my past failures in pools, I came to share the view of Phineas, from John Knowles's *A Separate Peace*, who said, "Swimming in pools is screwy anyway. The only real swimming is in the ocean." One fellow I met ranked ocean swimming easier than pool swimming and thought fresh-water swimming in a lake was the toughest. He was right, for compared to the pool at school, I was a much stronger swimmer in the ocean. Looking for new challenges, I fell into a routine of swimming the 1,000-meter buoy line that stretched north from Humiston Park. Upon reaching the buoy line end, I either swam back or ran down the beach before bicycling home. I felt gratified after these workouts, and Humiston Park became my favorite swimming spot.

More than a year has passed since Clermont, and I am now lost, driving along in the pre-dawn hours on a Sunday morning. Making a right off the main highway and then a left onto a side road plunges me into a mishmash of campers and mobile homes. I pass two women who stand next to the road. One appears to be holding up the other. Obviously headed in the wrong direction, I turn around. When I am passing the pair again, the one who was having difficulty standing grins and beckons me to stop. "It must have been quite a Saturday night for those two," I think.

My situation is embarrassing, if not desperate. My entry fee will be wasted if I miss the triathlon start. On the third time by, I turn into Winter Haven's Cypress Gardens to ask for directions. An attendant motions me on, and I catch sight of the bike transition area down in a circular hollow. I feel like a fool for not knowing or guessing Cypress Gardens, "The Water Ski Capital of the World," was the race site.

I have only a short time for a swim warm-up. Physiologically a lengthy warm-up is probably not that important, but I know my psychological state improves, the longer I am in the water. Not surprisingly, I will again suffer "swimmer's panic," during the one-half-mile swim in the Cypress Gardens water ski venue, Lake Eloise.

While stroking out from the beach with my wave, I feel my bowels turn to liquid just past a water ski ramp. Stopping, I gasp for air. Swimming on, I find that each stroke is agony. Looking to escape the murky lake, I eye the nearby grassy bank on my left. Unable to swim, I tread water and watch my wave leave me behind. Oddly, I feel no pain; neither am I out of breath. "What is wrong with me?" I ask myself. I try to compose myself by taking a few tentative strokes, but seize up again. Feebly breaststroking, I make little progress while watching swimmer after swimmer exit the water over by the

NOW A TRIATHLETE

grandstand. With only a few stragglers remaining in front of me, I resume swimming a choppy, nervous stroke.

Turning right at a green buoy, I am unnerved by the chop created by waves reflecting off a buoy line of old car tires. Eventually calming down, I find the nerve to swim strong onto the finish.

Staggering out of the water, I note with disgust my time on a large digital clock. My bike leg is decent, but forgetting to pin my race number to my shorts earns me an official DNF, despite a good push over the last mile on the run.

On the drive home, I decide not to enter another triathlon until I purchase a more competitive bike, and more importantly, improve my swimming. The former will require only funds; the latter, much more intractable, will demand practice and resolve. Although I am no more than a mediocre, panicky swimmer, I am filled with pride, for I am a triathlete.

Two years will pass, though, before I dare enter another triathlon.

⟆⟆⟆

While I stand barefoot on the cold, wet sand, my eyes follow the narrow channel out into the lake. Moored sailboats, with their main sails furled and wrapped in blue cloth, are aligned in rows on both sides of the channel. A narrow aluminum gangway extending beyond the sailboats impinges into the channel to my right. Watching as a couple of triathletes wade into water, I assume the waterfront is now open, and I step off the beach into the cool water. The sandy bottom slopes away gradually, and walking deliberately, I scan the bottom for rocks and debris. With the lake water reaching my waist, I stop and study the ashen gray sky, wondering if I will see rain this morning. The lake is free of boats and its surface is flat. I look out over the lake, and the distant trees bordering it appear a dull blue-green. After fitting my goggles, I dive under, surface, and swim off, following the channel out toward the red buoy line.

CROSSINGS: A SWIMMER'S MEMOIR

The cool water revives me. Having awakened at three this morning, I drove through the predawn to arrive here at Saratoga Lake in the first gray light. While I swim through the brownish-green water, images from my trip pass before eyes.

Three fat raccoons waddling home after a night spent foraging freeze in place. One turns to face my headlights defiantly. Helpless, he holds his ground. All refuse to move until well after I have stopped, and I feel sad, knowing why seemingly whole families are seen slaughtered along the roadways.

Albany's red roofed gothic Capitol reflects light off the low clouds.

The wide-awake truck traffic on the New York State Thruway presses me into the far right-hand lane.

Like lemmings, sedans and SUVs with triathlon bikes lashed to trunks and roofs rush along with me, downward toward the lake.

Reaching the first buoy, I stop swimming and slide my goggles up to my forehead. Treading water, I survey the two parallel lines of red buoys extending out into the lake. Estimating distances over open water is difficult. Almost every swim course looks short to me from land. This course is advertised at just under a mile. After swimming on to the next buoy, I stop and float on my back. My wetsuit buoys my legs, and I recline as if in a bathtub. The last of my morning grogginess gone, I feel reinvigorated. After rolling onto my stomach, I swim some drills: one arm stroking, catch-up, and breathing every other stroke. Eying swimmers from the first wave gathering on the beach, I swim back in.

Back on the beach, I gather with the other triathletes for the pre-race instructions. There are more than two hundred competitors gathered. All wear identical yellow swim caps marked in black with their wave number. I am in the last wave this morning.

After instructions, the first wave is sent off. Aside from the few who have galloped ahead and are swimming, the main pack trudges slowly through the shallows. Garmented in their black wetsuits and yellow

NOW A TRIATHLETE

caps, from a distance the throng could pass for a group of religious adherents marching off in unison.

Walking along the beach to my right, I reenter the water for more warm up. I stop swimming to watch as each wave of swimmers is sent off. Other triathletes join me, but an official motions us back to the beach. Wishing to have remained in the water until my start, I reluctantly walk up onto the beach.

The splashes from the staggered waves of swimmers are visible along the buoy line. Some stragglers lag far behind, their yellow-capped heads barely moving. The starter announces thirty seconds until our start. I take a few deep breaths, adjust my goggles, and check the timing chip strapped around my ankle. More comfortable breathing to my left, I move to this side of the wave. The lead swimmer from the first wave approaches the channel. Those around me worry aloud, "We might swim into him." The countdown begins: three, two, one, and I am off.

I am moving well near or at the front of the wave. I am taller than most triathletes; my legs allow me to sprint farther out into the lake before repeatedly porpoising (repeatedly diving and surfacing like a porpoise). Faster than swimming, porpoising is fair and gains me time. The water level rises to my chest. I make one last dive, surface, and begin stroking.

My first few strokes are wild and my legs feel numb after running across the lake bottom. A trailing swimmer grasps my feet and ankles, but I kick hard to move ahead. A fellow on my right is swimming too close and persists in pushing me toward the buoy line. I try to swim ahead, but he keeps pace, oblivious to our collisions. Making matters worse, the strap attached to my wetsuit zipper has detached itself from its Velcro tab and wrapped itself around my neck. Seeing a way to solve both problems, I swim up onto the fellow's back and fall off into open water on his right. I then pause for an instant to toss the strap over my shoulder before resuming swimming. Lifting my head up every few strokes to sight my direction, I stay relaxed and focus on my stroke.

More than six years have passed since I was first seized by panic during the Clermont Triathlon swim. Sometime after the Cypress Gardens Triathlon, I mentioned my panic to another triathlete. He related also being so distressed while swimming through weeds during one triathlon that he swam back to shore and received a DNF, despite completing the bike and run legs. Apparently my problem was not unique, but I needed to find a solution, if I hoped to progress as a triathlete. My initial hunch, back then, was that my swimmer's panic was manageable, if not curable.

Analyzing a triathlon's start, I saw that although there was ample time for a warm-up before the start of the swim leg, I reentered the water only after standing around for some time. The shock of immersion and my reflex action to gasp for air me was causing me to lose my head. A missed breath, a mouthful of water, along with being jostled, kicked, or grabbed only added to my angst. Hypersensitive, I was a victim of my flight-or-fight instinct. The simple act of putting my face in water while under duress was enough send me into a panic. As a new swimmer, I had no experience swimming laps in choppy water with other swimmers, and neither had I practiced what swimmers call breath control—skipping breaths.

Sometime, about when I was struggling with my triathlon swimming, I happened to watch a TV show about people trying to overcome various phobias. One woman had a fear of driving over bridges. After working with a psychologist, she was able to complete a jittery drive over a span while her psychologist coached her from the passenger seat. Another spot depicted a group of individuals who were terrified of flying. They also eventually worked up the nerve to embark on a flight replete with champagne. I took a clue from these; I would desensitize myself to swimming in a pack.

My wave has spread itself out along the buoy line. Separated from the other competitors, I have found my stroke. The water feels heavy and viscous when I am swimming well. There is a sense in my arms extending down through my hands much as if I were walking. On each stroke, I reach out, and planting my hand, I take what feels like a big step. Perhaps because I learned to swim so late in life, this sensation takes some time before manifesting itself, but when felt, it is exhilarating. The pace clocks at the pool where I swim prove it is no illusion for I am truly swimming fast. Alone in the pool, I have no more than my breathing, the blue pool bottom, and this wonderful sensation for company. Like an addict, I am continually seeking new sensations that might lead to better swimming. My progress as a swimmer has gone hand-in-hand with my heightened feel for the water.

I have fallen in behind a fellow who is swimming well. Following his bubble trail enables me to stay tucked inside his wake. Drafting is a well-known strategy in triathlon swimming. I felt like a real pro the first couple of times I was able to draft off another swimmer. Occasionally my hands find his feet or ankles. I am tempted to pass, but sensing the increased drag when I swim to his side, I remain behind him.

Seeing another red buoy glide by gratifies me. My speed is in part because of the wetsuit I am wearing. Crafted from neoprene rubber, the suit buoys me and reduces drag. Only an odd few out here are swimming without a wetsuit this morning. In order to compete successfully in a triathlon, a wetsuit has become a necessity for all but the fastest swimmers.

Being purists, open-water swimmers frown on wetsuits. A legitimate English Channel swim, one that would be recognized by the Channel Swimming Society, does not allow the use of wetsuits. Legendary English Channel swimmer Ted Erikson—who Conrad Wennerberg chronicled in *Wind Waves, and Sunburn,* his book on marathon swimming, as the one of only two swimmers to complete a sixty-mile race across Lake Michigan—said of wetsuits, "If you need help to cross the lake, get in a boat." Roger Deakin, in his book *Waterlog: A swimmer's journey through Britain* wrote, "Wearing a wetsuit is sensory deprivation," and by "preventing the full force of your physical encounter with cold water," a wetsuit "is against nature and something of a killjoy." Reversing positions, Deakin later writes, "I tell myself each time I struggle into the rubber, not a drop of water ever actually touches the skin of the otter. The inner fur is so fine and tight together that the water never penetrates it." A duck's feathers, along with the layer of insulating fat beneath the skin of whales, porpoises, and penguins are other examples one could cite to rationalize wearing a wetsuit.

The water temperature out here is in the low seventies. Most, including me, would be comfortable swimming without a wetsuit. Triathlon rules allow the use of a wetsuit up to seventy-eight degrees; far from the hypothermic low-sixties-degree temperatures encountered during an English Channel swim. A triathlon, though, is more than just an open-water swim; it is three events, the last two contested on land. A test of an athlete's speed and endurance across three disciplines, a triathlon, unlike an open-water swim, is not (or at least aims not to be) a battle against the elements. Just as a lean triathlete might turn blue in cold water, a beefy, barrel-chested marathon swimmer, well suited for swimming hours in cold water, would no doubt struggle on the fast-paced bike and run legs of a triathlon. A wetsuit allows triathletes to focus on their swimming and not be hampered by overly cold water. A wetsuit is not a panacea, though, as swimming speed will always tell. At swimming competitions, almost everything is held to a standard, including the pool temperature, to ensure the fairest swimming conditions. A wetsuit only does the same for a triathlon.

I have passed the fellow I was drafting. The pair of buoys marking the turnaround are not far now. Upon rounding these, it will be a sprint back to the beach. I used to be unnerved when swimming so far from land. This morning, though, I have dodged my swimmer's panic. Little concerned with the deep water or how far I am off shore, I only care about passing the swimmer ahead me.

After moving from Florida to Connecticut, I was happy to discover the sport of triathlon flourishing throughout New England and New York State. I joined a fitness club with both an outdoor and indoor pool for year-round swimming. In a year's time, I had enough funds to purchase a competitive triathlon bike.

Two years after my debacle at the Cypress Garden triathlon, I entered a late-season Olympic distance triathlon. Although a mild case of panic hampered my swim and hamstring cramps slowed my run, I was nonetheless encouraged after this race. To improve, I needed to ratchet up my cycling, run without cramping, and somehow overcome my panic in the water. While I knew of a local triathlon club, it was not until the following summer before I began competing in the club's weekly triathlons.

Here is what became a Tuesday ritual for me: I cleaned my bike and oiled its chain; removed the tire pump and water-bottle cages; packed my wetsuit, racing flats, and other gear into a pack that I shouldered on the short bike ride to a nearby park. There, week after week, on hot and muggy evenings, I dove into the weedy lake with eighty or more other triathletes. Absorbing kicks, slaps, collisions, and mouthfuls of water, it was in this lake where I finally became a triathlete. Swimming the same course with the same competitors, I allowed the lake and surrounding roads to become my triathlon classroom. I honed my transitions from swimming to cycling and cycling to swimming, strengthened my legs on the hilly bike course, and learned how to run fast despite my legs feeling as heavy as tree trunks after the bike leg. I had found a way to desensitize myself to triathlon swimming, and if not always comfortable swimming in a pack, I nonetheless reveled in the competition and looked forward each week to an improved swim time.

The Tuesday evening triathlons emboldened me to enter longer, sanctioned triathlons. Each race brought a new swimming experience. I endured numbing fifty-seven-degree water temperatures in Maine's Casco Bay, imagined myself a salmon while swimming against the current after overshooting a buoy in the Hudson River, watched from Idaho's Lake Coeur d'Alene as a pontoon plane took to the air, bobbed like a cork in the buoyant salt waters of the Long Island Sound, peered at the ghostly image of a sunken boat in the aqua waters of a Pennsylvania quarry, swam a quarter mile before realizing my goggles were still pushed up on my forehead, rounded a small island by pulling myself along the rocky lake bottom, watched steam rise off shoulders and backs the other triathletes after a frosty morning swim in early October, and saw Dick Hoyt of Team Hoyt push his disabled son Rick across the finish line in a wheelchair.

Nowadays I often have dreams about triathlons. Some are vexing, frustrating episodes where I endlessly fumble with my gear and miss the start. Others, often repeated, have me either swimming around what resembles a blue running track, diving into a grassy green canal, or swimming ahead of a pack of swimmers in a clear icy pond surrounded by leafless hardwoods. I have no recollection of dreams involving cycling or running, though.

Having made the turn, I can see the beach in the distance. Swimmers are scattered about in front of me. Swimming well, I pass one after another. I begin playing with short bursts of swift kicking and quick strokes. These leave me breathless, and I slow my cadence. There is something pleasurable in this exhaustion, and I repeatedly hurl myself against the water. Having seen others swim with an overhand windmill-like stroke, I experiment with this motion, wondering if I am swimming faster. Many swimming breakthroughs—when I happen upon some small change in a hand or body position leading to an improvement—occur on extended swims like this. I relish these moments, and when back on land, I reenact the mechanics, hoping to internalize the motion.

I see those up ahead wading toward the beach. I have the urge to be up there with them, but the last stretch of water ahead compels me to keep swimming. Entering the channel, I see and hear those gathered on the aluminum gangway cheer and wave. Triathletes are coached to keep swimming until their hands touch bottom. Thinking I might sprint out of the water, I instead stumble to my feet and run slowly through the shallows onto the beach. My watch tells me I have been swimming for thirty minutes. Feeling that I had a strong swim, I am disappointed. My swim split always outweighs my bike and run times. I have even thought that winning an age-group medal off a fast bike or run leg is somewhat underhanded.

The truth is that while a slow swim can lose a triathlon, a fast swim is almost never enough to win.

Finding my bike in the transition area, I peel off my wetsuit. After strapping on my helmet and fastening on my shoes, I run my bike out into a parking lot. Sidestepping a couple of muddy spots, I hop on my bike and pedal out onto the main road.

My body will soon make the transition from swimming to cycling. My breathing will level out, my legs will come alive, and the rushing air on my bike will dry me. All outward signs from my swim, except my cast-off goggles, yellow swim cap, and damp wetsuit lying in crumpled heap will have vanished. The swim leg is over for me, and so, in some sense, is this triathlon.

I am driving back to Connecticut; an attractive cherrywood mantel clock for winning my age group rests next to me on the passenger seat. My swim leg was faster than I thought; I finished second in my age group. Nearly at September's end, this was my season's last race. The fellow who came out of the water ahead of me will spur me on to return to the pool this winter in search for more speed. I passed the half-century mark a few months ago, and my trophy attests to winning a war of attrition as much as it does my progress as a triathlete. Besting several cadets up from West Point this morning is no small source of pride, though. There is a mania nowadays among triathletes to compete in ironman distance triathlons, but for me, this morning's Olympic distance triathlon was long enough. The race over, I can enjoy the remainder of the day with all my faculties intact. Not to detract from those who complete these long-distance triathlons, but from a swimmer's perspective, the focus of these all-day affairs is the bike and run.

Being a triathlete is synonymous with living the triathlon lifestyle: eating right, training for three disciplines, purchasing and maintaining equipment, and traveling to events. It is the traveling that Janet and I enjoy together. When I enter a triathlon in some scenic spot, we will rent a campground cabin and then have the weekend to explore, do touristy things, or just relax. After the triathlon is over, it is a pleasure to drive the roads or gaze out over the waters where only a short time before, I swam, cycled, and ran.

There are many known benefits to being a triathlete: a lean and muscular physique; improved fitness and self-confidence; lower blood pressure; reduced chance of cancer, heart disease, and osteoporosis—the list goes on—but perhaps its best benefit is what dancer Merce Cunningham attributed to dance. "It gives you nothing back, nothing but that single fleeting moment when you feel alive."

CHAPTER 8

A Season on the Farmington River

Issuing forth from earth, sand, and rock, every river is a miracle.

Tomorrow is the last day of March. The winter has been long and cold with more than six feet of snow. Today, though, feels like spring. The temperature has soared into the sixties and the afternoon sun, although muted by the sky's milky-blue haze, feels deliciously warm. Having run the launch's bow up onto our dock, I sit on the aft bench studying the new engine's manual. The choke closed, the engine idles smoothly. Taking a break from reading, I dip my hand into the murky water. Repelled by the icy cold, I wonder that town kids will soon be flying off the rope swings on the opposite shore.

Our shells are slow coming down from the boathouse. I suppose Kim is taking her time teaching the novice rowers nautical terms and boat-handling skills. "Port means left, starboard right, but since you face the stern, everything is reversed. And remember, never lift a boat by its riggers; lift it by gripping the gunwale," I can hear her saying.

Acquainted with the engine workings, I look out over the river trying to discern how the opaque green water changes into its distant steel color. There is a smooth melding, but the burnished waters entice my eyes forward, and the river appears in two shades. I leave the problem to painters, when I hear a red-winged blackbird call. "Konk-la-reee," he shouts from atop a riverbank maple. Adorned in the colors of Germany's national flag—the *Bundesflagge*—I envision the weeks to come watching this fellow and his cousins flitting about the riverbank brambles.

Leaving my German general, I turn and face the sun in the bluing sky. Half reclining with eyes shut, I ruminate on the color blue: blue is the color of doctors' waiting rooms, sagging spirits, spent blood and death; it is also an aristocratic color, the color of royalty and of baby boys. Usually thought of as placid, gentle, and sedative, blue is a winter color and the color of repose. Blue is the chosen color of the morally correct, the profane, and the northern Yankee. The sea and sky are mostly seen as blue, but finding blue in the earth's flora and fauna can be as rare as seeing a blue moon. Over the past winter months, I have lived with all shades of blue: Tiffany blue, sapphire blue, and October sky blue; all has been colored a watery blue. *"Coach J., how do you do the breaststroke kick?"* asks Monica from the light-blue pool.

It is only the second night of swim practice, and I am scrambling for explanations. "Draw your heels up together, flare your feet outward, and kick back and around," I say, demonstrating with my hands and arms.

"But I don't get it," says Alex.

"Oh well, watch this," I say.

Lying flat on the damp pool deck, I repeatedly draw up my shins and throw my feet back. Uncomfortable on the deck, I am relieved when Monica says, "That's good, Coach J.; now I understand," but Emily quips, "You remind me of Shamu."

"Yeah, pretend you're Shamu; be Shamu," says Tiffany.

Now all four are huddled with their elbows on the deck waiting to see Shamu's next trick. Not to disappoint, I place my hands on the small of my back and, keeping my feet together, I flex up while emitting a couple shrieks. Amid the giggles and laughs I hear, "Throw him a fish."

Standing, I ask, "Who first swam the English Channel?"

"I don't know," says Alex.

"Englishman Captain Webb in 1800s."

"How far was it?" asks Tiffany.

"Twenty-one miles, but he was in the water more than twenty hours, so he swam a lot farther because of tides. The channel is also much colder than this pool. Do you know what stroke he used?"

"Freestyle."

"No. The breaststroke. Back then the English were crazy about swimming, so they kept tubs of frogs near their pool when learning the breaststroke. They called them 'swimming frogs.' Maybe I'll bring a frog to this pool for you guys to watch one night."

"No way. That would be so cool," says Monica.

I see Kim walking along the earthen dike that leads from the boathouse to the dock. She walks ahead of rowers, who are staggered in alternating pairs, each shouldering a section of an emerald-green racing shell. The aluminum gangway clinking and rattling, the rowers make their way onto the dock. "Rowers, stop," barks Amanda. In measured intervals, she then commands, "Up overhead. Ready, up. Toe to the edge of the dock. Ready, walk. Roll to waist. Ready, roll. And out and over and down into the water. Ready, down. Starboards, hold. Port rowers, get your oars."

Never needing more than these few terse commands, five high school girls have cleanly set a forty-two-foot racing shell into the river. Hoorah! The crew season is under way.

We row on a three-quarter mile stretch of Connecticut's Farmington River that was dredged years ago for its sand and gravel. The river has its source in the Massachusetts Berkshire Mountains and flows out of these northwest hills into Connecticut's Central Valley. On a beeline toward the Long Island Sound, the river bends in the shape of a horseshoe just south of here as if redirected by the north-south-running Matacomet Ridge. Flowing northward, the river eventually breaches the ridge, where it ends its life in the Connecticut River north of Hartford.

Our crews row coxed-fours—a coxswain and four rowers pulling on alternately set single oars. Sweep rowing—the predominate style of rowing practiced in America's schools, colleges and clubs—conjures up Cecil B. deMille-type images of torch-lit, fetid ships manned by rows of scruffy, manacled slaves rowing rhythmically to a drummer's beat, two slaves per oar. A missed stroke would earn lashes from the galley master. The rowed slave ship is a popular image of rowing; our old boat trailer had a sticker affixed that asked, "Have you flogged your crew today?"

Beyond the requisites of strength, grit, endurance, and a high pain threshold, the analogy between a slave ship and sweep rowing breaks down with the incorporation of the sliding seat into today's racing shells. An innovation from the nineteenth century, the sliding seat transformed rowing from an upper-body motion to a vastly more powerful leg-driven stroke. With rowers sliding back and forth atop plastic wheels set in narrow tracks, the popular saying, "get your back into it" should be recast as "brace your back and drive with your legs." Since sliding-seat rowing is much more unstable than rowing on fixed thwarts, as in a rowboat, Kim and I will devote hours coaching correct posture and slide control in the weeks ahead.

In our boats, the coxswain (taken from "cockboat" meaning a small boat and "swain" meaning servant) reclines low, tucked inside her boat bow. Steering with a tiller and speaking through battery-powered speakers set inside the hull, she is both her boat helmsman and captain. As with jockeys, it is a widely held view that a coxswain need only be diminutive, but just as not every lightweight man makes a good jockey, not every petite girl make a good coxswain. A good coxswain must know her rowers, be decisive, be a great tactician, and above all be able to steer a straight course. She must be competitive to the bone, have a sense of humor, and most importantly, she must be well liked, if not loved, by her crew, for then and only then will they be willing to endure any suffering for her. With her calls and shouts sounding, a coxswain must be able to inspire torpid minds, cajole weary bodies, and spur on burning limbs. In a dead sprint, with the red finish line buoys wafting tantalizingly across the water, a coxswain's words must somehow break through her crew's pained, despairing minds, to offer hope that they might still somehow prevail.

Our coxswain and her rowers taken together bring to mind the Roman god Janus, the god of two faces—one facing the future and the other, the past. More than bearing a resemblance to this god of beginnings and endings, our rowers and coxswain are his adherents. Rowing under his auspices, they hope and pray for each stroke's clean start and smooth finish.

Kim sees off our rowers and clambers into the launch. After taking her seat, I back the launch off the dock and motor off toward the waiting boats. Ahead is a bulge of land that rowers over the years have named Mullet Point for the short-in-front, long-in-back coiffure seen on some of those who haunt its wooded banks on warm days.

The moniker Mullet Point, with its association with tattooed forearms, Pontiac Trans Ams, and doublewide mobile homes, smacks of classism. And no doubt those looking in on rowing would concur—crew is an elitist, upper-class sport.

With oars, racing shells, launches, engines, and boathouses tallying thousands, even millions of dollars, the body of water and leisure time needed to row, its long practice at the English universities Oxford and Cambridge, and its high regard in our Ivy Leagues, rowing is often seen as a sport for the privileged. This view is also not infrequently heard. "There is no bigger preppy sport than crew; it's a sport for rich people," an acquaintance once said to me. Along with polo and yacht racing, rowing might even be viewed conspiratorially as an attempt by the upper classes to create a sport where the artisan, mechanic, or laborer could not afford to compete on equal terms, or in some cases could not compete at all.

What was true for English amateurism (keeping the classes separate) might have been true for the rowing, but even if only partly true, the perpetrators of this snobbery and social exclusiveness have paid dearly, for the practice of rowing is brutally egalitarian. Social class has never protected any rower from burning lactic acid, blood blisters, or enduring long hours of freezing rain. Surely, the true reason for rowing's lasting popularity among the gentry is its capacity to toughen young gentlemen with its leveling naval discipline. Rowing is taxing, painful, and often savage. Requiring Napoleon's instantaneous two o'clock-in-the-morning courage, rowing hammers weakness into strength, raises silliness to sensibility, and bends self-aggrandizement into humility.

On the water—away from wealth, status, and connections—all rowers become nameless bodies. Superstars are not found in the seats of a championship crew boat, for a boat must row as one to win. Being non-weight-bearing and using most muscle groups, rowing flat out can induce blood-lactate levels unmatched by any other endurance sport. For a novice, this fact can make their first hard row as sobering as a near-death experience. Other sports, such as swimming and cross-country running, can serve the same purpose, but crew, with its short apprenticeship, alluring but confining boats, and one-for-all spirit, finds the mark sooner for greater numbers. Primitive tribes have had their rites of passage for their adolescents—spells, incantations, hallucinogens, vision quests, bloodletting, and self-mortification—but here in New England, we have rowing.

No matter its past, rowing now aims at breaking down barriers, both real and perceived. Rowing clubs nowadays offer open houses, where novices can give rowing a try. If a boathouse is unavailable or one just wants to row alone, there is single sculling: one person, one shell, and two oars called sculls. Weighing no more than thirty pounds and garfish thin, a single scull rides nicely atop a car rooftop, allowing the sculler to do without a coxswain, other rowers, or a boathouse. A captain of her ship, a single sculler charts her own course, be it solitary contemplation, fitness, or competition. Single sculling is oarsmanship at its purest, and its Olympic champions are deemed the world's best oars persons. Alone on the water, a sculler can experiment with her stroke, feeling how the smallest movements can affect the boat balance and run. The sculling stroke, unlike in sweep rowing, is symmetrical and is the first stroke taught overseas.

Barry Strauss, an academic who took up sculling in midlife and found it redemptive after an inglorious little league baseball career, wrote on why he sculls, in his book *Rowing Against the Current: On learning to scull at forty*. "Because it's beautiful. Because it's challenging. Because it's escapist; when I'm on the water, I'm on the water and nothing else matters, not the kids, the bills, or the students or the committees, not everything else that takes away time day after day."

Rowing has also been a boon for women in recent years. In 1996, the NCCA declared women's rowing an emerging sport, and in adherence with Title IX (a 1972 federal law prohibiting sex discrimination in educational institutions), colleges and universities have used rowing to maintain number parity with men. Colleges and universities row mostly what are called eights—a rowing shell with eight rowers and a coxswain. With nine women per boat, women's crew is known as women's football, in reference to its large team sizes. Unlike in other heavily recruited sports, women walk-ons fill many of the seats in collegiate crew boats. A fast time on an indoor rowing machine (known as an *erg score*) can lead to a rowing athletic scholarship or may give a girl a boost in college admissions. With top colleges able to pick and choose, students can become harried performers, each one vying to stand out beyond the requisite academics. Our school's only Harvard admittance each of the last three years has been a rower.

A few years ago, one of our students approached me saying, "I want to go to Harvard and plan on using rowing as my hook." She added, "I need a good erg score in Boston this February."

"No problem," I said. "If you're willing to work, I'll get you your erg score." Three months later and tens of hours spent on indoor rowers, I screamed myself hoarse as Katie, racing against forty other girls on indoor machines, rowed herself into exhaustion.

Standing before her as she lay in a stupor on a cot next to other spent rowers, I asked the paramedic taking her blood pressure how she was. "Ah, I've seen worse," he said laconically. There were nine stronger girls who rowed that morning, but I doubt if any of them had pushed themselves so close to the edge.

A committed, passionate athlete is precisely what this coach wants, no more and no less. To train in solitude, to fortify oneself without fanfare day in and day out, aiming to be one's best for one competition on just one day is what keeps bringing me back to coaching. Whether on the water or indoors on a machine, I like rowing. Rewarding those who are willing to work hard, rowing leaves one nowhere to hide any lack of fitness. Edison's adage, "There is no substitute for hard work" is true for most things and truest for rowing.

We float still in the water to our two crew boats' starboard sides. Sycamore trees crowd the banks on the far shore. Standing tall atop narrow trunks, they appear to have sprung up fast. Looking like Christmas tree ornaments, golf-ball-sized brown seed pods hang from their upper branches. Back toward the dock, the trunks of the sycamores growing along the bank have a soft greenish-yellow color; it is the only color seen amid winter's drab browns and grays.

A SEASON ON THE FARMINGTON RIVER

Returning rowers fill the seats in our third boat, but graduation and attrition have put three novices in our fourth boat. Kim and I have a daunting task. In three weeks, these girls who never before today sat in a tipsy, racing shell will be expected to row hard, yet cleanly, up Boston's Charles River. It is true; we would never expect a swimmer to race a quarter mile in a pool only weeks after getting wet; neither would we expect a bicyclist to negotiate a busy street after first balancing a bike, but we expect the equivalent from our girls. Fortunately, rowing is a simple sport—a linear motion repeated ad infinitum. Aside from blistered palms and aching muscles, staying focused will be the toughest challenge facing our novices. Kim's words in past seasons states their task. "It's hard to concentrate on one thing for very long, but you all have to do it."

Today and on subsequent days our novices' minds will be filled with questions:

"Am I leaning toward the rigger?"

"Is my outboard shoulder higher than my inboard?" "Did I drop my hands at the catch?"

"Do my legs go down first at the catch?" "Am I rushing my slide?"

"How is our boat's set?"

Only in time will rowing approach the automaticity of riding a bicycle, walking, or breathing.

Playing the engine between forward and reverse, I keep us abreast of the boats. Kim, with megaphone in hand, is about to start the first lesson. "Where do I begin?" she asks half-jokingly.

"I don't know; there is so much to tell them. Why not start with safety?"

"Yes, I'll do that. Rowers never let go of your oars, or the boat will flip over, and if the boat does capsize, don't try to swim to shore. Hang onto the boat, and we will come and get you. Also the oars will float, so if you can't get to the boat, hang on to them. Remember, the water's real cold, so pay attention. Okay, let's talk about the outboard hand."

Kim continues the lesson, but the warm sun on the flat river causes my mind to wander.

It is the middle of October, a few weeks before I had found myself playing Shamu on the deck of Trinity College's pool. I am sitting in a New Jersey hotel ballroom listening to Bob Bowman. He is not too tall and a bit on the heavy side, with short brown hair. His wire rim glasses make him look analytical. Still flush with pride from coaching Michael Phelps to his gold medals at the Athens Olympics, Bowman is speaking about the butterfly stroke. The hundred or so swim coaches sitting in the dimly lit ballroom could not care less about stroke technicalities, though. All here want to hear only about Phelps, the swimmer Bowman coached and mentored at the North Baltimore Aquatic Club.

In time, Bowman traces his coaching career and how he and Michael met.

"When Michael came to me, he was a kid full of energy who loved to compete," says Bowman. "As a coach, I always liked to be the first to the pool for morning practices. When Michael figured this out, it became a competition between us who would arrive first, until one morning at 4:30, I put a stop to it."

My vision narrows and I feel the goose bumps as Bowman begins recounting one of Phelps's superhuman swim workouts. "All right, Michael, to break that record, you will need to swim a set of thirty one-hundreds."

The boats are moving slowly, and I keep pace off their starboard. Kim has the stern pair rowing easily, while the bow pair sits motionless, balancing the shell with oars splayed on the water. A rower's oar is like a tightrope walker's bar. Lose control of the oar, and the boat will lose its balance, or what is called its set. Should our rowers draw in their oars, their shell will roll over as if on cue.

How ironic, even fraudulent, a lifelong aquaphobe like me should have been found listening to Bob Bowman at a swim-coach clinic. What qualified me to coach swimming? Nothing more than what qualified me to be a crew coach. I never rowed in high school or college. Before I came to Connecticut, my brushes with rowing were limited to seeing sculls and long-hulled eights on Philadelphia's Schuylkill River as boy, and many years later, hearing the coxswains' shouts while running along northern Manhattan's Spuyten Duyvil Creek.

Upon arriving in Farmington, I discovered the indoor rowers in our school's fitness room, and I became possessed by the machines. They set my mind ablaze with the promise of new levels of fitness. Noticing my efforts, Brian, our head crew coach, approached me, saying, "We think your talents are being wasted during the spring. Would you consider helping out with the crew team?

"But I've never rowed," I said.

"I don't care. You have passion, and the knowledge can be gained."

My rowing education began when Brian lent me David Halberstam's *The Amateurs* and Brad Lewis's *Assault on Lake Casitas*. Written from different perspectives (Lewis's the rower and Halberstam's the journalist), each book looks in on the lives and training of U.S. rowers leading up to the Los Angeles Olympic Games. While Lewis's book details an athlete's internal life and Halberstam's is researched and broad, both reach the same conclusion, that rowing can be heartbreaking, because one's seat in a boat is never guaranteed.

Later, traveling with our team to a Virginia reservoir for their pre-season practice, I experienced what it is to sit for hours in a launch as cold rain fell. During the ensuing summer, our school funded a stay for me at a sculling camp in Northern Vermont. In the evenings, after twice-a-day sculling sessions, I read Joe Paduda's *The Art of Sculling*. "Sculling is the rarest of vocations," he wrote. "Without fail it provides a reward precisely indexed to the amount of effort invested."

I came to enjoy the instant before my sculls found the water, a mix of yin and yang. Reaching forward with my arms outspread, I crouched and tottered before dropping the blades into the water. Initiating each stroke with my abs braced, I felt the sculls tug up through my chest. The shell accelerating, I was cheered by the water's rippling sound off the boat stern. With my hands crossing left over right at a stroke end, I pushed the sculls down and listened for their telltale plucking sound as they left the water. I twisted each scull a quarter in its oarlocks, and the sculls were in their oarlocks. My balance never certain, I planed the scull blades, while my seat's rumbling wheels took me forward for yet another stroke. Slips, imbalances, and my over anxiousness made no two strokes the same. Frequent capsizes became an odd source of pride as I grew adept in hauling myself out of the cold lake and back into the shell. Sculling captivated me, perhaps too much, for only strips of white tape allowed my pained, blistered hands to grasp the sculls at the end of my stay.

I was chatting one afternoon with another camper named Bob, a doctor from New Jersey, when he said he thought that with my tall, lean frame and decent erg score, "sculling might just be my sport." In another lifetime, he would be right. There are only so many sports one can pursue without becoming a dabbler. Besides, I had already swum too far to turn back from swimming. Rowing also demands muscle and lots of it; my aerobic fitness would take me only so far.

I like the supple, sensuous freedom of swimming and how it affords me the opportunity to undulate, drift, and explore water in all dimensions. Rowing requires a machine, and as such, must necessarily be linear and confining. I suppose what one imagines when looking out over water is what sets a rower and swimmer apart. Sitting here in the launch, watching the water glide by, I feel water's pull not to row, but to swim. I wonder what it would be like to drop overboard and stroke madly through the icy cold.

Late afternoons at the camp were free, and I would walk down from where I bunked to brave the cold, greenish lake for a swim. Fellow campers were out sculling for a third time, and from lake level, they looked like giant water bugs skimming across the water. My swimming was not strong back then, and I was content to stroke along a stretch of pine- and birch-treed shoreline.

My journey toward water is an old story for those who have read this far. For me, everything has run toward water; coaching crew is yet another facet.

Both boats are moving now, but our fourth boat is wallowing. "Catch together. Keep your eyes in the boat," Kim shouts in the megaphone. The megaphone is an old-fashioned, but effective device. Sound spreads out over water, but by placing a megaphone to your ear, one can hear what a rower says remarkably well.

Brian's boats have turned around and are beating down along the opposite shore. His boats are filled with returning rowers. They are rowing well, having rowed down in Virginia last week. A few years back, the *New York Times* ran a piece on our crew team. The writer noted Brian was "a man who brooks no nonsense." With a benefactor's support, he has built a successful crew program over the years, but not—as was noted in another *Times* article—without some resistance and controversy. To understand the rumblings about our crew program, it is helps to know that ours was once a staid girl's school whose intellectual history, in its own way, paralleled western civilization.

Fueled by classical learning, the school shone from its founding before the Civil War until the end of the World War I, when a school circular stated, "The course of college preparation is given up for the next few years." According to the school's written history, those few years ran into several decades. Gaining a reputation as a finishing school for wealthy young ladies, the school slipped into a sort of Dark Age, including subjects such as deportment, carriage, diction, and curtseying. Today, though, our school stands on firm academic footing with strong college placement.

Not having any competitive athletic past, our school's commitment to athletics cannot be called a renaissance, but it has the energy of one. Championship banners adorn our gym. Every girl is required to compete on a team before graduation. Women athletic professionals and Olympic medalists speak at our annual Women in Sport Day, and statistics are recited on how sports can lessen depression and improve a girl's self-esteem.

The growth in women's sports makes it easy to forget the time when women had little opportunity to play sports. Marathon swimmer Diana Nyad, in her swimming autobiography *Other Shores*, observed, "The physical domain is the last bastion, and female athletes are still untouchable visions to be stared at with wide eyes and open mouth." She also stated, "Probably the weakest realm left is the physical one, and ironically enough in this age of technology, the fulfilling of her physical potential is one of the biggest steps a woman must take toward commanding the fifty percent in all domains."

Women's participation in sports is not only recent; it is also tenuous, for the battle over what constitutes feminine beauty rages on. On one side stands the fit, athletic, and even the muscular, and on the other, the wan and wilted. Twiggy-esque models ceaselessly jump out from glamour and fashion magazines; photographers' cameras, flashing like strobe lights, illuminate tall, skeletal women thumping bone on bone along the catwalk; inane tidbits such as "television makes you look ten pounds heavier" are passed off as knowledge; and styles such as heroin chic are popularized. "That's what sells," said a friend in reply to my remarking on today's svelte starlets. Perhaps, but it might be more accurate to say, "That what's being hyped." The voluptuous Venus paintings painted by the masters show that feminine beauty is not static. From a more heroic age, the unknown sculptor of Venus de Milo envisioned the goddess of

A SEASON ON THE FARMINGTON RIVER

love and beauty as womanly yet muscular, with a serene, forthright face. Should our rowers' conversation, as it often does, turn to some gangly movie star, I like to toss a rock at their glassy-eyed talk by offering something such as, "You know. She wouldn't be worth a damn on an erg or in a boat, for that matter."

None of this really matters, other than it matters immensely to adolescent girls.

Regular visitors to the river, several gulls float atop the water up ahead. The flotsam of winter's wreck—twigs, branches, and hefty snapped-off limbs denuded of bark—are scattered about. Our coxswains need to be alert, for such debris can break off a shell's small rudder called the skeg. A brownish-white hawk sits perched atop a sycamore on our right, scanning the riverbank for a meal. To him we are new, but undoubtedly unwelcome guests. On the far bank, protected from the sun, lie a few isolated patches of snow. Winter's last remnants, this snow will soon be gone.

Trinity College's pool has been shut down for more than a week, and every pool in the area is booked. Running, calisthenics, and tae bo videos are no substitute for swimming, but that is all our team has been able to do. Today though, we have a pool.

Walking out on the dark pool deck, Wendy, our head coach, shouts, "Let's get some lights on."

"I've tried," says a swimmer.

Looking up, I see most of the fluorescent lights are burned out. Down on my knees, I work with a swimmer in setting up the lane lines. "Wow, this water is warm." I mutter. I find a couple of pace clocks and place them out on the deck. The girls settle into their warm-up swims.

"Coach J, the water is so warm. Could you open the door?" says a swimmer.

"Sure," I say.

Walking across the pool deck, I prop a pair of glass doors open with a kickboard. A couple inches of fresh snow covers the ground outside. The icy air rushing in soon raises a thick fog over the water. Like apparitions, the swimmers glide through the mist.

"Wasn't this a scene from Macbeth?" I ask.

"I don't know, but can't you do something about the heat?" asks Emily.

"Keep swimming," I say.

Leaving coaching for another day, I focus on counting swim caps, but the complaints continue. Having an idea, I say, "I could you get you guys snow from outside."

"Yeah, get us snow!" I hear.

Grabbing a kickboard, I walk out through the doors. The sun having just set, the January sky is colored a dark red. I am wearing only a T-shirt and jeans, and the wind chills my skin. "Fire and ice, it's a damn sauna in there," I think. Taking deep breaths, I flush my lungs. "Wasn't chlorine gas used during the first World War?" I think.

I return with a kickboard heaped with snow. "Pack it under your swim caps," I tell the swimmers. They stroke off with their caps bulging.

After a few laps Alex stops swimming and says, "You know, it really helps."

"Could you please get us some more?" asks Tiffany.

"Yeah, I will. You know, a lot of heat is gained and lost through your head, blood flowing through a large area of exposed skin and such."

Four or five swimmers gather about the kickboard, rubbing the snow on their arms and faces.

Tasting some, Monica asks, "Hey, Coach J., is it safe to eat snow?"

"You know, when I was a kid I used to eat snow, just like you're doing. I suppose it is still okay—pollution probably being no worse," *but unable to resist the puerile, I add, "I always tried to avoid the yellow stuff."*

Monica thinks for a moment, and glaring at me before swimming off, says, "You're gross, Coach J."

Those days without a pool were exasperating, yet interruptions and delays are an integral part of high school coaching. We should have been rowing here days ago, but heavy ice on the river tore the dock out, and we had to wait while maintenance reset it.

We have reached the end of the navigable river. Up ahead, the river narrows into some gentle rapids. An old railroad bridge, reclaimed as part of a Rails-to-Trails walkway, spans the rapids high above. Before the bridge was rebuilt, I made my way across the bridge's fire-blackened ties one winter day. Forced to inch along the rusted rails as if I were doing pushups, I can still see the white-gray water running between the ice-covered banks below.

Where the rapids end is a popular spot for fisherman after trout season opens. The river froze to more than a foot thick during my first winter here in Farmington. I walked across somewhere here on a bright sunny morning. All the way down to our dock, the river appeared as one white expanse spotted with fisherman brooding before their ice holes.

"Way-nuf," Kim shouts at the rowers. Short for the old nautical term "weigh enough," *way-nuf* means stop rowing. "Coxswains, spin your boats," she says.

Motioning toward our novices, I say, "We have some work to do."

"You're telling me," she says.

Most of what I have learned about coaching crew has come from our time together in the launch. Kim rowed in high school. I have listened to and absorbed her words over the years. Next year, Kim will move on to coach an Ultimate Frisbee team she is forming. I will then be alone in the launch, the rowers my sole charge.

CROSSINGS: A SWIMMER'S MEMOIR

On the far shore there is short dirt incline used by jet skiers to trailer their craft into the river. Accompanied by Janet in our kayak, I will swim from our dock to this incline on summer evenings. I was surprised to hear metallic pinging of the jet skis underwater and to feel the river's cold current the first time I made the swim. Only when I swam in the river was its true character revealed. A novice rower once asked me if the stretch of water where we row was a lake. With its placid, wide expanse, it was easy to understand her question, for the river here looks very much like a lake, but who is to say if her first impression was not correct? For conversely, cannot the Great Lakes—Superior, Michigan, Huron, Erie, and Ontario—be viewed as one long river, leading to the ocean?

When our rowers become proficient, the end of the river here will be the start of their countless full-pressure rows down to the dock. Known as race pieces, these rows are key to building boat speed and for sorting out rowers. Crew is an anomaly in our digital world, because changing water and wind conditions makes times almost meaningless. A few years ago, we had a small propeller mounted to the underside of the hull of one our shells. Intended to relay boat speed, it soon was lost, and I later heard, "It never really worked."

There will be no racing today, as Kim says, "Ready, all row." The two boats moving slowly, she shouts, "Fourth boat, catch together!" Moving ahead, our third boat's green hull reflects the water as an illuminated crosshatch pattern. Facing to the east, I enjoy the sun's warmth on my back. A month has passed since I first sensed winter was ending.

After dropping my swimmers outside the pool, I park the van in a lower lot. While I am walking up a steep snow-covered path, the sun rising over a ridge warms me, and a pine scent fills the air. The pool is built into the side of a low mountain, and to my back lie the pastures and farms of the Massachusetts Pioneer Valley.

I am happy with my first year as a swim coach. Obeying Hippocrates,

I have aimed at doing no harm. Monica has developed into a good freestyler, Emily has improved her breaststroke and tried other strokes, Tiffany has persevered with the backstroke, and Alex, my best all-a-rounder, has an excellent start and is now a fine butterflier. As often happens, the new coach and his swimmers have learned together.

Inside the pool, I look for the four. Not seeing them, I walk toward the locker rooms.

I turned down a narrow hallway, and all of them, with Alex in the lead, rush toward me. "It was horrible. We saw everything," says Alex.

Tiffany, smirking, says, "Mr. J., what kind of meet did you bring us to?"

"What are you talking about?" I ask.

Pointing at door upon which a makeshift Girls Locker Room sign is affixed, Alex says, "In there, a naked old man. It was so gross."

"What?"

"Yeah, my stuff is in there," says Alex.

"Mine is in there too. Could you go in and get it for us?" Monica asks.

Gingerly pushing the door open, I see an elderly man clothed in boxers and a white T-shirt sitting on a wood bench. He is drying his white hair with a towel.

"They can come in in a minute. I'm sorry. I didn't know there was a swim meet here today," he says.

"Yes, it's confusing. Boys lockers turned into girls lockers and girls into boys," I say.

"At least they will have something to talk about in the next two weeks," he adds.

Nodding to him, I gather up their bags and manage to keep a straight face back out in the hallway. "Sorry about that. The poor guy was just getting dressed after his morning swim. You all can go in a few minutes."

With Emily and Tiffany laughing, Alex—her brown eyes staring intently at me—says, "No way. You're not getting me to go back in there."

"Mr. J., where do you expect us to change?" asks Tiffany.

"I don't know, but we have plenty of time. Let's go and see who's in charge," I say. Out on the deck, other teams are arriving, and I find a coach.

"Sorry that had to happen to your girls," she says. "I'll get someone to straighten it out."

Shaking her hand, I say, "Don't worry about it. Thanks for putting on the meet; my girls are thrilled to be here."

It is late in the afternoon, and I am waiting in the van outside the pool. Despite the morning miscue, we have had a good meet. Alex swam her first 200-yard IM, Monica finished second in her fifty-yard freestyle heat, and all four won their heat in the 200-yard freestyle relay.

Alex's mother, up from New Jersey, spots my van and walks over to introduce herself.

"I'm glad you could come and see Alex swim," I say. "She was so happy to see you in the stands. She has really become a fine swimmer."

"I can't tell you how much she has enjoyed this season. Thanks for being so kind to her. She has really enjoyed having you as her coach," she says.

"Yes, we have had our times," I say.

Working with teenagers suits my juvenile nature. As most might recall, incidents such as the above emerge almost miraculously from the humdrum of school life and are not lost on me. Energy and curiosity is what is best in a child, but teachers do their job too well, for the giddy, careless freshman almost always becomes the mature and responsible senior. This is at a cost, as a sophisticated dullness supplants what was once a bright-eyed curiosity. Perhaps life's proper workings require this regression, but not wanting to see this curiosity die, I like to play the jester and involve my students in my readings and odd quests. "Oh, grow up" and "Don't be so foolish" are common refrains, to which I reply, "But why should I?"

A while back a perceptive student said to me, "You are one of us."

Smiling, I replied, "Yes, but probably not for long."

H. L. Mencken was correct (but failed to see any value) when he wrote, "The truth is that the average schoolmaster, on all the lower levels, is and always must be next door to an idiot, for how can one imagine an intelligent man engaging in so puerile an avocation?"

A wooden ramp on our right ends abruptly at the river's edge. Up from the ramp is a pair of corrugated metal containers that house the local public school boats. "Farmington hasn't got its dock in yet," says Kim. The relatively small section of the river that we are able to row on here forces us to stagger practice times with them. Rowing fast-moving eights, their races consist of two lengths—down the river and back up with a turnaround near our dock.

Our third boat glides ahead. "Coxswains, keep the boats together!" shouts Kim.

We will be faced with deciding boat lineups in the coming weeks. Crew is possibly the least exact of all racing sports. What makes for a fast rower or boat is never clear. Erg scores are helpful, but they are often red herrings. Seat racing—where two boats are raced for a set time and the race is then repeated with a pair of rowers swapped—is the commonest, and in practice, the only way to choose between rowers. Fatigue, changing conditions, synergy, and even rower sabotage can turn seat racing into guesswork, though. Boat changes are never pleasant, when they occur. Sullenness and tears are often the result of a lineup change. No one, particularly an adolescent, enjoys being removed from his or her group, and an inseparable group is what every boat inevitably becomes. Cold and impersonal, the term-seat racing conveys a rower's unimportance. Rowers may come and go, but a boat seat is a constant to be defended and fought for. Seat racing is a harsh reality of crew and as such seems good preparation for what our rowers will face later in life.

We are nearing the end of today's practice. Paralleling the riverbank is a trail popular with hikers and joggers. Janet and I have cross-country skied there in past winters. Clearings along the bank allow quick descents out onto the frozen river. The trail has enough dips, turns, and run outs to rivet the attention of a novice skier such as me. Other than coaching crew, I never thought myself very much tied to this river, but today's musings have proved otherwise.

We float a short way up from the dock. Looking back up the river, I see Grier's JV boats are still out.

Seeing Brian's boats being shouldered back to the boathouse, Kim yells, "Amanda, bring it in." Feathering the throttle, I motor the launch's bow up onto the dock. The dock is old, and should too many rowers congregate on an end, the river water will climb their ankles.

Kim walks off to catch our boats. Hauling the launch out of the water and onto the dock, I empty it of oars, cushions, and my toolbox. What will be a daily ritual for me, I lift the engine onto a dolly and begin wheeling it up the gangway. After sitting for so long in the launch, I enjoy the engine's tug.

Up on the dike, I trudge toward the boathouse. A small lake created by more dredging lies on my right. Kim and I held a practice there on a warm day last year, but today, a whitish-gray ice sheet covers half its surface. Mergansers float near the ice sheet. During the summer and fall, I swim here too. When someone steps off the bank, the water drops off to untold depths. The small lake is mostly lifeless, other than the occasional smallmouth bass seen darting off into the green water.

Nearing the boathouse, I pause and wait until Brian's boats are racked inside our boathouse. I think back a few weeks to the end of swim season.

I was little enthusiastic when I awoke and looked at the sky's gray pall out my motel room's window, and as I am driving through coastal New Hampshire's melancholy winter landscape, my spirits are no better. Exiting the expressway, I follow the frozen Squamscott River as it winds through light brown marsh land. Finding the school, I drop the swimmers off outside the athletic center. I park near an imposing brick smokestack, and thoughts of steam, hissing pipes, and black smoke flood my mind. Glad to be out of the cold, I find our team on the pool deck. After dropping off my backpack, I climb to the top of the concrete stands and gaze down on the many swimmers frothing the water below.

I am here for the New England Prep School Swimming Championships. My swimmers having swum their last meet last week, I expect only to do catchall duties such as filming, timing, and shuttling swimmers back to the motel. The pool below will be everyone's focus today, but there is an older pool hidden somewhere in the school's labyrinthine athletic complex. I hope to find it today.

The morning heats are nearing an end, and I have captured some good video of our swimmers. After I arrive home tonight, I will edit the tape in time for tomorrow's assembly. Always trying to discern what makes for fast swimming, I have enjoyed the races. The front crawl is an unbalanced and disfigured stroke, and I think it is ironic with its contorted breathing that it is the fastest. The butterfly has potential, though. Perhaps another John Trudgen—who revolutionized swimming back in England with a stroke he learned from South

CROSSINGS: A SWIMMER'S MEMOIR

American Indians—will appear someday and swim the butterfly faster than anyone can imagine.

Later, at lunch, I listen as the other coaches discuss the morning and how their teams have fared. One coach, recalling his times competing here, remarks how he "enjoyed the solitude of the warm-up pool." Tempted to ask for more details, I say nothing.

I am in the athletic center's older section now. I walk across a tennis court that was laid out over an old basketball court. The odor of chlorine hints that a pool is near. Pushing through a pair of doors, I walk down some cramped stairs and out onto a narrow deck. Light shining through translucent glass only faintly lights the space. A student lifeguard sits reading a magazine while a lone girl swims. The pool is narrow, and not having any lane lines, its surface is a jangle of sharp waves. The light blue water lies several feet below the deck and conjures for me the image of a well. At one end, a couple of water polo balls and nets lie in a pile. The coach at lunch was right; the pool offers a respite, even if a forlorn one, from the noisy competition pool. No records are affixed to its white walls, but I recall one broken here years ago.

On your mark, go! There was a complex moment when his body uncoiled and shot forward with sudden metallic tension. He planed up the pool, his shoulders dominating the water while his legs and feet rode so low that I couldn't distinguish them. A wake rippled hurriedly by him, and then at the end of the pool again, his position broke. He relaxed, dived, an instant of confusion, and then his suddenly and metallically tensed body shot back toward the other end of the pool. Another turn, and then up the pool again—I noticed no particular slackening of his pace. Another turn, down the pool again, his hand touched the other end, and he looked up at me with a composed, interested expression. "Well, how did I do?"

A SEASON ON THE FARMINGTON RIVER

I looked at the watch; he had broken A. Hopkins Parker's record by .7 seconds.

Our rowers seated in the van, I drive us out along an undulating dirt road. A cornfield covered with patches of snow lies on my left. Spring rains make for treacherous driving down here. While swinging wide to avoid a large puddle last spring, the van's rear wheels sank deep into the sodden ground. A tow truck was needed to extricate us.

Turning onto the pavement, I gaze up at a high dirt embankment. Come May, its face will be pockmarked with hundreds of round holes, each a swallow's nest. Resembling bats, the swallows will stream out on their way to the river.

On our drive east, we are stopped by traffic. While Kim answers questions about the upcoming season, I reflect on the old pool up in New Hampshire.

The excerpt above is from John Knowles's novel, *A Separate Peace*. During the Second World War, Knowles was a student and swim team member at the school where our swimming championship was held. I thought it might be interesting to see the pool he might have had in mind when his Phineas broke the school's hundred-yard freestyle record.

Although his book is not particularly great literature, I nonetheless admire it, for aside from its few pages devoted to swimming, the book depicts an adolescence that is guileless, ebullient, and vigorous. Set against a looming war, Knowles's novel follows the tragically intertwined lives of two schoolmates—Gene and Phineas—during a summer and subsequent year at the fictional Devon School.

The preparatory school world, with its expectations for life's orderly progression and future successes, has not surprisingly been the source of books chronicling sensational, but predictable tales of adolescent failings. Many of these works twaddle and muck about with the worst of adolescence, yet *A Separate Peace* offers what Knowles himself has called "a gorgeous world." Nowadays, many of our young have lost his world, and I believe it is in part because they have simply stopped moving. Youth is movement, and Knowles's Gene and Phineas are never at rest. They initiate a snowball fight, break a school swimming record, bicycle to the New Hampshire seacoast for an ocean swim, organize a winter carnival, and train for the 1944 Olympics. Knowles's novel is at about action, vigorous action.

I have heard veteran elementary teachers lament their students' loss of fitness and coordination. While I do not advocate a return to illiteracy, shouldn't this slide spur action? If in promoting the Special Olympics, we see the benefits of vigorous activity for our challenged children, why not require the same for every child? Besides improved health and warding off a jaded sophistication, physical activity's inevitable knocks and blows may even be necessary for our mental development. A mind no less than Isaac Newton attributed his mental awakening to his mashing a schoolyard bully's nose into a church wall as retribution for the painful kick he received from the tough guy.

The unabashed impostures and outright stupidities youth perceive in the adult world can be their undoing. They imbibe life deeply, and this, along with their black-and-white morality, leaves them poorly equipped to handle life's grays. Nihilism, cynicism, apathy, depression, and misguided rebellion are the despairing responses one often sees after a first contact with an adult world. Sports, though, are tangible and direct. They can offer adolescents the clearest picture of themselves and others. In the pool or gym, on the track, playing field, or back on the Farmington River, everyone's character is laid bare; pretense is exposed; injustices are righted; and almost everything is resolved decisively. Of course, competition is not for everyone, nor it should be—there are substitutes.

I have stopped the van in front of our school's main building. "Don't forget. We meet tomorrow afternoon at three-thirty, so don't be late," says Kim.

Opening the doors, I feel the van rock as each girl steps down. "Thanks, Coach J," and "Goodbye" are heard as they pass by.

Kim, exiting last, says, "Well, that's day one."

"It's going to be an interesting spring," I say. "No doubt. See you tomorrow."

Closing the doors, I pull out and merge into traffic. In the van mirrors, I catch sight of the rowers. Their brightly colored water bottles in hand, they walk off in groups of two or three. I know they may not realize it today, next week, or even at the season's end, but more than a mere source of satisfaction in the prosaic years to come, their recollections of their times on the river will gladden their hearts and embolden their spirits. The Farmington River's waters abide.

")))"

More than eight weeks have passed since that first day on the Farmington River. Standing here at the bridge center, I can trace the outline of Lake Quinsigamond's north basin. Spotted with a few snowy clouds, the sky is colored a brilliant blue. A cool breeze blows out of the northwest. Today is one of those pleasing days when hot and cold magically mix to raise goose bumps and make one shudder with delight.

A mile distant, I can discern the next heat's boats maneuvering into a position. Puffs of wind are made visible by the shadows they cast across the lake. Spectators throng on the shore to my left. A judge's hut housing video equipment is set out on an island down from the crowd. Everyone there is focused on the finish marker across the lake.

The boats are aligned, and I can make out their first few strokes. The race under way, the coxswains, after stepping their rowers through the start, are calling power tens or twenties. From here the boats appear minuscule, without color, and seem propelled by rhythmic, easy strokes. Like watching a silent film, the muted, placid scene belies the rowers' heaving chests, the clunking oarlocks, the blades' quick splash, and the coxswains' exhortations.

"Your boat looks to be ahead," says a coach.

"Yes, but there's a still a long way to go,'" I say.

The boats are now in sight of the spectators. I hear cheers, shouts, and a clanking cowbell. What looks like a long oil slick trails each boat. I begin to wonder at its persistence, but my attention is drawn to a woman holding an orange flag. No more than twenty strokes remain, and our first boat is ahead of a fast-moving crew on its port side. The two boats driving toward the finish, I see in quick succession the flag swing down and then up. First and second places have been claimed. The flag will fall and rise as the other boats finish, but the race is over for Brian's first boat. It has won its heat and qualified for the afternoon's grand final.

Our first boat sits dead in the water close to the bridge. The four in the boat sit slouched forward, gasping for air. Cupping my hands, I shout, "Way to go!" A couple of them look up and return small waves.

"Nice race," says the coach.

"Thanks. The pain is always easier to take after a win. Is your boat in the next heat?"

"Yes, it is."

"Wish I could watch, but I have to catch up with my rowers," I say.

Turning away, I walk along the bridge's raised walkway. The fast-moving traffic makes me cringe, and I break into a jog. Exiting the bridge, I enter Regatta Point Park. Here, cradled in aluminum-framed boat slings, repose the boats from New England's grand old prep schools. I pass Andover's and Kent's dark blue eights, Groton's bright yellow fours, and Deerfield's new sinister black double-hulled boats. Eschewing carbon fiber, purist St. Paul's light-colored cedar eights are a link to rowing's past. When I first began coaching crew, I studied racing shells. Now, knowing any boat can be fast given the right crew, I spend my time sizing up rowers.

I pass some closely packed tents pitched on the land back from a small beach. Spacious, with their peaked roofs, most tents have their school name emblazoned above their open fronts. Inside, parents, rowers, and coaches shuffle along white-clothed tables covered with salads, sandwiches, cakes, and pies. Outside many of the tents, bluish-white smoke rises up from grilling hamburgers and hot dogs. The lengthy time between races allows, if not encourages, an all-day-long picnic.

When I find Kim, she says, "I'm going to take the girls back to the hotel and let them rest before their race. I thought you could save my parking space, while I take them in my car."

"Fine; what time should I meet you?"

"Give me an hour or so," she says.

I move the van forward after Kim drives off. Slipping off my deck shoes, I lace on my running flats. I have time for a run before Kim returns.

Setting off slowly, I start up a long hill. Glad to be moving, I am on my way up to the defunct Worcester State Hospital's grounds. I discovered the old asylum during a run last year and enjoyed its solitude. The noisy traffic and sunlit sidewalk whitewashing my mind, snippets from our season intrude on me.

Not long after our first practice, a new ash-gray, plastic dock appears, and melting snows up the Berkshires brindle the river with enmeshed leaves, twigs, and branches. . . . *The river—flickering with an electric light—silhouettes rowers at the start of a predawn practice. . . . The day is gray and drizzly as we motor along Boston's grassy-banked Charles River. Turquoise, maroon, and gold cupolas rise above Harvard's ivy and red brick. The first boat race is under way, but I* am uneasy. Earlier, after the host school's coach nearly ran our launch into a bridge arch, I took over the tiller, but having regained her seat in the stern, she is now too close to the launch ahead. Motioning to her, she veers off and finds smoother water. While passing under a bridge arch, she has again encroached on the launch ahead. None of us can foresee the wave that reflects off the bridge walls. In an instant, our bow plows under an ocean wave. Kim, sitting in the bow, is washed off her seat. I fall back and slump into the boat hull. The coach next to me somehow remains seated. Our launch lurches, balks, and trembles, but somehow stays afloat. Saddened to see the crews race off to the finish line, I am surprised by how warm the Charles River feels for April. A swim would not at all be unpleasant. ... Back on the Farmington River, a hawk wheels above, and a skunk stink later fills the air. Kim and I motor over to see three red-faced turkey vultures gathered about a kill. Brownish-black and larger than a rooster, the vultures stare back at us defiantly. ... Blue-backed swallows arrive and burrow into the high sandy embankment. Swooping and skimming inches above the river's surface, they swerve just before impacting the launch. ... Starting our crews off on a warm-up row, and a river otter, looking like a seal, pops his head out of the river. Wearing a happy grin, he locks eyes with our coxswain Amanda, but before she can cry out or Kim or I can raise a voice, he is gone.

 ... A second autumn has come. Buds of gold and crimson color the trees along the riverbank before giving way to a lime green haze. ... It is a cold, wet afternoon on a lake in western Connecticut. Low gray clouds have been rolling in from the south since we arrived. Brian motors around the point in a flat-bottomed, green launch. Both his boats have won their races. Kim and I jump onboard, and we speed off. The opposite shore, visible all afternoon, soon vanishes beneath what looks like a low cloud. Not long after, we are enshrouded in thick fog.

A SEASON ON THE FARMINGTON RIVER

The lake shores obscured, Brian says, "I don't like this. We need to find our crews."

"Hopefully, the other launches are with them," says Kim.

The throttle wide open, we speed over the flat water. Pockets of dense fog dampen my face; I can see nothing but gray water and white mist. Today, though, we are lucky, as a shoreline filled with docks, pleasure boats, and cottages emerges out of the fog. We veer right, and like an apparition, one of our boats appears, rowing toward us. It is such an ancient sight, a sight gratefully seen by countless mariners over the centuries. They lead us to the other crews. The races are postponed; later all are canceled, because of high winds.

Winds blowing the lake's length have been fetching large waves at the start all morning. The first few hundred meters have been unrowable at times; some crews have been nearly swamped. After contesting only one of the final races, the regatta organizers are gathered in launches about a pontoon boat in the lake center. Strong gusts, flattening and darkening broad swatches of the lake, threaten to scatter their boats. "I'm ready to cancel this fucking regatta," booms across the lake. Soon after, a decision is reached; the regatta is over. On the drive home, I wonder whatever possessed me to get involved with such an unforgiving sport.

It is our last day on the Farmington River, and my little German general—the red-winged blackbird—flits ahead of my van. We have overstayed our welcome, and he happily escorts us out.

Reaching the asylum, I find an old maple to sit under and stretch. When I stumbled upon the abandoned buildings last year, I guessed they were part of an old hospital. Later I learned they were what remained of the Worcester State Hospital, built in the 1880s. Large sections were torn down after a fire, but the remaining structures are remarkable. An ominous clock tower, with its blue-green roof and red-brick-framed windows, brings to mind images of Prague.

Nearby, looking like a giant yurt, stands a rotunda. Silent and serene, the buildings and grounds speak nothing of the troubled, tortured souls who once resided here.

I like this high place. With a breeze rustling the maple leaves, I think how torn I am between high places and water. Both are twin loves of mine. When driving past some hill or mountain, I will feel the urge to pull over and bound up its slope. Perhaps it is a strange compulsion, but I am not alone. The corpses littering Mt. Everest and other high peaks attest to mountains' pull. Over the years, I have cycled, hiked, and run up peaks in the Berkshires, Smokies, and White Mountains. Always, upon return, I have felt improved. Mountains' salutary benefits have long been known. Back when a classicist friend and I both had homes in the piney flatland north of Houston, he noted that even "the ancients recognized the healthfulness of residing on high ground."

I am wary of water, though, for simply being near it predisposes one to venality. A walk through the New Orleans French Quarter or along Key West's Duval Street shows life there devolving into decadence. Sin City Las Vegas (The Meadows, in Spanish) was once an oasis in the Mojave Desert. Holland's windmills and dikes have kept the water out for centuries, but perhaps the sea has already claimed seedy Amsterdam. Water, life's source, is not to be trusted. Water is not only perilous, it is also soft and seductive. Whereas spiritual enlightenment can be found on mountaintops, listlessness and a bad case of sunburn usually result from a day at the beach. Familiar is the image of self-reliant mountain man, but beaches always have their bums.

Vigorous sports such as swimming and rowing are the best safeguards when near water. Whenever I visit a beach littered with sunbathers, I am surprised to be the only one person off shore, swimming alone. I wonder how so many could have failed to see water for what it is: nature's universal solvent.

A SEASON ON THE FARMINGTON RIVER

The clock tower's frozen hands remind me of the unfinished business in the basin below. Standing, I run off, on guard.

Maybe because we have spent so much time together in the launch, Kim stands a ways up from me on the narrow beach, barely a football field in length, manmade, and quite insignificant as beaches go.

I hear a crowd roar and see our third boat—a streak of black—sprint from last place to claim a second-place medal. . . . It's then Brian's emerald green boat fending off another crew's late rush to win our school's only New England Championship. ... Now it's my daughter's boat, flying in the far outside lane, holding on to win first place. ... A year later, on a cold rainy morning, her boat fades, not even qualifying for the afternoon final. She and her fellow rowers sit motionless, slumped in their seats. They add their tears to the many others who have filled this lake.

Breaking in on my reminiscences, the public address system sounds, "And they're off. It's a clean start with all boats moving well."

The third boat finals are under way. This race is our only chance for a medal, as our fourth boat failed to qualify for its final this morning. The canceled regattas have made choosing boat lineups difficult this season. Our third boat lineup was finally set only ten days ago, when we winnowed four rowers from eight during two hours of seat racing. Defying erg scores and coaches' prejudices, all of the four rowing out there won their seats where it mattered most—on the water.

The announcer has us among the early leaders. Hearing this, Kim looks back and raises a clenched fist. I wave and nod in her direction. Like the Holy Trinity, what makes for a fast boat is a mystery of mysteries. The four out there, Ama, Andi, Pauline, and Hoppy, did not have the fastest erg times and at times did not seem particularly hard working, inspired, or focused; neither did they have the best technique, but when it counted, they rowed fast together, really fast. I am not surprised to hear we have a lead over Deerfield.

I can see a boat appear in the far lane. The other five boats soon come into view. The press boat drops off, its last report being, "Deerfield might have regained the advantage." The crowd is pressed against the shoreline. Loud shouts are heard and cowbells clank. Moving across my field of vision, our boat and Deerfield are wrapped in battle. Green against black, it is now a two-boat race. Like boxers exchanging blows, each boat is looking for that one stroke that will separate it from the other and seize victory. "Don't quit! Come on. Come on, pull," I hear myself growl. The crowd's roar reverberates in my chest, and time slows as both boats drive toward the finish. After crossing the line, the crews check water and come to rest before the bridge. The angle is deceptive, but I know; we missed winning by maybe half a boat length. "So close," I think. "They had a better sprint than us. Maybe if we were gutsier in the mid-race, we might have gotten them." I catch sight of Kim bounding down the beach.

Reaching me, she is all smiles and yells, "Yeah!"

Slapping her hand, I say, "Not too shabby, coach."

The first and second boats will row their races later, but our medal will be the only one won today. The spring has not been kind.

Brian, Kim, and I are busy loading the boats on the trailer. I like this after-race ritual; pressing the shells overhead, placing them on the trailer's racks, and hearing the hulls creak and groan as the cloth straps are pulled tight. Securing the boats grounds me after a regatta's ups and downs.

The oars and riggers loaded and the aluminum boat slings stacked and lashed, the rowers and coxswains stand huddled in twos and threes. They seem happy to be going home. Their season is over, and the afternoons will be theirs again. There will be no more five a.m. wake-up calls, rain-soaked rows, screaming ergometer sessions, bloody blisters, or aching backs to suffer. Their muscles and tendons can soften and slack, their nerves can relax, and their pulses slow. And although a few will spend a week or two at some rowing camp, most I suppose will laze the summer away with family and friends. But if not this summer, then one day, all will surely come to share the regret expressed in the lines of Rudyard Kipling's "Galley Slave," knowing well what it was to have rowed, and more, what was lost:

> But to-day I leave the galley and another takes my place; There's my name upon the deck-beam-let it stand a little space. I am free-to watch my messmates beating out to open main, Free of all that Life can offer-save to handle sweep again.
>
> By the brand upon my shoulder, by the gall of clinging steel,
> By the welt the whips have left me, by the scars that never heal;
> By eyes grown old with staring through the sunwash on the brine,
> I am paid in full for service. Would that service still were mine!
>
> It may be that Fate will give me life and leave to row once more— Set some strong man free for fighting as I take awhile his oar.
> But to-day I leave the galley. Shall I curse her service then?
> God be thanked! Whate'er comes after, I have lived and toiled with Men!

CHAPTER 9

Walden Pond

The life in us is like the water in the river. It may rise this year higher than man has ever known it, and flood the parched uplands; even this may be the eventful year, which will drown out all our muskrats.
—Henry David Thoreau

Things were not going well for him. His life poorly planned, his way had narrowed and then suddenly came to an end. Over the years, there had been hints and words that might have helped him, but he chose to ignore them. Preferring fantasy and escapism, he let opportunity after opportunity to find a way through slip by, and now he was gripped by malaise, a malaise that was broken only by debilitating hypochondria and shattering panic. He had taken to calling his malaise an emotional flu. "Yes, I have an emotional flu," he would say to himself. His malaise was not new to him. Troubling him off and on since his youth, it was no more than an annoyance back then. Like a cold or fever, his malaise would run its course over time, but as he aged, his bouts became more severe, so much so that he had sought help beyond the general practitioner's office.

As of late, he had undergone weekly sessions where, still dressed in a shirt and tie from work, he crawled into what looked like a gigantic white egg. There, before the upper half of the egg was lowered, he donned headphones and reclined on a water mattress. Engulfed in total darkness, he listened to a tape on which a soothing voice retold a popular children's story or asked him to imagine some bucolic scene before dissolving into a pair discordant voices.

His doctor, named Dr. G., was very hopeful. Dr. G. spoke of the power of the unconscious, sensory-deprivation chambers, and the relevance of the movie *Altered States* to his case. He had never seen or heard of Dr. G's movie and had no experience with what seemed to him a form of hypnosis or subliminal suggestion, beyond the time a hypnotist visited his psychology class back in high school. That experience—besides being some years ago—only left him feeling groggy and with a mild headache, despite his expectations for some sort of revelation. Desperate for relief, he too shared Dr. G's optimism.

As Dr. G. explained, the first few tapes would enable him to relax and lay the groundwork for the later ones. These would in turn energize him and help him realize new goals for his life, and it was true, for those first few weeks, he did experience an easing of his malaise. He was sleeping better, and he believed he was more productive at work.

Cruelly paradoxical, he knew from past bouts with his malaise that it was his free time—his leisure hours—when he suffered the most. Unable to relax, he would feel his throat tighten and his chest constrict, and he awakened with night sweats. He often felt what seemed like an electric current pulsing through his body. Other times he felt dry and brittle, as if his body might crumple like a withered leaf. When he was out for a walk, the ground sometimes felt as if it were moving under his feet. Feeling unsure of his next step, he would stop to right himself before proceeding. This embarrassed him, and he wondered if others noticed. There was also his sensitivity to fluorescent lights and bright colors, which produced a sense of unreality, suffocation, and claustrophobia in him. Even worse was the fear that he might faint or suffer a heart attack when he was out shopping at a crowded mall or market. And yet he hated being at home, resting, for an impossible desire to flee his body would often grip him. His malaise symptoms were variegated, and if someone would listen, he could recite a litany of them. His malaise had become his own private Hydra; it was his omnipresent monster.

Unfortunately for him, the palliative effects of Dr. G's tapes lessened over the weeks. He thought it curious, how listening to the tapes had somehow rechanneled his panic. When feeling anxious or panicky, he no longer hyperventilated to the point of lightheadedness. Instead, when beset, he found that his breathing became heavy and labored, his lower jaw gyrated involuntarily, and his eyes watered. As he embarked on the last round of tapes, a sense of exigency came over him. He felt more driven at work; he took more upon himself and hatched grand plans in his mind. He felt a pressure, an energy, pushing him, but all this came to an end as he grew weary and became fatigued. His insomnia returned, and he was again not able to taste his food. These symptoms added to his worry, as he was certain he was losing weight. "I should have just stuck with those first couple of tapes," he lamented to himself.

He began to seek relief in odd places. In the afternoons after lunch, he escaped into his office building stairwell. There he sat on a landing and attempted to console himself. Occasionally the odor of a lit cigarette would waft up from someone sneaking a smoke some flights below. Hearing footsteps above or below sent him fleeing back to his desk. At other times, he climbed the stairs up to his office building's roof. Amid the roaring evaporators, he sought to numb his pain. It was then June. The warm weather, blue skies, and a spectacular view of the city should have gladdened him, but an empty wall might have been in front of him, for he felt nothing. He was only filled with a sense of dread, as if some sort of disaster seemed imminent.

Before coming under the care of Dr. G., he had tried traditional talking cures with Freudians. They had prescribed tranquilizers for him, which he was glad to take, and although these pills did provide some short-term relief, he did not like taking them, because he soon became dependent on them; dependent to the point that he could not leave his apartment without having a full bottle in his top coat pocket. Like those who in times of need clutch and knead a rosary, he busied himself by opening and closing the pills' bottle cap.

He had discussed the tranquilizers with Dr. G. early in his treatment, and of course was warned of their danger. Nonetheless, he still possessed a good number of the pills, and as he slipped further, he resumed taking them. He hated himself for doing this and would often stare in the amber bottle, jostling the pills around, before giving in and swallowing a couple. Perhaps it was a blessing as he soon found that the pills, like the tapes, offered him little respite. He could no longer deny it; he was spent, emotionally exhausted, if not burned out. He sought out a general practitioner who dispensed some salve for a minor infection in his left eye. This doctor, hearing of his troubles in the course of his examination, remarked, "You're probably someone who cannot take a lot of stress."

Despite the beehive of physicians swarming about him, he soon found what seemed like a new bump on his nose and was sure it was cancer. There was no means to stave off his downward slide.

Hearing that he had resumed taking the pills, Dr. G. knew the man was a lost cause and decided that it would be best to be done with him. Knowing the embarrassment he felt about his condition, Dr. G. asked him during a phone call whether he would be willing to be part of documentary on his experience using the tapes. Back before the time when it was common to make every private woe public, his doctor's proposal appalled and angered him. Words were exchanged, and their conversation ended with idle talk of a lawsuit. It was a sad, strange end to his relationship with Doctor G. The doctor, so happy to woo him away from a Freudian only a few months before, was now no less glad to be rid of him.

Back at work things grew worse. He spent more time out of his office, often coming in late. Always a teetotaler, he began having a few glasses of wine after work, thinking these might help. The wine did help him fall asleep, but he failed to sleep through the night, always awaking in the early morning hours. After getting dressed, he wandered about the apartment until it was time for his commute. He started skipping lunch to stave off the gagging sensation that usually followed a meal. He did not really mind not eating, as the food had no taste. He lost weight, but so as not to alarm anyone, he kept the information to himself. Despite his being exhausted after a day at the office, the disorienting sense of panic he felt on the subway ride home sometimes caused him to miss his stop. There was one crowded ride when another rider, noticing his distress, took pleasure in tormenting him with talk of "crashes, flooded tunnels, and fires." Too distressed to move, he stood in place, tightly holding onto a support pole. After exiting the car, he walked quickly toward the stairs leading to the street. He did not get very far before he was doubled over by an attack of dry heaves.

When the Fourth of July came, he bought some sparklers and bottle rockets to entertain the kids back in his neighborhood. This purchase was odd, for he had no interest anymore in such things. Perhaps he hoped the sparklers' bright light and the rockets' hiss and crack might lift his spirits. The holiday came and went. Back at his office, he gazed out his window and wondered if anyone in the neighboring high rises would notice if he launched a rocket. The image of a tiny rocket lost in the canyon of buildings made him feel sick to his stomach and brought a bad taste to his mouth.

Later he traveled to Florida with his family. He sat in a large amphitheater to watch marine animals perform. Killer whales (orcas) were the star attraction. Watching their endless circling in their large tank, he wondered about their flaccid dorsal fins. He knew from photographs that killer whales' fins stood tall in the wild. He saw them as martyrs for their race, and supposed they missed the open ocean. The killer whales' black-and-white colors attracted him more than the water's sapphire color. Before the start of the show, he walked down to peer through the tank glass. Like apparitions, the orcas suddenly appeared and then as quickly vanished behind what looked like a wall of blue. Feeling weary, he rested his hands on the metal frame atop the glass. He was finding some amusement when he heard, "Sir, please remove your hands from the tank." Stepping back, he turned and felt assaulted by a young female attendant's upset look. "I was all right; I could see them," he said before walking off.

His malaise marred all things. Driving to the seaside with his wife and young daughter for a few days' stay, he had not traveled far before he was forced to exit the expressway. Leaving his wife with his daughter in the car, he wandered off toward some bushes, away from the roadway. There he was overcome with such panic that his body convulsed and his vision blurred for a time. This epileptic-type episode was cathartic, though, and when back on the highway, he thought he had somehow exorcised his demons. Although he did feel better for a time, much like with a dose of food poisoning, his malaise returned again, undiminished.

Not long after his break with Dr. G., the crisis he felt powerless to prevent overwhelmed him. Quitting his job, he abandoned his wife and child in the city in the hope that a more rural life might provide him some relief. It was an awful, shameful time for him, and perhaps he should have chosen hospitalization instead of fleeing, but he could not even contemplate, let alone do something like this. Having always seen himself as strong, without weakness, that he might now need help was hateful to him. He instead blamed his troubles on the city, never considering that his malaise might have some psychic or organic origin.

It is difficult to describe his first month outside the city. His life smashed and torn apart, he lived in a twilight world of fear and remorse. The days passed, but he had no more than a hazy sense of the summer dying about him. Having a fondness for landscapes, he took some joy in again seeing the rise of the land, a far-off hill, or a distant line of trees on a ridge. At other times, just basking in the late summer sun seemed to help revive his spirits. Besides his malaise, he was also struggling with his addiction to the tranquilizers, and weeks would pass before he shook the urge to swallow any. He visited yet another doctor, who performed a physical on him. Other than his blood work indicating that he was run down, the doctor found him physically sound.

October morning frosts and the barking of far-off dogs brought back some pleasing memories. Feeling restless and wanting to be of use, he found work emptying out a department store. Scrutinized by the foreman, he was surprised to be among those asked back the next day. He then moved on to making deliveries for a warehouse and later ran a plastic injection-molding machine. The owner planned to expand and wondered if he would head up the operation. Fearful that his malaise might return, and missing the outdoors, he instead moved on to work with a paving crew. Happy to be working outdoors, he felt renewed. He liked hearing a shovel slice into gravel, feeling the weight a pickax, and smelling the scent of fresh pine. He found the strain of carrying buckets of tar strangely gratifying. Years had passed since he done such labor; he saw that his body needed to be worked.

Away from the cubicles and his frigid air conditioned office back in the city, his malaise began to abate. Nonetheless, he was living an isolated and joyless life. He harbored tremendous guilt over his failure in the city. Like an escaped convict, he was mum on his past life, should he be found out. Occasionally others would notice there was something not right with him. An empathetic fellow at the warehouse asked him why he was so sad, and there was the time in a hair salon when the young woman who was cutting his hair, unable to contain herself, blurted out, "Please stop it! You are so depressed, it is freaking me out." Off with the paving crew on a job in the mountains, he and coworkers were amusing themselves throwing stones at lot signs. The mood changed when he picked up an oversized rock and hurled it crazily, cracking the wood. "Hey, man, take it easy," said a coworker. Having lost some sense of his outward demeanor, he was taken aback. There were still times when he felt as if he were suffocating, and after lunch, his eyes often watered and he gagged, but relieved to be sleeping again, he was grateful for the long hours of work.

He was sad when winter put an end to his work with the paving crew. That work suited him, but believing he needed more challenging work, work that might lead to a career, he took a job in a metal shop. Here, amid the clunking of presses, the flash of welding arcs, and the acrid smell of spent corundum paper, he fell into a routine of ten-hour days. Cognizant of the Middle Age craft guilds and their tightly guarded secrets, he imagined himself privy to some ancient arts. Shoring up his belief was Jim, one of the two brothers who owned the shop. Jim lamented, "No one wants to do this type of work anymore," and "ours is a dying art."

Adding to this was a welder's remark, "I hope you realize how special this shop is."

Over the months, he came to like the cold, heavy feel of metal in his hands. The exactness, orderliness, and repetitiveness of his new job encouraged his introspective nature. There was ample time to ruminate on his past. Standing before a press with calipers in hand, he nudged and tapped a jig to keep tolerances within a few thousandths of an inch. The rolling, bending, drilling, and grinding of the steel, aluminum, copper, and brass were a revelation to him. He borrowed an old book from the shop on developing sheet metal patterns. Recalling the patterns his mother had used in dressmaking, he comprehended for the first time the term *metal fabrication*.

To someone looking in from the outside, his job choice might have seemed random. It was if he had cut out classified ads from the newspaper, scrambled them, and after blindly choosing one, he announced, "Yes, this is what I'll do." If he had chosen any other work, this might have been true, but he had learned mechanical skills from his father, and there was the strong influence of a longtime friend, who on a canoe trip with him, waxed lyrically over the compound curve of their craft's aluminum bow. To his addled mind, working with metal had some exotic attraction, but perhaps the real reason for his choice was that it was something he needed to do. He had felt his job in the city was stultifying, even unmanly; he felt he had missed some important rite of passage. Like the metal he worked, he too needed forming.

He still worried about himself, though. Relieved of much of his malaise, he was functioning, but he often wished to be old and done with his life. At other times, the realization seized him that he was nothing but a jumble of atoms and could melt into the earth. This thought terrified him, and attempting to flee, he suddenly would walk off or fidget. A bright spot for him, though, when work dragged, was a fellow named Jack. In his late fifties, Jack ran a press in the back room. Jack mostly kept to himself. There was a thoughtful irreverence about Jack that he liked. During his breaks, he liked to sit and chat with him. "This type of work attracts a lot of drunks," Jack told him. Suffering from kidney failure, Jack left work early three days a week for dialysis treatment. Seeing Jack come in on Mondays well rested but leave Fridays stooped and haggard emboldened him.

Away from work he was happy to rest, lest his malaise return. He donated most of his books tied to his life in the city to the local library, parted with his stereo system, and lit fire to his many notes and papers. These things that had once been so important to him seemed inconsequential as they smoldered and flamed in an open field. He intuited that by slowing down and casting off his life's detritus, he might begin to heal. Not only were Dr. G.'s tapes rattling around in his head, so where the sounds and images from countless books, movies, newspapers, ads, and family and friends. All was so much noise to him; he began to relish his solitude.

Having regained some of his equanimity, he looked for ways to fill up his hours after work. No longer interested in newspapers, radio, TV, and the like, or feeling much like exercising after standing long hours, or wishing to pick up a new hobby, he began to read. An inveterate reader since his high school days, his life in the city had left him little time for this pastime. The books he donated were tied to his old life, and that life had ended. He now sought books suited to his increasingly introspective nature. He was slowing down, becoming more pensive, and he did not want to feel rushed or hurried. He was not seeking any sort of payoff and did not want to adhere to any timetable. His malaise having quashed his ambitions, he felt freer. When before, he might have felt he was wasting time, his thoughts now were, "Maybe it'll take me months to finish this book, but so what?, I'm not going anywhere." He had been holding onto so many dreams and aspirations that it was unnerving to let go, but slowly, he loosened his grip.

How he obtained a copy of Robert M. Pirsig's *Zen and the Art of Motorcycle Maintenance* is lost, but this was the book he settled on. He had a curious history with this book. Published when he was a teen, the book created enough buzz to reach his ears one afternoon while he was perplexing over the source of an intermittent short in a friend's motorcycle. "You should check out that book," said Rick.

"Oh, yeah," he said, before returning to the problem. He was an avid motorcyclist then, and when not riding his Honda Twin, he was working on it. Several years passed before he followed Rick's advice and picked up Pirsig's book, actually three books in one. He skimmed the book chapters on his first read, interested primarily in the cross-country motorcycle trip Pirsig took with his son. His mind shrank and retreated from the philosophical digressions and Pirsig's mental collapse. Viewing the book as unfinished business, he looked now to read deeper.

He was soon drawn into Pirsig's contemplative, if not self-absorbed book. He meditated on Pirsig's struggles with mental illness and the concept of quality. Having never been exposed to philosophical writing, he roamed happily over what seemed like a new world. Employing scant quotes or references, Pirsig built what was for him an imposing edifice of thought. He was drawn to Pirsig's discussion of art and technology and the grand synthesis Pirsig claimed to have achieved between Eastern and Western philosophy. He read that Pirsig also had periods of "drifting laterally." His malaise having turned his focus inward, he empathized with Pirsig's sufferings. Not caring or even cognizant of what the world thought of the book, he read in isolation. By reading slowly and reflecting on what he read, he discovered the book had a therapeutic effect on him. He felt a lightening in his chest and a certain joyful relief upon reading some passages. Pirsig's book—if not curing him—was at least ameliorating his malaise. He believed he had hit upon something that might help him. Back at work, he put into practice what seemed the essence of Pirsig's book—thoughtful, caring workmanship. When faced with a lengthy or repetitive job, he amused himself by experimenting with the sequence of operations required to complete the task. For most tasks, certain motions could be simplified or completely eliminated to speed things up. Being nothing more than simple time-and-motion analyses, these discoveries were not great, but they were his finds, and better, they lifted his mood. Sometimes he became so engrossed that he needed to be reminded to take a break or stop for lunch. Pirsig had it right; when faced with a tedious task, one should not tune out, but rather immerse one's self, all the while being vigilant for the untried or new. He was embarrassed and felt sorry for himself that he had not realized this fact long ago. He felt that he existed in a pit, a hole so deep that it would take a lifetime to climb out.

He had no communication with his wife until he was served with a divorce summons one evening. He was charged, naturally enough, with abandonment. His wife loved the city and wished to remain there. The summons added to his malaise and shame. Feeling like an abject failure, he nonetheless believed he could transform himself, if he only had the time. Needing to retain an attorney, he traveled back to the city. The day was cold and clear, and although apprehensive, he was surprised to find the city innocuous. "Perhaps I am changing," he thought. He later found work tutoring high school students a few nights a week. Near the end of the winter, he restored his old ten-speed bicycle. His plan was to bike to work when the weather warmed.

On the lookout for new insights, he was receptive to anything that resonated with him. At work, the vapid songs that played ceaselessly on the radio were an annoyance, until he heard Dylan intone the following:

> You used to ride on the chrome horse with your diplomat
> Who carried on his shoulder a Siamese cat
> Ain't it hard when you discover that
> He really wasn't where it's at
> After he took from you everything he could steal.

He began renting movies on the weekends. His mind haunted by Indians and how their way of life might offer him an escape, he took to John Boorman's *The Emerald Forest*. This movie—the story of a tribe of Amazonian Indians who carry off a young white boy in order to save him from ecological destruction—rattled around in his mind for weeks. Watching Ryuzo Kikushima's *Runaway Train,* he listened intently while Eric Roberts (playing an escaped convict on the run with fellow convict Jon Voight) screamed at Voight, "You're an animal!"

"No, worse. Human!" rejoined the razor-edged Voight.

Given to extremes and struggles, he reread James Dickey's novel *Deliverance.* Allying himself with the novel's themes of self-reliance and physical endurance, he reflected on Dickey's introductory biblical quote, "The pride of thine heart hath deceived thee, thou that dwellest in the clefts of the rock, whose habitation is high; that saith in his heart, Who shall bring me down to the ground?" Tying this passage to Dylan's lyrics, his felt his self- awareness grow while his egotism dissolved. Like a balloon returning to the earth, he too was settling. His was the commonest of journeys, but for him, all was an epiphany.

Setting aside Pirsig's book, he next turned to a collection of Emerson's essays. There was no apparent reason for him to choose Emerson. True, he once watched a dramatization about Henry Ford, where Ford, on his deathbed, shouted out, "I believed in Emerson." And from what he knew, Emerson embodied the hardy Yankee spirit. But perhaps his choice arose from simply proceeding alphabetically through the stacks. Whatever his rationale, leaving the local library with the thick book tucked under his arm did much to lift his mood.

He spent months reading and meditating on Emerson. He liked Emerson's aphoristic style. Eschewing the abstract, he combed each essay, always on the lookout for the practical and useful. With a dictionary in hand, he became a prospector of sorts, panning for nuggets—nuggets not of gold, but insight. The well-known titles such as "Self-Reliance" and "Spiritual Laws" stirred him, but also the out-of-the-way pieces such as "Farming" helped liberate him from the city.

The glory of the farmer is that, in the division of labors, it is his part to create.

WALDEN POND

The city is always recruited from the country. The men in cities who are the centres of energy, the driving-wheels of trade, politics or practical arts, and the women of beauty and genius, are the children or grandchildren of farmers, and are spending the energies which their fathers' hardy, silent life accumulated in frosty furrows, in poverty, necessity and darkness.

Cities force growth and make men talkative and entertaining, but they make them artificial. What possesses interest for us is the nature of each, his constitutional excellence.

Absorbing each line, he was captivated by Emerson's sweep and grandness. Emerson's dogmatic, almost preaching style transformed his psyche. Exalted and uplifted, he began to look down on life from a higher ground. Discovering the power of philosophy to transfigure reality, his malaise lessened. His troubles were all leveled and made trite. It seemed to him everything that once was terribly important could now be dismissed. Somewhere along the way, Dr. G's tapes ended up in the trash. "These too were paltry and hollow," he surmised.

On Sundays, he arose early and set off on long, solitary bike rides. Mulling over his readings, he enrolled himself in the peripatetic school—riding replacing walking. Each week, he found new hills to climb. His gaze always directed upward, he sought to escape the lowlands, to command a more lofty view.

There was a downside to all his reading. Without a foil, a sounding board to bounce ideas off, he became unbalanced. Emerson's writing became an *idee fixe* for him. He could hardly hear someone express an opinion before the phrase, "Emerson said..." pounced upon him. This was all harmless, and with the weather warming, he put down Emerson's essays to spend more time outdoors.

After purchasing some fishing tackle, he looked to revive an old hobby from his youth. Braving a snow squall, he returned empty handed on the opening day of trout season. Later he set off on early mornings, but he had no better luck at various lakes and streams. Considering himself a fair fisherman, he was perplexed by his lack of success. More troubling was the fact that the thrills he felt on seeing the morning mist on the slack water or making the first cast were gone. Something in him had died. He felt put off, even repulsed by fishing. The oily smells, mucky shorelines, grubby fisherman, and suffering worms became so distasteful that on his last outing, he put away his gear and set off to scale a nearby mountain. Scrambling over numerous large boulders that he supposed were left behind by some ice age, he was happy to be moving higher. The lake far beneath him, he left the water and all that it promised behind.

Although he was now working long hours, he was still not well. He often felt sick to his stomach and at other times a sickly taste arose in his mouth. And then there was the gagging and the sense of unreality that gripped him after meals. Imagining that no one is one hundred percent, he kept his pains to himself. Socially he was still isolated, if not crippled.

During the spring he attended the funeral of his great aunt in Canada. His relatives looked at him askance, no doubt concerned over what might become of him. Reinforcing all this was that he viewed himself as a monkish outcast, and he played the part well.

The weather warming, he meditated on the *Tao Te Ching* and "Bhagavad Gita." Themes such as humility, simplicity, detachment, flexibility over rigidity, and suppleness over strength did much for his mental state. Like mortar, his readings over the last year had begun to fill chinks and cracks in his psych. The Bible was, of course, recommended to him, but he read little of it. The Psalms were no more than moaning to him. The endless weeping, cries, and calls for vengeance put him off. He sensed there was something physically weak, unheroic about the writing. Perhaps he was guilty of heresy or plain oversight, but he could not stomach them. Was he the only one who thought this? He knew any talk of the Bible was off limits, as people's minds froze or retreated whenever the topic was broached. Religion was also taboo, so he supposed there was nothing to be gained from discussing it. Besides, always one to be different, he would not be happy unless he was reading something more esoteric. There might be something for him in the Bible, but he did not have the time to pore over its many pages. Needing practical insights and visions, he set his Bible aside.

His finances received a boost when he found work teaching a night class at a nearby college. Now working three jobs, he felt more self-satisfied. On his bike rides to work in the predawn darkness, the only sounds he heard were the whirring generator, the tire hums, and his deep breathing. Catching glimpses of deer as they crashed through the woods, he wondered, "Isn't this Emerson's ideal?" Here he was making his living using all his faculties—both mental and physical. He saw himself as Emerson's self-reliant, New England lad "who in turn tries all the professions, who teams it, farms it, peddles, keeps a school, preaches, edits a newspaper, goes to Congress, buys a township, and so forth, in successive years, and always, like a cat, falls on his feet." And yes, he was "worth a hundred of these city dolls," he thought. If he was not leading a balanced life, his work at least gave him some gratification and better—he was making a contribution. He nonetheless was not well, and compounding this fact, it was against his nature to work so many hours. He never questioned what might be driving him, though. Perhaps he hoped for some awakening or transcendence.

A reconciliation was eventually made with his wife, and she made plans to join him in the countryside. Having suffered a lengthy hospitalization during his absence, she probably made her decision based more on necessity than choice. On one of his last visits to the city, he babbled on about the immorality of burning fossil fuels for transportation and other environmental issues. His wife remarked on how he had changed, but she surely must have seen that he was not well.

The shorter days signaled the start of another fall. Although free from most of his malaise and pain, he took less satisfaction in his job at the metal shop. Added to this, the stress of working three jobs left him feeling numb. Wishing to learn more, he felt stunted and grew restless. Jack had told him "most guys move from shop to shop to learn new skills," and it surprised Jack that "he had hung around so long." Jack's remarks played on his competitiveness, and feeling stronger, he felt the need to make up for lost time. Reading the classifieds at lunch, he was determined to make a change.

A couple of months into the new year, he jumped to a much larger shop—in truth a factory. Initially he felt liberated by the job change. His raise in pay was also a sign to him that he was recovering. The weather warming, his bike rides became longer and more strenuous. Seeking even a greater range, he acquired a new road bike and an expansive plastic relief map of his and neighboring counties. Studying the map peaks, he dreamingly traced each weekend ride. Buying a second car and enrolling his daughter in a preschool that his wife had selected added to his sense of progress.

In the evenings, he turned to a volume of Thoreau's writings. Beginning with *Cape Cod*, this littoral travel log led him to read Thoreau's essay "Civil Disobedience," and then, naturally enough, *Walden*. He was attracted to Thoreau's cold, Hindu-like detachment. In *Cape Cod*, he read of Thoreau's visit to the site of a "wrecked brig from Galway, Ireland, laden with emigrants. On the whole, it was not so impressive a scene as I might have expected. If I had found one body cast upon the beach in some lonely place, it would have affected me more. I sympathized rather with the winds and waves, as if to toss and mangle these poor human bodies was the order of the day."

And when reading "Civil Disobedience," he seized upon the following:

The night in prison was novel and interesting enough....It was like traveling into a far country, such as I had never expected to behold, to lie there for one night...It seemed to me that I never had heard the town-clock strike before, nor the evening sounds of the village.... It was to see my native village in the light of the Middle Ages, and our Concord was turned into a Rhine stream, and visions of knights and castles passed before me.

Reading *Walden* was a singular experience for him. Other than the *Walden* quotes he had read in high school yearbooks over the years, he had never given the book much thought. Perhaps *Walden* was too homely, unsophisticated, for him during his more heady days. Along with Thoreau's philosophizing, he liked Thoreau's irreverence and strong individuality. He came to see Emerson as the joyless puritan, whereas Thoreau was the free-spirited Indian. He was pleased that spring to be reading *Walden*. During his idle hours, there was nothing, outside spending time with his family, that he enjoyed as much. There was a time when he sat on a bench waiting for his daughter to finish a preschool class. The trees were coming into full foliage and a cool breeze fell upon him. Engrossed in his reading, he was at once happy; it would also be one of his last contented times before a great darkness descended upon him.

~~~~

The August sun is strong as I walk west along Beacon Street. I have an hour or so to explore a little bit of Brookline while Janet takes her tai chi lesson. Having swum across Lake Champlain last weekend, I am filled with satisfaction and no less enthusiastic about our planned visit to Walden Pond later today.

I can count on only one hand the number of times that I have been to Boston, and now an approaching green trolley underscores the quaint, orderly aspect of the city that I have felt when here. Watching as the trolley comes to a stop and riders step down, I think by way of contrast the numerous hours I spent riding the noisy, aluminum-clad trains back in New York. The trolley is heading off toward downtown, so I walk on.

Neat stone-faced walk-ups and balconied apartment buildings hug the sidewalk on my left. There is not much to interest me here, and I think of walking up to the Waterworks by Boston College, but I see that I do not have the time. Stopping at a small market, I buy a bagel along with some energy bars. Sitting on a bench outside the market, I pass the time watching the shoppers come and go. I have always found it soothing to be near where people are busy and about. When sitting in malls, department stores, or wherever there is a bustle, despite all the activity, I want to do nothing more than steal away to some vacant corner, stretch out, and sleep. In *Walden*, Thoreau, writing about his trips to nearby Concord, notes those who "can sit forever in public avenues without stirring." Whereas these fellows were out to hear the latest news, I would be happy just to doze.

Back at the tai chi studio, Janet is in the foyer talking with her instructor, Bill. After Janet introduces us, Bill and I step into the cavernous studio to chat about the building's history. After so many years of participating in endurance events, I am struck by the baby-like softness of Bill's skin. Bill is about my height, and his hair is blondish gray. He carries a small paunch and wears shorts. His legs down to his bare feet appear doughy and pliable. I am impressed by Bill's almost boyish aspect. Janet had told me that Bill, like me, is about fifty years old, and now the tanned, taut skin on my face, arms, and legs makes me feel old and worn out compared to him. The thought of what I might have done to myself with all my training and racing makes me cringe.

WALDEN POND

Janet, having gathered up her belongings, joins us out on the light-colored wood floor. She mentions our planned trip to Walden Pond and wonders if Bill could help us with directions. After a moment or two of thought, Bill outlines a route. Barely knowing Boston, I leave it up to Janet to decipher his directions. After Janet sets a date for her next lesson, I shake hands with Bill and thank him for showing me the studio.

Out on Beacon Street, we find our car and set off for Concord. Winding our way through the mesh of roads and multi-way intersections, I mull over Bill's youthful appearance.

"After seeing Bill, I think I understand more of what you've being saying about the seventy-percent principle and being soft and supple," I say.

"He has been practicing a long time, and I guess it shows," says Janet.

"I felt odd standing there with him. I'm so used to everyone at races looking lean and intense."

"You're too much yang," says Janet.

"I know. You've told me. But only when it comes to training and sports. You've heard me talk about reading the *Tao Te Ching*, and how the book made a big impression on me."

"True. You follow the Tao better than I do."

"I wasn't always that way, though. Something changed in me years ago. Maybe I'm not really following the Tao, though. It could be that I've just become lazy and like to procrastinate. Either way though, there does seem to be something in letting things work themselves out, as you say, organically, but when it comes to exercise, I just can't seem to relax and let go of the all my hard training. Les down in Florida, you remember him? He always said that I wasn't happy unless I was training, and do you know what? He was right."

"But all that hard training might not be good for you," says Janet.

"I know, and after meeting Bill, I sort of wonder. I enjoy working out so much that I'm not sure I could give it up, unless I had to. There is probably a little something off about me." Janet laughs and tells me to follow the signs for Route 2.

Merging with the traffic, I reflect more on my predilection for strenuous exercise. I note the sense of strength and vigor and the sense of accomplishment it bestows, how it lifts my spirits and relaxes me afterward. It serves as an outlet for my natural competitiveness and brings me closer to the fit and cut man that I forever aspire to be. I recall the few times I attended a tai chi class Janet was teaching. Like those times when I mediated, I felt an increased focus and an inner calm afterwards. I did not practice regularly, so my gains were soon lost, and I fell back into my old ways of rough exercise. Janet also practices a slow, patient form of tai chi called Wu Style tai chi, and I doubt if I could keep my nervous, impulsive nature in check for very long. Sometimes I see myself as this fidgety schoolboy bursting with energy who cannot remain seated for long.

Not paying attention, I drive too far west and miss the exit for Walden Pond. After stopping to ask for directions, I turn around and head back toward Boston. Our route takes us through grassy wetlands filled with tall stands of purple loosestrife. I imagine the land here drains into the Concord River. This river was the subject of Thoreau's first book, *A Week on the Concord and Merrimack Rivers*. Perhaps it is my excitement to be finally visiting Thoreau's famous pond that makes the wetlands shimmer in the afternoon sun. Seeing a sign for the Walden Pond, I turn left, drive up a short hill, and find a shaded parking spot in a cramped lot.

I feel a sense of urgency as we step out of out of the car. With swimming suits and towels in hand, we rush pass a bronze statue of Thoreau set outside a replica of his cabin. "We'll see these later," I say. After walking a short distance, we find an entrance and walk down a steep concrete access road. Through the thick growth of trees, the pond comes into view. I am struck by its size. A half-mile across to the far shore, the pond could easily pass as a lake. "I thought it was a pond," must be a comment heard from first-time visitors.

We reach a small beach that has a tiny section roped off for swimming. What I soon notice is that there are a fair number swimmers far offshore. "I can't believe this. Look at those people out there," I say. A lifeguard informs us that swimming outside the roped area is at your own risk. Walking back up the beach, Janet says, "That news should make you happy."

"I've never been to such place; it's a swimmer's dream," I say.

I had chosen to travel here today because a local group has a swim scheduled for this afternoon. Believing they had permission to swim, I thought I would swim with them on my first visit. Knowing now that the pond is open to anyone, I drop my plan. Watching the swimmers crisscrossing the pond, I want nothing more than to be out there with them, but Janet, who has noticed a footpath off to our right, says, "Let's go explore the pond; we have time." I am reluctant at first, but with the sun still high in the west, I agree.

Thoreau surveyed the pond in 1846, and a copy of the map he drew up is included in my edition of *Walden*. Bringing to my mind the outline of a pig minus the rear legs, Thoreau's map includes numerous soundings. Thoreau lists a maximum depth of 102 feet and a circumference of 1.7 miles. In Thoreau's time, Walden Pond was popularly thought to be bottomless. Debunking this premise, Thoreau writes, "Many have believed that Walden reached quite through to the other side of the globe. But I can assure my readers that Walden has a reasonably tight bottom at a not unreasonable, though at an unusual, depth. I fathomed it easily with a cod-line and a stone weighing about a pound and a half." Having been formed by retreating glaciers, Walden Pond is what is called a kettle pond.

We head off in a counterclockwise direction along the pond underside. Shaded by a mix of pines, oaks, and maples, the trail has a mild camber. Here and there, where the path nears the pond, I see stone steps leading down to the water. The water in these places has a surprising aqua hue. Reaching Thoreau's cove (the pond's forelegs), we follow a sign to the site of his cabin. A large cairn stands near a stone marker ring that outlines where his cabin once stood. The pond being our main interest, we linger only a short while before returning to the trail.

After rounding the pond head, we reach its shoulder. Here we scramble up a steep rise to survey a rail line in Thoreau's time known as the Boston-Fitchburg Railroad. I listen intently and place my hand on the tracks, but fail to detect any approaching trains. It was this railway that led Thoreau to write, "I have learned that the swiftest traveller is he that goes afoot," and "to make a railroad round the world available to all mankind is equivalent to grading the whole surface of the planet." I was struck by the insight and prophecy of these lines when I first came across them in *Walden*. Back on the trail, it is not long before we return to the beach—the pond hind quarters.

Over the course of a year, Walden Pond sees more than a half million visitors. Today, with only a scant number of people scattered about the beach, it feels as if we have the pond all to ourselves. Up a small rise from the beach, we find an aged, cramped bathhouse in which to change. "This must be a horrid place on a hot summer weekend," I think upon exiting.

Back down on the beach, I wade in up to my waist and wait for Janet. The water feels a little cold after our hike, but it will be ideal once we start swimming. Janet joins me and we warm up with few short swims outside the roped off area. Like many other women, Janet is a born swimmer. Women are often thought to be naturally better swimmers than men because of their higher body fat and shorter stature. Although this fact might be true, any advantage they have might also be because of their innate sense for the water. A woman approaching swimming for the first time might be more patient than a man and less inclined to struggle, resist, and try to out-muscle the water. Every good swimmer is also a sensuous swimmer. A feel for the water is immeasurably more valuable than any physical strength; it is the female (yin) triumphing over the male (yang.)

We settle on swimming the pond perimeter in the reverse direction of our hike. I fall in behind Janet as she swims off. Although she turns her head too far to the side when she breathes, her stroke is sound. Curiously, Janet employs principles from her tai chi practice when she swims. She talks in terms of not breaking her four points, swimming from her kua (hip), and when one thing moves, everything moves. Watching me swim, she noticed that I was "breaking my rectangle" and suggested that I try not to overreach. Her suggestion (apparently missed by swim coaches over the years) quickened my stroke and improved my speed in the pool. Although tai chi has its origins in fighting, Janet practices—as I noted above—an internal martial art. Internal martial arts (as opposed to an external martial art such as karate) combine energy development with slow fighting movements. Some of Janet's forms—a full set of prescribed movements—can take more than a half hour to complete. Perhaps Thoreau would be pleased that a spirit from the East has come to swim in his pond this afternoon.

As we arc to the west along the pond back, the sun flashes make sighting difficult. Flipping over onto my back, I swim ahead of Janet, who follows my bubble trail. Reaching deep to catch the water, I take slow and purposeful strokes. I enjoy swimming backstroke, because once I find my rhythm, the stroke becomes almost effortless. Up ahead, a boy and a man—I suppose the boy's father—are fishing, their lines crossing our track. I angle away from the bank. "The perch swallows the grub-worm, the pickerel swallows the perch, and the fisher-man swallows the pickerel," writes Thoreau.

Swimming with Janet has settled me. Rolling side to side with each stroke, I feel a calmness overtake me. The usual urge to push myself while swimming has vanished. Content, I gaze about at the sky, the encircling woods, and the receding beach. Familiar sights from other open water swims, these all now appear fresh and new. "Who can make the muddy water clear? Let it be still, and it will gradually become clear," says the *Tao Te Ching*.

We round to our left and enter Little Cove, one of two small coves along this stretch. Here the invasive purple loosestrife blends in with lime-green grass and the tall cattails all along the bank. We glide by a shirtless, shoulder-length-haired fellow who stands alone on some steps just above the water and who is unperturbed by our swimming. With his eyes closed, he basks in the last afternoon rays. "I find it wholesome to be alone the greater part of the time. To be in company, even with the best, is soon wearisome and dissipating. I love to be alone. I never found the companion that was so companionable as solitude."

Leaving the cove, I aim for the pond's far end—the snout. More than half mile into our swim, Janet's swimming looks to be smooth and relaxed. Nearly two decades have passed since she lost control of her car on a patch of ice one winter day and crashed into a tree. After a Massachusetts rescue squad extricated her from her car, she remained in a coma for more than a day. After she regained consciousness, two weeks would pass before she was cleared to leave the hospital. She eventually returned to her job as a project engineer, but persistent pain and vision problems forced her resign after only a few months. Although she did not understand all the ramifications at the time, she had suffered what is called a traumatic brain injury. In the ensuing years, she has gone from doctor to doctor in search of relief. Eventually she received disability benefits, but not before subsisting on food stamps and living in public housing. When I first met her some years back, she had already hit upon and was receiving great benefit from practicing tai chi.

WALDEN POND

Janet composed the following, modeled after Dr. Suess's *Horton Hears a Who!*, not long after her accident:

"When she got here she was comatose and could have been dead, Then combative and angry, so we tied her to the bed.
We had no idea how much she could have swelled and bled,
So we watched her in ICU and took pictures of her head."

"This is a good one," they raved and moved her up to the floor.
A few pictures of her spine, "That's good enough; no more.
There's nothing more we can do. We'll just watch her," they all roared.
Some physical therapy and time and back to work," they all swore.

Now I became aware that something was not quite right.
There was a tremendous pressure in my head and my scalp felt very tight. My left eyelid drooped shut and dim was my sight.
Blurry shadows moved around me and loud noises gave me a fright.

I knew I was somewhere. I knew not the cause.
I was not really frightened. I was here. It just was.
Bits and pieces would come to me out of the fuzz.
Sometimes the shadows would talk to me, their voices all abuzz.

First a wheelchair, then a walker, then a cane. I had no fear
That even in my fog, I could get out of here.
I was only there for two weeks, but it seemed like a year.
Then I was jetted down to Florida, and things started to become more clear.

At first things moved quickly. Freedom from my cane I had won.
In six months I was back with my friends and I was fun.
But little did I know my trial had just begun.

CROSSINGS: A SWIMMER'S MEMOIR

The pressure in my head did not subside. I became a prisoner on the run.

...

I swim ahead of Janet and stop here and there to probe the pond by letting myself sink below the surface. Although I am not far from the bank, I fail to touch bottom and begin to sense the pond depth. Janet swims by, and I fall in behind her. We are nearing Long Cove, the pond's crown. Having found her stroke, Janet is swimming really well. Following her bubble trail, I wonder at her zest for health. She has a snapshot of herself taken not long after her accident. Her face appearing flaccid and swollen, she bears little resemblance to the woman I know today. Much like a restorative mineral spring or a healing hot bath, perhaps Walden's waters will afford both of us more than recreation this afternoon.

Out of Long Cove, we enter Ice Cove, the pond's snout and its farthest extent. Janet swims over to a level wood-chip-covered spot on the bank. Scrambling to her feet she says, "I think I have had enough. I'm going to walk back to the beach."

"That was a great swim! You did really well; we went nearly a mile," I say. "I'll follow you along the trail," she adds.

After watching her walk into the woods, I swim off slowly, staying close the bank. The rise of land up to the old Boston-Fitchburg Railroad shades me. Rounding to my left, I swim off toward Thoreau's cove.

Swimming out into the brilliant sunshine, I see Janet keeping pace on my left. Years ago, it would have been impossible for me to imagine myself here, swimming where Thoreau swam. "After hoeing, or perhaps reading and writing, in the forenoon, I usually bathed again in the pond, swimming across one of its coves for a stint," he writes. But having swum in so many other New England ponds and lakes, Thoreau's pond, no matter its history or beauty, feels now rather ordinary.

So much can and has been written about Thoreau. Eminently quotable, his works are readily available in print or on the web. Although long the staple of high school English classes, *Walden* is not an easy book. With its convoluted nineteenth-century prose, classical allusions, and philosophical bent, *Walden* is surely more referenced than read. Personally I have encountered few who have read the book, and even fewer willing to discuss it. A colleague of mine—an English teacher—thought *Walden* was best read after the age of thirty. Curiously, Thoreau was about thirty when he ended his two-plus-year stay here. Reading being onerous for her with her double vision, Janet listened to a recording of *Walden* a while back. Less moved than I would have thought, she did take delight in some of Thoreau's observations and generally found him an amusing character. Thoreau has his devotees, though. The large cairn next to his cabin site attests to his high esteem. Nowadays, both a society and an institute exist dedicated to his works and environmental conservation.

Besides being a writer, Thoreau was also a man of action. "There are nowadays professors of philosophy, but not philosophers. Yet it is admirable to profess because it was once admirable to live," he writes. *Walden* documents his experiment in living simply. Beyond what I have written above, *Walden* interests me as Thoreau personally tackled the universal concerns: sustenance, shelter, and earning a livelihood. Despite our advances, these concerns are no more resolved in our time than they were in Thoreau's. Reminiscent of the Spanish moss (an epiphyte) I observed hanging from live oaks and telephone wires when living in the South, Thoreau wished to subsist on nothing more than air and water, to be free and unburdened. Pointing at his toiling neighbors, he deplored, "Why should they begin digging their graves as soon as they are born?" In *Walden*, Thoreau makes repeated appeals to our higher, more spiritual natures. An ardent individualist and free thinker, it is remarkable to me that Thoreau could have emerged out of Puritan New England. Thoreau's spirit and beliefs are fragile, though. His singular mindset has never been universal, and it needs regular cultivation if it is to endure.

Thoreau anticipated today's environmentalism and many ecological discussions or works often begin with some lines from *Walden*. He influenced Mahatma Gandhi and Martin Luther King Jr. with his essay Civil Disobedience. Their successes perhaps affirmed Thoreau's belief that "a tide rises and falls behind every man that can float the British Empire like a chip." I could of course go on, adding sentence after sentence. I best pause here, and not delve into any of his other works, his journal's two million words, or rehash what so many others have written. Everyone should be left to find their own ways into *Walden*. I have come here with Janet to see where Thoreau lived, to swim in his pond, and to tell something of our lives, our own experiments. "I, on my side, require of every writer, first or last, a simple and sincere account of his own life, and not merely what he has heard of other men's lives."

Swimming into Thoreau's Cove, I catch sight of what looks like a small cairn on the pond bottom. On doubling back, I see nothing more than the water's yellowish-green hue extending downward. "What was that?" I ask myself. Whenever I visit some historic site, I like to look for an old tree or structure that might be a connection to the past. Wishing to find something tangible from Thoreau's time, I suppose my mind fooled me.

Up ahead, Janet waits for me in the cove. Swimming in close to where she stands, I stop and ask, "How is walking barefoot?"

"You have to pick and choose where to step; there are some sharp rocks," she answers. "I'm going to swim on to the beach. I'll meet you back there. Be careful," I say.

"I'll watch for you."

Swimming out of the cove, I shake off my sluggishness as my yang nature reemerges. I kick and pull hard, and my breath deepens. I see the beach; it's maybe a quarter mile off. With each stroke, I feel and hear the water gurgle past my ears. My face feels flush and my shoulders and arms are hot. Swimming close to the bank, I see tree after tree glide by. Driving myself on, I feel myself lift up as if I were a skiff hull planing across the water.

Catching glimpses of Janet, I hear her shout, "Go, peeps!"

A couple of years ago, a house wren built her nest atop our front porch light. After her eggs hatched, we were beset with endless "kah-cheeps." Parroting the hatchlings, our "kah-cheeps" eventually were shortened to "peeps," which is how we now endearingly refer to each other.

Coming up to the beach, I slow my cadence. Rounding around to my right, I glide along the rope outside the guarded area. Coming to a stop, I hunker down. My breathing slows, but my heart races on. Looking back over the pond, I am happy with my swim. Janet joins me in the water with her camera in hand. Framed against the low sun, we take turns snapping photos of each other swimming.

Some years have elapsed since our visit to Walden Pond, and I should relate something about our own experiments. As I write this, Janet and I now reside in Virginia, outside of Richmond. Curiously, our rental home originally served as a one-room schoolhouse. This, though, is not as quaint as it might first seem. Public schools were segregated in the South up until the early 1960s. Our schoolhouse was one of the more than 5,000 constructed throughout the South in the early twentieth century for the education of African American school-age children. The story behind of these schoolhouses is affecting, as it involves the collaboration of two individuals, Booker T. Washington and Julius Rosenwald, a onetime president of Sears,

Roebuck and Company. Since relating the story of these schoolhouses would be too large a detour, I will refer those interested to the web. Because of its tin roof and tall windows, more than one person has referred to our schoolhouse as an oversized cabin. And although there is no Walden Pond nearby for us to swim in, we, like many in Thoreau's day, warm ourselves in the winter with a wood stove.

Janet continues to practice her tai-chi and as of late is experimenting with acupuncture. She has also gone on to embrace the whole-food movement. She regularly purchases raw milk and grass-fed meats from local farms, grinds her own grain, preserves the vegetables she grows or buys, and has a brood of layer hens that spend their days happily scratching and pecking the grounds about the schoolhouse. When my food choices came under her review a while back, I felt as if my world was being overturned. But seeing Janet's increased vitality and learning more about the ethical and environmental issues associated with our modern, industrial food production, I now wonder at my blindness.

For my part, I continue to experiment with ways to forgo fossil fuels. With proper clothing and studded tires imported from Finland, I discovered it was possible to commute by bicycle through a snowy Cleveland winter. Each passing day, week, or year seems to afford us with some new insight or idea that removes yet more of our ignorance.

Returning to Thoreau, he cared more about his neighbors than what might commonly be believed. He had no desire to be a hermit or to avoid others. Instead, he went to the woods seeking answers. What discoveries he made, he recorded in *Walden*. Thoreau earnestly hoped that his neighbors, if not all of New England, would live more exalted lives. He sought to be Concord's morning chanticleer. I know of no more inspirational prose than *Walden*'s concluding chapter. The quote at the start of this chapter is taken from there. Anyone who has been through *Walden* can easily discern the book's influence on me. That fellow in this chapter's first part also had a strong affection for Thoreau's writing. He is still around, and although he is no longer my constant companion, I do occasionally bump into him. Fortunately, though, nowadays when we do meet, our time together is brief. To be fair, though, I should not be flippant. It is just that with any illness or painful time, the passing years have softened those unpleasant memories. Also, whenever one's spirit and vitality returns, memories of those hurtful, distressing times are quickly replaced by lighthearted, if not boisterous, thoughts and feelings.

So one might ask: to what do I attribute my seeming turnaround? What cure prevents that sour fellow from spoiling my days? I wish I had more to offer other than the story told here. I should note, though, as with garlic's purported use in warding off mosquitoes and vampires, so too has modern pharmacology provided me with the like. I have been told by those in the know that I have been fortunate, and never doubting this, I am grateful. For many, a return to health is not easy or even possible. Believing nothing of value would come from adding more, I will stop here.

So Henry David ends, "The light which puts out our eyes is darkness to us. Only that day dawns to which we are awake. There is more day to dawn. The sun is but a morning star."

CHAPTER **10**

Champ

We're related to each other in ways we never fully understand, maybe hardly understand at all. —Robert M. Pirsig

After dropping a couple of slices of whole wheat bread into the toaster, I depress the lever and stare vacantly into the deepening glow. Clare is asleep upstairs. I should wake her, but knowing she was out on the lake late last night, I choose to let her sleep a little longer. The house is quiet, as the other college kids she lives with are off somewhere this weekend. The refrigerator's soft rumble and the toaster's clinking are the only sounds I hear while standing here in the kitchen. The toaster pops, and after fishing some peanut butter and jam from the refrigerator, I smother the slices for a calorie boost.

Between bites, I stow energy gels, bars, and several cans of sport drink into my backpack. I feel a sense of unease, for I am not sure if I brought along enough food and drink to see me across the lake. Hearing Clare about, I return to finishing my toast.

Stepping into the dining room, I shoulder my sack. I then walk down a steep flight of stairs and out into the morning air. Opening my Civic's trunk, I find a place for my pack, and before closing the lid, I mentally check off again what I'll need for the swim. I note my inflatable kayak, my swim cap, a couple pairs of goggles, and a tub of zinc oxide cream. There is one more item, my wetsuit, but I do not plan to use it today.

Back in the house I find Clare poking around in the kitchen. "How were things last night on the lake?" I ask.

"Okay," she says.

"Was that a big boat you guys went out on?"

"It was pretty big, I guess."

"Being nighttime, I guess you didn't know how far offshore you were. And now I'm dragging you back out there. I hope you can make it through your shift tonight."

"I'll be fine. Let me get a few things upstairs, and I'll meet you down at the car."

Once I am back outside, the sun is up and the air is clear and cool. There is no traffic, and the houses on both sides of the street are quiet. At a little past six on a Saturday morning, it is much too early to expect anyone to be up and about. In addition, Burlington, Vermont, is a university town where afternoons become mornings for some.

Clare meets me at the car and we drive off. Leaving the side streets, we find College Street, and I am presented with a panorama of Lake Champlain. With the sun rising behind us, the lake and the jumble of blue mountains on the New York State side of the lake stand out in clear detail. The eight-mile stretch of water appears deceptively short. Appearing even nearer is little Juniper Island. Three miles offshore, the island looks almost within reach. College Street, like most of Burlington's east-west streets, slopes steeply down to the lake.

"I have to ride my bike back up this hill every day after work," says Clare.

We pass Church Place Marketplace's red brick pedestrian mall. New England's town colors, red and white, predominate here.

"That looks like a fun place to hang out," I say. Clare says little; she is no doubt tired from last night.

CROSSINGS: A SWIMMER'S MEMOIR

Lake Champlain dwarfs Burlington. On my first trip here to drop Clare off for her summer internship last May, I was overawed by the lake. I had little interest in the locals, shops, restaurants, or the University of Vermont's pristine campus. My attention was fixed on the lake and the land's tilt. Any sizable stretch of water elicits thoughts of swimming from me, nowadays. Only after coming across the local YMCA's advertisement for its Annual Lake Swim, did I seriously consider crossing the lake here.

We cross Lake Street, and I find a place to park in a lot on my right. After unloading the car, I remove my kayak from its bag and splay it out on the asphalt. We have arrived early, but I nonetheless scramble around filling the kayak bladders. The plethora of miscues consequent to adventures like this invariably make me frantic. Clare wants to help, but there is nothing for her to do.

The kayak inflated, we toss in our packs, oars, and my wetsuit. With me at the bow and Clare at the stern, we carry the kayak down to the marina. On our left is the aquarium and science center where Clare is interning this summer. The rising sun and the kayak's unwieldy load raise perspiration on my brow. Walking onto a deck outside a small shop, we set the kayak down. I give Clare a few bills and ask her to purchase a disposable camera in the shop. One of the swimmers gathered here relates that the pre-swim meeting will soon take place.

I double check the kayak air pressure and arrange the backpacks so that Clare will be comfortable and safe. After finishing these tasks, I walk over to the deck railing for some easy stretching. New York on the lake's opposite shore appears deceptively near; I spend the next few minutes attempting to persuade myself that this is actually so.

Today is a perfect day for the swim. The water appears calm and the air is still. My main concern, though, is the water temperature. I have confidence in my fitness, but I am unsure how I will do in the colder water up here. A week and half ago I stopped off to see

Clare on my way back from the World Swimming Championships in Montreal. Before heading home, I drove over to Burlington's North County park and swam a mile or so. The water surprisingly was not much colder than the Connecticut lakes and impoundments I was used to swimming in.

After the swimming in the lake, I dropped by the YMCA to fill in some details about the swim. Coincidentally, Josh, a reporter from *The Burlington Free Press*, was also there gathering background for an article he was writing on the swim. Tad, the Y's aquatics director, asked if I would agree to be interviewed. I saw no problem, but I found it amusing to be in the local press so soon after arriving in town. I added, "An outsider like me who comes to town and ends up in the local paper would normally expect to be just another item in the police blotter."

Clare has returned with a cup of coffee and a camera in hand. She seems revived. Tad arrives and calls everyone together for a meeting. I see there is a small number of swimmers entered, no more than fifteen, all told. We learn every support kayaker needs to have a cell phone and will be expected to call in a report every hour or so. Police water rescue boats will be on the lookout and a sailboat regatta is scheduled for later in the morning. Tad, motioning in the direction of a thirty-plus-foot white cabin cruiser, indicates that it is time to load up the kayaks for the ride across the lake.

After climbing on board, Clare and I find seats on the bridge, behind the boat owner and captain. The rough handling my kayak received when it was stowed with the other hard shells made me wince. As it seems to retain its shape, I turn my attention to the lake ahead. After the cruiser clears the breakwater, our captain—who is heavyset and probably in his late fifties—relates that he has ferried swimmers across the lake since the swim's inception eight years ago. His well-tanned wife with her shock of white hair sits off to his right. He notes it will take forty-five minutes to reach the swim start at Willsboro Point, New York.

The cruiser now well underway, I smear globs of zinc oxide on my arms, legs, face, and torso. Clare reluctantly coats my back. We make good progress, and I enjoy what feels like a cool onshore breeze. The lake up ahead is a dark metallic blue. The cruiser's smooth ride lulls me, and up high here on the bridge, away from the water, the upcoming swim loses its import.

Sitting behind us is a middle-aged fellow with heavily bleached blond hair. He reviews a laminated copy of his feeding schedule. I am intrigued by the schedule details, which shows a regimen of breaks for coffee, energy bars, or sport drink every twenty minutes. After I comment on his log, we compare notes on the swims we have completed. He talks of completing the 4.5-mile Chesapeake Bay Bridge swim, and I mention my 12.5-mile swim around Key West last June.

"I've heard about that swim. How was it?" he asks. "Not bad until the last couple of miles, when I sort of died."

"It's a lot longer than this swim," he says.

"True, but the water was a lot warmer."

He wears a wetsuit and asks, "Why aren't you wearing a wetsuit? The water up here is too cold for me."

Putting on brave face, I say, "I'll be all right."

The fellow returns to reviewing his schedule with his kayak support, and I notice we have passed Juniper Island, which rises above of the lake behind us. "It will not be long now," I say to Clare.

Despite my outward display of confidence, my unease about the lake's cold water returns. I have trained well, but my swimming has mostly been in pools or warm impoundments. I should have been up here for a few trial swims this summer. A week ago, Janet paddled beside me while I swam a couple miles in the Farmington River back in Connecticut. The water was much colder than I was accustomed to, but one cold-water swim is not enough. To help ease my jitters, I smear on more zinc oxide.

Without warning, our captain slows his engines. Glancing up, I notice there are people gathered on a point of land to our left. Tad starts barking commands, and I watch as his YMCA staff begins lowering the kayaks. Clare and I climb down from the bridge, and I move toward the boat's stern. Clare is soon called to board her kayak. I pass down a paddle, our packs, a couple of towels, and my wetsuit to her.

The bleach-blond fellow, pausing on his way past me, says, "There is nothing to you. You'll never make it across."

I am at a loss of words as he jumps off the low platform into the water.

The water around the boat is littered with swimmers and kayaks bobbing about. I lag behind, as I feel hesitant to enter the water. Clare maneuvers the kayak off the cruiser's port side. Awaiting my turn, I fall in line with the few remaining swimmers. Having entered the lake off the point of land, I watch as a fellow in a full-sleeve wetsuit strokes purposefully toward us. "That is one way to get to Vermont," I mutter to myself.

It is now my turn. Feeling the cabin cruiser wallow under my feet with the lake's gentle swells, I forgo the low platform and leap off the cruiser's stern. Upon surfacing I bicycle pedal while fitting my goggles. The water does not feel too cold. Clare is a few strokes away, and I swim over to her.

"Is everything okay?" I ask.

"Yeah, I'm ready."

"Can you see those large white tanks Tad told us to sight?" "Yes."

"I can too."

"It's a long paddle. Are you up to it?" I ask

"Dad, don't worry. Remember, I rowed crew back in high school."

"Oh, yeah. I'm going to warm up some," I say.

I swim off, but I am not at all comfortable. My high spirits when

I first entered the water are gone. The cold water slapping my face makes me gasp when I try to swim. Swimming with my head out of the water, I take a few strokes, but soon stop. After all my triathlons and open water swims, I should be better at getting used to water, but I'm clearly not. I always seem to need the longest warm up, and my speed usually does not pick up until the second part of a swim. I am not too concerned, though, as there will be some time before the start.

A sense of urgency grips me, however, when the cruiser horn blasts.

"Damn! They didn't give me enough time. Let's go. Paddle on my left," I say to Clare. I take few strokes and then stop. I re-fit my goggles and try swimming some more. Stopping again, I tread water. Feeling desperate now, I watch the other swimmer-kayak pairs recede into the distance. I swim a few more weak strokes only to stop once again.

"I'm so cold. Maybe I should put on my wetsuit, but I don't want to," I say. "Dad, you're in northern Vermont," says Clare.

"This spoils it. I'd wanted to make this an honest swim," I say.

"Well, the other swimmers are getting ahead. You have to get going," she says. "Okay. Pass it to me."

Clare hands me my suit and it floats flat in the water. I have never tried putting the suit on in water, but my legs slip into it easier than on land. After wrestling the suit up my torso and over my shoulders, I zip the back. After making a few more tugs here and there, I swim off. Clare soon joins me, paddling along on my left. We are finally underway, but for me, the day's swim across Lake Champlain is tainted.

My wetsuit is sleeveless and not the best quality, but nonetheless it warms me as much as if I had put on a coat after stepping outside on a wintry day. Actually I am overstating things. The water here is in the high sixties, but compared to the English Channel, where the water can be in the low sixties or below, the lake is not that cold.

It's just that I have lost my nerve again. Maybe this time, though, I can blame the mammalian dive reflex for my failing. Observed in beavers, otters, seals, dolphins, and humans, this ancient survival response slows the heart and breathing, shunts blood to internal organs, and constricts the larynx, whenever cold water contacts the face. Unable to do much more than feebly breaststroke, I could never quite manage to relax during another cold water swim down in the Long Island Sound some years ago. No matter the cause, I console myself knowing that eight miles of open water swimming still remains.

After my miscues, I settle into a nice rhythm. From the rate of Clare's paddling, I suppose I am moving well. Breathing to my left, I maintain my distance from the kayak. Because of the wind's fetch, the water is choppier here on the New York side of the lake. The swimming is relatively easy, though, and I look forward to even flatter water up ahead.

I catch up with a fellow named Lou, who swims with a bright green snorkel and fins. A not-too-tall, stocky fellow, Lou was also interviewed by Josh for his story on the Lake Swim. Picking up a copy of the paper yesterday, I learned that Lou is sixty years old and travels up from Florida every summer for the swim. While waiting for our interview with Josh, Lou described how sea lampreys have latched onto him during past swims. "I just pull them off; they only leave a small red mark," he said. According to Mike Winslow in his *Lake Champlain: A Natural History*, "The sea lamprey lack a jaw and are among the most primitive organisms with a backbone." Winslow also notes that unlike Lake Erie, where the sea lamprey entered by way of the Welland Canal, "genetic research suggests the sea lamprey here are actually native to Lake Champlain, having likely become established when the lake held a saltwater sea, following the last glaciation." Most recently, pesticides and trapping have been used to limit their reproduction.

Clare motions to me, and I stop swimming. Her cell phone is

ringing. She answers, and it is one of the YMCA staffers over on the Vermont shore checking in. Clare assures the caller that we are fine.

"I'm not really hungry, but I'd better eat something," I say.

"Here are a bar and a bottle," says Clare.

Resting my left forearm on the kayak, I take few bites out of the bar. "If you can keep track of the time for me, I'll swim thirty minutes before taking break," I say.

"Sounds good," says Clare.

After washing down the last of the bar, I pass the bottle back to Clare. Fitting my goggles, I ask, "Are you all set?" Clare indicates she is ready, and I swim off.

My swimming is strong now. Small waves occasionally break over me, but I hold my stroke steady. Clare also appears to be paddling more smoothly. When I committed to this swim, I viewed it as just another physical challenge that Clare, residing here in Burlington this summer, could help me meet. But Clare is now twenty years old, having just finished her second year of college. With her graduation, internships, jobs, and new relationships looming, it occurs to me that today's swim might likely be our last shared adventure.

Clare shepherding me across the lake takes me back to when she was in kindergarten. I had landed a teaching job at a private school in Bradenton, Florida, that also afforded me a place for Clare. We lived in an old white Spanish-style apartment building only a mile and half from the school. For various reasons, one of them monetary, I chose to do without a car that year. In place of a car, I planned for us to get around town on our bikes. In the weeks before school began, I repeatedly ran beside Clare on her tiny bike, to right her wobbles and catch her near spills. My right hip grew tender because of always running to her left. No pain, though, could diminish the satisfaction I felt one evening when I finally saw her ride off solo. When the school year started, our current positions here in the lake were reversed—I rode on the left and Clare on the right—on our bicycle commutes. When riding, I would sometimes reach out with my right hand to steady her, whenever I sensed she was unsure. Over time, this morphed into what Clare coined "super-fast." By placing my right hand on her shoulder and pedaling while Clare coasted, we were able to jet along and regularly cycled ten or more miles. Florida's sunshine and Bradenton's slow pace back then afforded us a couple years of speedy and safe cycling. We no doubt made for an odd pair, with me sitting up high on my road bike, reaching down to propel Clare along on her little pink bike. In later years, when she became more aware, she remarked, "You know, Dad, that wasn't too normal."

I suppose thirty minutes has passed, as Clare has stopped paddling.

"That fellow with the snorkel. His name is Lou. Have you seen him?" I ask.

"Yeah, he's back there," says Clare.

"With those fins, he should be faster," I say. "He stops too much," says Clare.

"That Juniper Island is still so far away," I say. "You'll get there. Dad, I'm going to pee," says Clare. "Okay. I'll rest some up ahead," I say.

After taking a few strokes, I stop to count the kayaks in front of us. Lou and I seem to be the stragglers. Although Burlington's detail is still unrecognizable, I can trace the land's sweep north of the city all the way out to Colchester Point, which juts out into the lake on my left. The rise of land on which Burlington is constructed appears puny compared to the backdrop of Vermont's distant Green Mountains. Mount Mansfield, Vermont's highest peak, and to its south, the distinctive Camel's Hump, are both visible.

My quiet is broken when I hear Clare call out. Swimming back around to other side of the kayak, I find her treading water.

"What happened?" I ask. "I slipped out," she says.

Before I am able to say anything, I catch sight of her backpack and a towel floating nearby. I quickly retrieve them, and after tossing them into the kayak, I say, "We have to get you back in without flipping." While thinking about the best way to get Clare back on board, I spot a gray police boat bearing down on us. With its blue-and-white emergency lights flashing, an officer stands outside the wheelhouse ready to assist us, but before the craft can come any closer, I am able boost Clare over the kayak's port-side gunwale. After Clare finds her seat, I feel relieved to wave them off.

"That was a little bit of drama," I say.

"Yeah, it was. Other than getting wet, I'm okay," says Clare.

"Did you lose anything?" I ask.

After some cursory checking Clare says, "Everything seems to be here. Do you want to eat or drink?"

"No, I'm good. Let's get going," I say.

Although parenting any child is replete with crises and challenges both large and small, nature ensures few of us are able to sidestep (even if one so desires) begetting the next generation. Like any parent, I have experienced the unease bordering on fear hearing Clare say, "Dad, my throat is sore" or "I think I have a fever." But other than the usual scrapes and bruises and the broken collar bone she suffered when she fell out of hammock back in the sixth grade, the two of us made it through the years unscathed. I have sometimes attributed our apparent good fortune to cosmic justice, thinking. "Look at it this way. Clare lost her mother when she was five. Shouldn't that be enough for one lifetime? Haven't we paid our debt?" But observing others who suffer misfortune after misfortune, I always knew my rationalizing was nonsensical. More correct, it is has been Clare's natural good health, her innate equanimity, and my doggedness that have buoyed us. I won't say anything more here about Clare, but what about my doggedness? Simply put, I have endeavored to keep the superficial and inane out of our home. From antiquity, all the way down to our wired, connected age, thinking for oneself has never been easy. Distractions and overpowering influences abound. My single claim is that I have persistently (and I am by no means unique) tried to follow my own best judgment whenever it came to parenting.

Seldom have I received much credit for the person (and she is by no means a saint) Clare is today. "Oh, you are so lucky to have Clare," is typical of what I have heard over the years, but those commenting were not with us on those nights at home when we read or conversed. Neither were they with us on our pensive bike rides. Neither were they present for our countless other shared experiences. Of course, I have not raised Clare on my own; many other individuals—mostly female—have aided me immeasurably over the years.

A few years ago Clare was swept up with her friends in that sad college frenzy that grips many high school seniors nowadays. "Are you proud of where I'm going?" was what she asked after her college choice was made.

"Of course, I am," I said, all the while feeling a little sick that I needed even to answer such a question. Later, when she returned home on her Thanksgiving break, she described a solitary run along a wooded trail near the campus. "I suddenly realized that the place does not matter. I could be off running like this at any college. What I feel and think depends on me."

I said nothing, but thought somehow we had endured.

Clare stops paddling and waits for me to swim over. "It's been another thirty minutes, Dad," she says.

"I'm getting hungry," I say.

"You've caught up with some other swimmers," she says.

"I know. I can see them when I breathe. Better give me another bar, and we will get going," I say.

While I am finishing off the bar, an unusually high wave breaks rises up and breaks just ahead of the kayak bow.

"Did you see that wave? It's strange. There are no boats nearby," I say. "Maybe it was Champ," says Clare.

"That's funny. Let's go!" I say.

Similar to Nessie, the Loch Ness monster, Champ is the name for a large reptilian-type creature that reputedly lives in the lake. Champ has a big following on both shores. New York and Vermont politicos have each passed resolutions protecting Champ. Champ sightings apparently go back to Indian days. Although Champ's existence is still unconfirmed, Champ is a real-life, revenue-generating attraction. New York's Port Henry celebrates an Annual Champ Day, and memorabilia are for sale on both sides of the lake. Coincidentally, there is a special program on Champ today at the science center where Clare interns. We, however, will not meet Champ on the lake today.

Privately held Juniper Island appears much closer now. Topped with a uniform dense growth of pine and cedar, the island's high rock sides fall sharply into the lake. The cliché "It looks so close that I can almost touch it" is now very real for me, but no matter how vigorously I swim, the thirteen-acre island remains beyond my reach.

According to Winslow, northward flowing Lake Champlain fills what is called a *graben*— German for ditch. Created by faults in the earth's crust, Lake Tahoe, Russia's Lake Baikal, and the Dead Sea all occupy grabens. Having studied several charts before this swim, I know that with the lake bottom some 400 feet beneath me, I'm now swimming through the lake's deepest water.

Lake Champlain receives water from Vermont rivers Winooski, Missisquoi, Lamoille, and Otter Creek. Lake George, along with the Ausable, Chazy, Boquet, and Saranac rivers, all contribute from the New York side. Every acre of Lake Champlain receives drainage from more than seventeen acres of land. Winslow notes this is more than four times that of Lake Ontario and makes Lake Champlain a much more fragile ecosystem. For a brief time back in 1998, Lake

Champlain was officially recognized as the sixth Great Lake. This accolade was quickly lost as an uproar over federal funds from some Midwestern states overturned the designation. Vermont still retains some rights to Great Lake funding opportunities, though.

What of the lake's namesake, Frenchman Samuel de Champlain? Explorer, mariner, author, soldier, cartographer, and founder of New France, in his fifty-five years of life, Champlain explored most of the Caribbean, present-day southern Ontario and Quebec, coastal Maine, Massachusetts down to Cape Cod, Nova Scotia, and of course, Lake Champlain. According to historian David Hackett Fischer in his comprehensive *Champlain's Dream*, "From 1599 to 1635, Champlain probably made twenty-seven Atlantic crossings." Crossings from France to the New World were undertaken during the late winter or early spring. Unfavorable conditions could extend a voyage to several months. The vigor, resoluteness, and bravery of Champlain and his crewmates to have endured the frigid North Atlantic is incredible to me. According to Fisher, unlike many other European explorers, Champlain admired and was deeply interested in the Native Americans. "We see his grand design for New France as a vision of Indians and French living close to one another, preserving the best of both cultures."

Whereas Vasco Nunez de Balboa founded the first Spanish colonial town in present-day Colombia in 1510, it was not until 1607 that England established its first permanent colony in the Americas at Jamestown, Virginia. After several failures because of disease, financial troubles, and conflict with Indians, Champlain finally succeeded in founding France's first permanent colony at present-day Quebec City, in July 1608.

After the hard first winter, in which, according to Fisher, "of the twenty-eight habitants, eight remained alive, and half of those very ill," Champlain "with only sixty Indians and two Frenchmen at his side" led an attack on Mohawk warriors at the southern end of Lake Champlain near Ticonderoga, New York. According to

Fischer, on July 14, 1609, Champlain traveled up (south) the Richelieu River to reach a large lake. Champlain "spent two weeks studying the lake as the Indians" slowed "their advance, probably" to avoid traveling "until the moon was reduced to a small crescent and nights were dark again."

Fisher notes that Champlain's estimate of the lake length at 125 miles is roughly correct. Champlain was fascinated by "its fine woods, beautiful islands, open meadows, and vast abundance of wildlife." Champlain attributed the abundance of game to the absence of Indians living there. Long before the arrival of Champlain, the Iroquois Indians in what is now present-day New York were at war with the Indians living north of the Saint Lawrence River. Over the years, the land about the lake became a no man's land. Fischer writes of Champlain, "On all of his many maps, this lake was the only place where he put his name on the land."

Perhaps it is remarkable to be swimming in the same waters that Champlain and his war party paddled their birch bark canoes nearly 400 years ago.

I see Clare has stopped to answer her cell phone again.

"What did they want?" I ask.

"They wanted to know if we were okay, and how close to the island we were," Clare answers.

"We've come nearly five miles; we have a little more than three to go. It's taking me longer than I thought. I hope you are not going to be too late for your job at the gate," I say.

"Don't worry. I'll call when we get near the beach," says Clare.

"Since I'm not last now, I'm going to swim over to Juniper Island. It won't take long," I say.

Clare holds water as I swim off. Swimming briskly, I soon see the lake's light brown bottom appear beneath me. Reaching a shallow depth, I stand lightly on a large barnacle-encrusted rock.

"What do you see?" shouts Clare.

"You have to be careful. The bottom is covered by all these small shells. I don't know. Maybe they are zebra mussels. I'd like to explore this island; too bad there isn't time."

"We'd better go, Dad," says Clare.

The thought of taking off my wetsuit crosses my mind, but I decide against it. We are low on food, and the large number of calories I would burn without the suit could make the last couple of miles miserable. Signaling that I am ready, I push off, swimming toward Burlington.

The wind has slowed, and gentle swells lift the steel-blue water. The sun shines brightly through the cloudless, blue sky. Occasionally glancing back toward New York, I revel in seeing Juniper Island shrink in size. Feeling a renewed sense of resolve, I surge ahead. Throughout the morning, I have been practicing my flutter kick, and now my legs come unleashed. I kick until exhaustion overtakes me, and catching my breath, I kick again. Up ahead, tall-mast sailboats list while waiting for their regatta start. Their brightly colored red, white, and blue jibs puff in the light breeze. Glancing behind, I see Clare has dropped back to take some pictures with the camera she bought. The passengers on one boat—its sails striped in Australia's green and yellow—stare blankly at me as I swim by. I cannot imagine a more enjoyable time now than to be out here on this great lake, swimming among these sailboats.

I stop and float in the water beyond the sailboats. Clare then paddles alongside. "That was great swimming past those boats," I say.

"They looked at you like you were crazy," says Clare.

"Maybe they didn't know there was this swim today, but they must have seen the other swimmers," I say.

"Here is your last bar; you'd better eat now."

"I'm hungry; it's been a long morning. Do you want to swim some?"

"No way. Here is your bottle. Drink some, and let's finish this swim," says Clare.

After washing down the energy bar, I toss the bottle in the kayak and say, "Let's go."

Fifteen summers ago, I signed Clare up at the Bradenton Red Cross for her first swim lessons. While we were riding our bikes over to the pool on the first day, she asked, "They're not going to make me bob (fully submerging her head) are they?"

"No, not until you are ready," I reassured her.

Thirty years after my first swim lesson, it was my turn to watch with other parents from the pool deck as our children took to the water. Becoming more confident and comfortable with the water after the first few lessons, Clare made it clear to me that I was more of an annoyance than a help. As the lessons were held in a corner of the pool, I would slip away and find an empty lane to swim a lap or two in. As it was my first time in an Olympic-size pool, I spent what seemed like an eternity to swim just one length. Putting off the next lap's misery, but unwilling to rest, I treaded water. Recalling that Rocky Marciano, the heavyweight champion from the 1950s, trained in a pool to improve his endurance, I comically jabbed and hooked the water while keeping myself afloat.

In the ensuing years, Clare never took to competitive swimming; volleyball was her sport throughout high school and now in college. Clare did, though, complete a 500-yard lake swim to earn her lifeguard badge while in high school. Similar to the times when she faced other challenges, she sought me out only for a couple of pool practices before her swim test in the lake.

As I left some loose ends untied above, now might be the time to say more about my deceased wife and Clare's mother. Other than noting it was a ruinous time for us, I think it best not to elaborate further. Some of those who knew the details of our lives back then thought I might profit from telling my story. I doubted this, as there were already too many tales of woe out there. Besides, I was able bodied and could earn what is commonly called an honest living. In this tell-all world, I valued our privacy more than any monetary reward. Stage mothers notwithstanding, a caring parent guards his or her child from outside intrusions. There is always some cost involved; any increase in notoriety or fame is accompanied by some loss, be contentment, dignity, or freedom. Should any of what I write find its way into print, I want to ensure that I am the only one who might be troubled. Still the question remains: How does a person manage after receiving such a big blow? I am not sure if a person ever does. I have been noticeably derelict in dealing with any emotional fallout on Clare. Friends, relatives, and lately Janet have filled in here for me. I have instead aimed at getting on with life, never missing a chance to add to our emotional and physical reserves. Like the buildup needed to swim across this lake, over the years I have been busy preparing us, making us ready.

One surely wonders, though, what does it mean to grow up without a mother? Nietzsche said, "When one has not had a good father, one must create one." Is this also true for those deprived of a mother? I suppose the answer is yes. Tangentially related to this are issues surrounding a girl's developing psyche compared to that of a boy's. I never gave this much thought when I was raising Clare, but should I have? Perhaps. Day-to-day life presented me with more pressing concerns, though. As I have already noted, I always endeavored to do what I thought was best for us. More to the point, what does it will mean for Clare to have had me, an oafish, not particularly empathic man, as her primary role model? Maybe I can allay my concerns, as Clare once said to me, "I will avoid your faults and improve on your few good qualities." The questions go on; they are endless. Friends and colleagues have all assured me a child can grow up healthy with one devoted parent. I have never doubted this fact, though I once heard a retired airline pilot relate, "A dual-engine passenger jet can still take off, even if an engine fails." Yes. True. The plane still flies, but the flight will not be the most stress free.

What has Clare learned or garnered from me? Who and what else has had a strong influence on her? We imagine our choices are made freely, but so much of our lives are beyond our control. A seeming contradiction, our choices are often foisted on us. Parents, relatives, friends, books, clergy, counselors, advertisements, chance encounters, lines from movies—the list of imperatives is long. Of course, this is the strong liberal view that we are all products of our environment. For me, I always have sought out acquaintances who in some way might improve me. "My best friend is the one who brings out the best in me," said Henry Ford.

Despite the relatively short time that Clare knew and was with her mother, today I can see so much of her mother in Clare beyond appearances and mannerisms. When I learned news of her mother's passing, I had a strong sense—much deeper than the usual literal meaning—of her mother living on in Clare. Pirsig's quote at the chapter's start seems apt here.

> My hunger stops my swimming.
> "Is there anything left to eat?" I ask.
> "Only this last can of energy drink," she says.
> "I might as well have it and hope I last."
> "Burlington looks so close," says Clare.
> "Yeah. We maybe have a mile and a half to go. This will be the last piece," I say. I finish off the drink and toss the empty can in the kayak. "Here we go," I say.
> I have left my morning jitters on the other side of Juniper Island. With each stroke, Burlington and the beach adjacent to Oakledge Park — our landing, grows nearer. In my typical fashion, my swimming has improved over the course of the day. The term

negative split refers to completing the second half of a race faster than the first half. This is what I do when swimming in open water. Having been a runner years before becoming a swimmer, I used to enjoy running the first mile of a road race fast, sometimes not caring about my final time. With swimming, though, my confidence and comfort level only increase the longer I am in the water.

I am gaining on a fellow who swims without a wetsuit to my left. I recognize him from the morning meeting. He is nearly as tall as me, but his stout build is ideally suited for cold-water swimming. Clare motions to me, and I stop to hear her say, "You can beat him, Dad."

"Yeah, I know, but it wouldn't be fair; he's not wearing a wetsuit," I say. Taking up my stroke again, I match my speed to his.

Much like focusing a camera viewfinder, the people and kayaks grouped on the beach suddenly become distinguishable. Swimming on, I eventually spy a couple of old wooden pilings that stick up high above the water. I point myself slightly to their right. A heavyset woman wearing a black bathing suit stands inside the pilings. She waves to the stocky fellow, who soon stands and walks up onto the beach. Passing the pilings, I savor and wish to hold onto these last few strokes. The gurgling in my ears, the cool water, the blue sky, and the water's green tint—I am not ready to give any of them up. Up ahead, the woman is motioning to me. Swimming until my hands hit bottom, I find my footing and stand. Out of habit from competing in triathlons, I quickly reach behind and unzip my wetsuit. Reluctant to leave Champlain's lake, I trudge slowly up onto the beach.

Clare, having dropped back to take a few last pictures, paddles ashore. I walk over to help her out the kayak, and she says, "Dad, I have to go to work, but that was a great swim."

"Okay. Thanks. I'll see you later up at the gate," I say.

Walking up the beach, I pass the blond-haired fellow. As I now wear a wetsuit, I interpret his mildly perplexed look as an "I told you so."

Farther on up the beach, I come upon Josh, the reporter, who is jotting down some notes, "How did you do?" he asks.

"I was out there too long," I answer.

Chatting with him some more, I learn that a collegiate swimmer finished first. Josh asks, "Did you hear her scream at the start?"

"No," I answer.

"A lamprey bit her," he says.

"Well, it was a tough swim for everyone," I say.

Leaving Josh, I grab a couple slices of pizza and find a seat at a picnic table under a pavilion. Between bites, I overhear a muscular, brown-haired fellow talking on a cellphone say, "It usually takes thirty minutes from when we first spot a swimmer." He pockets his phone and enters into a discussion with other YMCA staff members. Before long a white power boat with a broad red stripe down its side motors in close to shore. The guy with the cellphone, a young lady, and the blond-haired fellow all climb aboard. The boat pilot backs the boat away from the beach, and after turning hard about, speeds off into the lake.

"Someone is having trouble finishing the swim," I think to myself.

After finishing the pizza, I load my kayak onto a YMCA pickup truck for the ride back to the marina. Once there, I spend some time deflating the kayak and stowing it and along with my other gear in my Civic. Pulling out of the marina lot, I drive around the block to find Clare, who in addition to her internship at the science center, also works as a parking lot attendant on weekends.

"Park over there, Dad," she says

Returning from the car, I ask, "Were you late?"

"It didn't matter. Someone filled in for me until I got here," she says.

"I'm still hungry. Do you want a sandwich or something?" I ask her.

"No, I grabbed some pizza back at the park. A bottle of water would be good, though," she says.

Leaving her, I walk away from the lake, toward downtown. After walking a couple blocks, I happen upon a small tourist shop. Walking up a flight of stairs, I find a deli inside where I buy a sandwich, water, and chips. Leaving the store, I pause outside its elevated entrance. The wind has picked up. I have a clear view of the regatta and watch for a time as the sails tack northwesterly across the lake.

Back at the gate, Clare relates that the program on Champ at the science center was pretty much a replay of a TV documentary aired a few years back. I spend the remainder of the afternoon and early evening visiting with her as she collects parking receipts. I enjoy meeting some of the regular locals as they stop by for a chat. One fellow, clearly lonely and with not much else to do on Saturday evening, enjoys his time bantering with Clare. "He is such a nuisance," she says after he leaves.

As the sun begins to set, I tell Clare that I should be heading back to Connecticut, but watching as the ferry to Port Kent, New York, departs, I leave her to walk alongside the ferry's mooring basin. Reaching a small grassy area at the lake edge, I come upon what looks very much like a light-gray tombstone. Dedicated to Champ, the stone marker depicts an oversized serpent-like creature—*Belua Aquatica Champlainiensis*—peacefully swimming in the lake. With the sun now hidden by the Adirondack Mountains over in New York, I follow the ferry's track across the lake. Hearing its distant drone, I scan the lake one last time for Champ. Turning, I walk back to say goodbye to Clare.

Our children are ours, but we cannot keep them.

CHAPTER 11

Cayo Hueso

The younger the pupil is in becoming familiar with the water, the easier it will be for him to learn to swim. —Captain Matthew Webb

There is not much life about this morning, as I drive east along Roosevelt Boulevard. Following the road as it bends to the left, I head north on A1A. When I come upon Smathers Beach, my eyes race across the white sand and fixate on the flat ocean. "The water looks good. Real good," I say.

Driving farther, I park in a small pull-off on my left. A tanned heavyset fellow who is helping out with today's swim assures me that where I've parked is fine.

Moving around to the SUV's rear, I raise the hatch and unload my kayak. Pulling the boat out of its storage bag, Les helps me unroll it and lay it flat on the sandy parking lot. After inserting the foot pump nozzle, I listen to the pump's telltale whoosh and slow sucking sounds as I start filling one of the kayak ballasts.

"I'm sorry there is not much for you and Emery to do until I get this kayak blown up," I say.

"Don't worry. We're fine," says Les.

Emery unloads our backpacks and several gallon jugs of water-sport drink mix and places them next to the kayak. Without any prompting from me, Les fetches the paddles out of the kayak bag and fits them together. Standing the paddles against the SUV, Les joins Emery, and both watch as I finish blowing up the kayak.

"There. She is ready to go," I say.

"Don't you check this pressure gauge here on the side?" asks Les.

"When I first bought the kayak, I did. Now I can tell by pressing like this with my thumb." After loading the paddles, backpacks, and jugs into the kayak, I man the bow and Les takes on the stern. Together we lift and carry the boat across the highway toward the beach.

Passing under some palm trees, we slip and slide, walking across the beach's deep sand.

A half-mile long and not even a football field wide, Smathers Beach is an unremarkable patch of white sand, but when it is compared to the rest of overbuilt Key West, I feel as if we've stumbled upon a little Eden.

Upon reaching the end of the dry sand where the beach slopes down to the water, Les and I set the kayak down. Over to our right rest several red hard-shell kayaks all aligned, ready for the swim. Other than an odd person or two out for a stroll, the beach is empty.

"It looks like we are here early," I say. "What do you want us to do?" asks Emery.

"I think you and Les should arrange things in the kayak and then go for a paddle; make sure you're comfortable. I have plenty of time; I'll start smearing on the zinc oxide," I say.

"Maybe I should go back to the hotel and get Janet. I talked to that fellow back in the lot; they have kayaks for rent. Janet and I could go together, and Les could paddle one of theirs," says Emery.

"I wish she could come, but she hasn't been sleeping well lately. Being out on the water in this hot sun for five or six hours would set her back," I say.

Walking over to the kayak, I fetch my tub of zinc oxide and

a towel. "You guys have fun out there. I'll be right over there under those palms trees," I say.

I am relieved to retreat under the stand of palm trees. The summer solstice occurred only a few days ago, and though it's still well before eight o'clock, the sun is already quite intense. Smearing globs of zinc oxide onto my legs and arms, I watch as Les and Emery affix a dive flag to the kayak bow.

I have been possessed by this vision of swimming around Key West since it came to me in a pool last summer. Janet's father, Jack, having been retired for many years, passed away last year in Brevard, North Carolina. He had made his home for more than a decade in that quaint town nestled in the Blue Ridge Mountains. Although his memorial service was held in Brevard not long after his passing, Janet and I returned to town again last August to attend a ceremony dedicating two music practice rooms Jack had donated to the Brevard Music Center. For the few years that I knew Jack, I always enjoyed our stays with him in Brevard. Looking remarkably like the white-haired actor Spencer Tracy, Jack was always a gracious host, and he often drove me over to a nearby fitness club so I could swim. On the day after the dedication, Janet dropped me off again at the club before going into town to finish up some business. There, after finishing my laps, I faced the afternoon sun and gazed up at the surrounding mountains. I thought about Jack and the times we spent in Brevard with him. I supposed Janet and I would not have any reason to visit Brevard again. With the summer ending, I wanted some challenge to inspire my training through the coming New England winter. My mind wandering, I recalled a lifeguard I used to join for ocean swims in Vero Beach. He had wanted me to be part of a relay team he was forming for an annual swim around Key West. Not ready for such a swim adventure back then, I declined. Little matter, though; a high bacteria count canceled the swim that summer. "Why not train to make the swim myself?" I now asked. The warm, buoyant salt water, a return visit to South Florida, and trip to the Florida Keys, which I've never visited, all seemed ideal to me. Like the onset of a fever, the vision gripped me. Yes, I would swim around Key West.

Being fair haired and light skinned, though, I knew that swimming five or six hours with my back and legs exposed to a subtropical sun posed a big problem. Given only one shot to complete the swim, there would be no opportunity to experiment with various sunscreens, so I took swim director Bill's advice and brought along a pound of zinc oxide. White, so it reflects all types of light, zinc oxide is an old-time wundercompound. Commonly seen smeared on lifeguard's noses, zinc oxide was standard issue for pilots in the Pacific during World War II. Nowadays zinc oxide continues to find uses for a wide variety of things, from soothing baby bottoms and enhancing cigarette filters to powering nano systems.

Les and Emery are well offshore. Les sits in the stern, and his strokes match Emery's. I have known Les for some years. We taught and coached at the same school in Vero Beach. He still teaches there. Les is not overly tall, but his tanned, well-muscled body, shaved head, flashing green eyes, and pearly white teeth makes for an attractive sight. An avid weightlifter, Les introduced me to medicine-ball training and the Olympic lifts: the snatch and the clean and jerk. His school's longtime strength and conditioning coach, Les preached, "Don't sit. Stand. Get that weight over your head." Seeing him deftly balance seventy kilos while bottoming out on a snatch lift spawned a childlike "I want to do that too" urge in me. Les says little. He was the best man at Janet's and my wedding, but passed on making a speech. I know no other Floridian I'd rather have in my kayak for support this morning.

We met Emery for the first time a couple of days ago. Les mentioned a few weeks ago that she would be visiting him and wondered if she could join our adventure. I thought there would be no problem, as we could always rent another kayak. Emery is in the Navy, training to be a surgeon. She and Les haven't seen each other since they graduated from Suwanee—The University of the South. Emery is a counterpoint to Les. Without heels, I doubt if she would stand five feet. She is garrulous, quick, zany, and seemingly not too athletic. We should have fun out on the water.

Some time has passed, and other than my back, which I can't reach, I've painted myself white. I imagine I look like a skin-and-bones version of Poppin' Fresh, the Pillsbury Doughboy.

A fair number of swimmers and support people are gathering on the beach. Les and Emery have paddled the kayak up onto the wet sand. I walk back out into the bright sun to join them.

"Hey. How did it go out there?" I ask.

"Fine," says Les with his smooth Southern accent.

Emery, who is giggling, says, "You look like a ghost."

"I know, but I couldn't reach my back," I say.

"Here, turn around," says Emery.

Feeling like a boxer getting a rubdown before his big fight, I study the ocean as Emery slathers my back with zinc oxide. An acquaintance up North who visited this beach had mentioned that a thick sea grass grows on the bottom not far offshore. Standing here, I suppose the water owes its murky green tint to the grass. There are none of the electric turquoise hues we saw along the Overseas Highway on the drive down yesterday.

"There, you're good," says Emery. "Thanks," I say.

Out of nervousness, I take the tub of zinc oxide from Emery and continue to smear in dabs here and there.

Bill, the swim director, stops by and wonders if we need to rent a kayak. A glance at Emery says to me that she wishes Janet were here, but I tell Bill we are all set.

Bill runs an evangelical ministry down here. A muscular Christian,

Bill is more than fifty and has won this Swim Around Key West numerous times. Bill is swimming again today. Although he is shorter than Les and trimmer, Bill's tanned, muscular, v-shaped torso tells me that I will be vying for second place in my age group today.

Bill's online posts of his experiences swimming the 12.5-mile loop have been invaluable to me in preparing for this swim. He gave an informative overview of the clockwise course around the island during a meeting at his ministry last evening. Bill is to be admired; his zeal for this swim is infectious. This swim and its organization might be his softest challenge, though, for saving souls is never easy, particularly down here in watery Key West where bars surely outnumber churches.

Sorry to wash off some of my sunblock, I leave Les and Emery and stride off the beach into the ocean. The tepid, soft water here feels almost decadent after having braved the hard, chilly waters back up North. Turning around, I study the oily slick from the zinc oxide mineral mix. A few more steps, and I feel the spongy sea grass under my feet. Fitting my goggles, I swim off.

Stroking out to where I can no longer touch bottom, I rest and float among the scattered kayaks awaiting their swimmers. With such a long swim ahead, I realize that I've had enough warm up, and pointing myself toward the beach, I swim back in.

"How did I look out there?" I ask.

"You're a lean mean fighting machine," says Les.

"You've not seen me swim in five years; I've been training hard, but let's see how I do." Pointing at the White Street Pier a mile off in the distance I add, "But even swimming to that pier will be a challenge."

Hearing this, Les shrugs and raises his eyebrows. I suppose he is disappointed.

The fellow we met earlier in the parking lot calls everyone together for a meeting. Nothing I haven't heard before is said, and during the prayer, I give thanks for the flat water and calm air. Prior to the swim, there were doubts about the water quality here. I e-mailed Bill, and he assured me the swim was still on. Thanks to providence, there is a lull in the hurricane season now. A week or so ago, tropical storm Arlene passed west of here. After returning home, I'll read about hurricane Cindy and the even stronger Dennis inflicting their own damage here. None of these storms will compare to the late-summer devastation that will be wreaked by hurricanes Katrina and Rita.

I am now standing in neck-deep water awaiting the nine o'clock start. Les and Emory float well offshore, beyond the other swimmers and most of the kayaks. The number entered is small; I count fewer than twenty heads bobbing around me. Les and Emory will paddle on my left, my favored side to breathe these days. I focus on the starter in a boat behind the field. He readies us, and with a single horn blast, we are off. In no hurry, I fall in behind. From here in the water, the swimmers appear as so many big-headed birds ceaselessly flapping their wings. Les and Emory are paddling my way. Just north of Cuba, the Tropic of Cancer slices through the Florida Straits, seventy miles to my south. *Florida: a watery land of citrus, palms, cattle-spotted savannas, towering A-bomb-like white clouds, and turquoise-pink sunsets; I succumbed to water here.*

Clare is five. We slog through the sugary white sand and find a vacant spot to set down the brightly colored shovels, buckets, and beach towels. A mother and her young daughter arrive. I chat with the mother while our girls shape dreams in the sand. "They will never see each other again, but for today they are best friends," she says. Leaving them, I wade off into the water. The slack Gulf water is an opaque green. Without goggles and wearing a baggy swimsuit, I haul myself between a pair of rock jetties. Soon fatigued, I walk back up onto the sand. Across from the beach, at a small store, I buy juice and snacks for the drowsy bus ride back home.

We live in Texas now. For seven days I attack an Olympic-size pool's enticing waters. The lifeguards' tips cannot help my gasps and burning sinuses.

Clare and I drive south, past Houston's glassy skyline, to a state park near Galveston. The Gulf's salt breezes and gentle waves little atone for the seaweed-littered brown sand, nettlesome jellyfish, and gray water.

I visit with friends Mary and Tom, beside their apartment's community pool. They are both swimmers. My race with Mary seems unfair, as she glides effortlessly ahead.

"What do you think? Could I still learn to swim?"

"Oh, you could learn to swim, but you probably have no fast twitch muscles left," says Tom.

Clare's summer camp bus is delayed. I pass time by watching two beefy swimmers about my age swim laps in nearby pool. "I am in better shape. Why can't I swim like that?"

Swimming haunts my readings. "I went swimming half a dozen times a day, beginning with white dawn, and ending after sunsets that set the whole lagoon ablaze with amethyst and topaz. Between friends, I will confess that I am not guiltless of often getting up in the night and popping silently overboard to swim for an hour in the clear of a great gold moon—plenilunio—or among the waving reflections of the stars, " writes J. A. Symons in his The Quest for Corvo.

Obeying water's call, Clare and I rebound like a pinball back to Florida.

Emery is waving to me. I stop swimming.

"You need to drink," she says. She passes me a bottle. "How long have I been swimming?"

"Forty-five minutes," she says.

"It doesn't seem that long. Have we cleared the pier?"

"Yes, turn around."

I look inland. "Oh, yeah."

Breathing to the seaward, I will see little of Key West today. No matter; I'm here to swim, not to gawk.

"Are you hungry?" she asks. "No. Let's go."

"Wait. Let me see your face." I float over, and Emery smears zinc oxide on my nose, cheeks, and chin. After refitting my goggles, I swim off.

The water temperature is in the mid-eighties; Emery was wise to have me drink. We ate at a Cuban restaurant after getting in last night. I devoured my dish, *arroz, frijoles, y carne de cerdo*—rice, beans, and pork. Les ordered for us; he speaks fluent Spanish, from what I can gather. He taught high school for a couple of years down in Cartagena, Colombia. He had a sweet deal, a maid and his apartment rent paid for. I asked him once, "Why did you come back?"

"I missed coaching football," he said.

Back when we worked together in Vero Beach, I used to film games for the football team. On a hot night down in Belle Glade, with mole crickets thick in the lights, an opposing player leveled our player Kelly. It was a brutal hit; I felt it up at the top of the grandstand where I was filming. "Did you see that hit?" I excitedly asked Les after the game.

"Yeah. That was something," he coolly answered. That is what I glimpse now on every breath—beneath his khaki safari hat, a calm, assured strength.

We must be nearing Key West's southwest tip. Fort Taylor, a nineteenth-century battlement, occupies the land there. The race director noted that the first five miles covers the deepest water. Other than a few glimpses here and there, I've not been able to see the sea floor. Evidently predators such as barracudas or sharks are not normally found this close in. Their habitats are the offshore flats extending out to the Marquesas Keys or the coral reefs seven miles offshore, but to quote from Thoreau's *Cape Cod*, "I have no doubt that one shark in a dozen years is enough to keep up the reputation of a beach a hundred miles long."

Now the water clears and I am flying over a canyon. Two large fish, seemingly far below me, rest aligned near the light-colored bottom. They might be snook, but looking down, I cannot see the telltale black medial stripe. When I first ventured into open water, underwater sights strangely upset me. My first few views of the brownish-green, barnacled concrete reef off Vero Beach's Humiston Park made me shiver and avert my eyes until I was clear. When I am swimming in lakes or reservoirs, the sight of an aluminum can or a submerged boulder can still make me shudder. During the swim leg of a triathlon held in an old Pennsylvania quarry, I was unnerved when I swam over a rusted, sunken car. Perhaps these feelings come from being practically naked and so vulnerable while swimming.

Again Thoreau:

There must be something monstrous, methinks, in a vision of the sea bottom from over some bank a thousand miles from the shore, more awful than its imagined bottomlessness; a drowned continent, all livid and frothing at the nostrils, like the body of a drowned man, which is better sunk deep than near the surface.

Today, though, I feel at ease. I have the urge to plummet to the bottom. As I swim on, I skip a few breaths to keep the fish in view. I am of the same mind as that once-famous Key West resident Tennessee Williams:

I want to go under the sea in a diving-bell

and return to the surface with ominous wonders to tell.

. . .

> Oh, it's pretty and blue
>
> but not at all to be trusted. No matter how deep you go there's not very much below
>
> the deceptive shimmer and
> glow which is all for show
>
> of sunken galleons encrusted with barnacles and doubloons, an undersea tango palace with instant come and
>
> go moons...

Tennessee Williams liked to swim. Sprawson, in his *Haunts of the Black Masseur*, quotes Williams's reason for moving to Key West as "I would be able to swim here." Sprawson, compelled to swim wherever Tennessee bathed, once "climbed over the rickety fence of Williams's deserted house here on Duncan Street to swim through the green slime of his pool." He even journeyed to New Orleans "to submit my body to the hands of the Black Masseur," from Williams's odd story of the same name about love and cannibalism. Perhaps it is true: water can well up odd urges in us.

The sun is to my back now. We have rounded the point, leaving behind the Atlantic; the Gulf lies ahead. The blue sky, the opaque green water, and rusted barges—everything appears so much brighter now. I notice that Les and Emery have become much more animated, talking and pointing at the waterfront sights to the starboard. My mood lifts too, and I surge ahead into Key West Harbor.

Cruise ships dock and depart from the quarter-mile concrete piers on my right. A short ways inland are Key West's famous bars: Sloppy Joe's, Jimmy Buffett's Margaritaville, the Green Parrot, and Hog's Breath Saloon. Up ahead lies famed Mallory Square, along with many nearby seaside bars and hotels. Amid the dancers, jugglers, and fire eaters, race director Bill can be found some evenings evangelizing on the square. I am on course to intersect famed Duval Street, if it were somehow extended into the Gulf. A sense of bacchanalia reigns on Duval Street most nights. One of the street's well-known sights is its promenading cross-dressers, transvestites, drag queens, or whatever one might call them.

With no real natural resources, Key West has long attracted those with an entrepreneurial spirit. The original Spanish name for the island is *Cayo Hueso* (meaning Bone Island.) Although this colorful term is still in use here, its origin is not clear to me. Perhaps the island's hard limestone made excavation difficult and skeletal remains did not stay buried long. Created to boost tourism, the term The Conch Republic is also another popular moniker for the island. Nineteenth-century Key West residents survived on what the sea provided: fishing, salvaging wrecks, and piracy. Later in the century, Cubans were successful in manufacturing cigars there. In 1912, Henry Flagler's East Coast Florida Railroad was extended more than 150 miles down to Key West. Known as the Overseas Railroad and christened the Eighth Wonder of the World, the line was in service until it was destroyed by a hurricane in 1935. I saw the remnants of the Roman aqueduct-like railroad on our drive down yesterday. I suppose Key West has its attractions for some, but the truth is this flat, overbuilt, claustrophobic, and sunbaked two-mile-wide by four-mile-long island has no real draw for me. I would probably not visit it, if not for this swim. The island is having its way with me, though. Being offshore and swimming in this sensuous dark green water, I am secretly enjoying my own Key West dissolution.

I am swimming really well now. We have passed Sunset Key and Wisteria Island off on our left. When I turn sharply to the right, the sun shifts again. We enter a narrow channel called Fleming Cut. To my left is manmade Fleming Island. The long, narrow island belongs to the U. S. Navy, and I am glad not to swim the three or more miles it would take to round it. The incoming tide sweeps me into the cut. I stop swimming for a time to watch big rocks set in the island bank, a concrete seawall, and an odd building or two glide by. As it is not quite noon, the waterfront restaurant decks over on Key West have few customers. The sunshine is brilliant.

Back in the late 1970s, a woman named Anna first completed this swim around Key West. She is swimming today, but her first rounding took her much of a day, while she treaded water waiting for the tide to change. With the help of a local boatman, Anna later deciphered the tides and established the route we are on. Crucial to her and my success today will be our two-and-half hour head start before high tide.

After passing under the bridge that connects Key West with Fleming Island, I am rocketed out of the cut. Stroking strongly, I set my sights on far-off Dredger Key. Occasionally I glance back and revel in seeing the bridge quickly recede. An immense sense of power fills my body. Like pedaling a bike in high gear, each stroke propels me far forward. The swim is nearly half over, and I am flying, sprinting on to the finish. I am a leviathan, a trident-wielding Neptune, god ruler of the sea!

My exuberance soon vanishes as the water turns slack. A couple of twenty-something guys on jet skis race across my field of view. I pause for a moment, but Les says, "They see you." We enter an expanse of water filled with anchored powerboats and sail craft. I sense the day waning with each passing boat. Manmade Dredgers Key sits tantalizing off in the distance, each of my strokes seemingly bringing it no nearer.

Clare and I snorkel over the ocean reefs off North Palm Beach. Yellow zebra fish dart about the white-gray coral. Out of season, three-foot-long snook impudently loll just out of reach.

The rising sun has colored the flat ocean a gray-green. Nearly imperceptible waves slap the shoreline. Clare and I snorkel north. Small black-and-silver-striped sheepshead hug the barnacle-covered concrete reef below. Tourists and the town's idle soon start appearing on the beach. We stop, and I hunker down, letting the water buoy my weight. Appearing first as black speck, a Coast Guard helicopter beats by in a streak of orange and white. Looking like some ancient Triassic grasshopper, an olive-green military helicopter soon follows. Its gnarled engine roar is deafening. A helmeted, dark-goggled soldier peers stolidly out the open bay door. Back on shore, hand-held radios crackle, people chat in groups, and a few, hoping for a better view, stand atop the beach access stairs. All look toward the cape, seventy miles to the north. Keen anticipation has replaced the day's boredom. I hear, "It's up." An interminable time passes, and then the shuttle Discovery, looking like a whitish-yellow road flare, rises above the clutter of condos and hotels. Followed by its white contrail, Discovery bends to the east, casts off its boosters, and vanishes into the faded blue sky. The show over, most of the people shuffle home, the burden of the day weighing on them again. We stay and listen. Minutes pass, and then, sounding like distant thunder, the blast arrives. Having no direction, the rumble permeates the air. The beach now empty, we snorkel out into deeper water.

Like shipwreck survivors, Tom, Clare, and I cling to a yellow kickboard in the clear waters off Fort Pierce's Pepper Park. A dive flag in tow, we futilely scour the sandy bottom for the wrecked Urca de Lima.

Fitting my snorkel and mask, I swim into the channel. Halfway across, I'm seized with a panic that begins in my throat and knifes down through my bowels. I flip on my back and gag. Mary shouts, "What's wrong?" More than words, it's her look of disgust that brings back my composure. I warily swim on. A porpoise surfaces for air seemingly within reach. Intently gazing about, I expect to see his happy face through my mask, but he is gone.

CROSSINGS: A SWIMMER'S MEMOIR

Both the day and summer are dying. Breathing heavily through my snorkel, I pull with abandon through the clear waters off Florida's Longboat Key. Later, rinsing off in the night air, I silently declare myself a swimmer.

My snorkeling adventures will contribute (to paraphrase Henry Adams) nothing to my swimming education.

I finally reach Dredgers Key, and we all need a break. Emery passes me a bottle, and she and Les paddle over to a patch of sand to stretch their legs. I float like I am in a La-Z-Boy recliner, sipping sport drink. Key West, Fleming Island, and now Dredgers Key; I have been ceaselessly swimming in and around these lone land masses all morning. Atolls, archipelagos, isles, keys, and such are usually associated with refuge, privacy, and bliss, but they also can imprison. Alcatraz, Rikers Island, and Devil's Island all have their watery fences. I side with the latter, when viewing islands. Islands embody confinement for me. I need a county, state, nation; no, better—a continent—to roam over. A few years back, Janet and I vacationed on Rhode Island's Block Island. By the third day, having bicycled and hiked over most of the island, I found myself longingly staring at ferries departing for the New England mainland. "Get me off this rock," I pleaded. Years before, I could never quite make my escape, despite the countless runs I made along the Manhattan waterfront.

Emery has taken her seat in the stern and Les sits in the bow. He passes me an energy bar and they paddle off to try out the new seating arrangement. But the kayak does not track well and they spin about. They paddle on past me, retracing our route. After finishing the bar, I swim on ahead. They soon come along side and paddle by. Losing control again, I see them spin. Upon reaching them, I find Les in the water swimming after the kayak. Emery giggles while keeping the kayak just out of his reach. Les and I match strokes for a time before he is able to grab the blue nylon cord hanging off the

CAYO HUESO

stern. Leaving them to sort things out, I swim on and at last round Dredgers Key.

The Route 1 bridge (the swim's nine-mile mark) connecting Stock Island to Key West is in sight. The water is noticeably shallower here. I need to be careful, for according to race director Bill, standing or touching the bottom will result in a disqualification. Of course, everyone swimming today is their own judge, but for personal pride and a true sense of accomplishment, I hope not to touch bottom or rest on the kayak. Except for these large beige funnel-shape objects, the sea floor is an empty expanse of sand. "Are these coral or sponges?" I wonder.

With Les in the stern again, he and Emery paddle alongside me. The barren bottom is endless. My mantra becomes "The ocean is a desert underwater. The ocean is a desert underwater. The ocean is a . . ." The slack water gives me no boost, but I continue to swim well.

Although I will be elated to complete this 12.5 mile swim today, I will not be guilty of false pride. Compared to other long-distance swims, such as the twenty-one miles across the numbing English Channel, this swim is easy. Also swimming here is hypocritical on my part. When I ran, long-distance events such as marathons held no interest for me. "Have you ever run a marathon?" was what I was asked. "No, but I've run twenty or more miles while training." I have never been able to make clear my distaste for the marathons wherein so many walk across the finish line or worse, lose control of their bowels, collapse, or require hospitalization. A matter of aesthetics, for me the speed, stamina, and strategy displayed in a mile, 5k, or 10k track race is unrivaled. Ethiopian gold medalist Haile Gebrselassie, who turned to the marathon and subsequently set a world record for the distance, when he no longer possessed the foot speed, thought a 10k race on the track much more difficult than running a marathon. True for swimming as it is for running, long-distance events are the refuge for the untalented. I persist without gifts, but game.

On the related notion of physical endurance, we accede too much. Upon their return, those who have surmounted or survived some ordeal usually have an absorbing story to tell that perhaps will inspire others, but for any great insight or wisdom, I find it lacking. In *Ultimate High: My Everest Odyssey*, deceased mountaineer Goran Kropp recounts riding his bike 7,000 miles from Sweden to climb the world's tallest peak without bottled oxygen. Other than being witness to the well-publicized tragedies on Mt. Everest during the spring of 1996, Goran's telling offers no more than a celibate night in a brothel, being shot at by Turkish soldiers, and throwing rocks at combative kids in Iran. Kathy Watson, in *The Crossing*, a biography of Englishman Matthew Webb, the first person to swim the English Channel, quotes Webb as saying, "Go to bed early, do not smoke, and if you have been accustomed to drink beer, one glass with your dinner and one with your supper will be more than sufficient." To what does Webb attribute his success swimming the Channel? "It's dogged as does it," he says. Eight years after his Channel success, Webb—broke at the age of thirty-five—drowned while trying to swim the rapids below Niagara Falls. Perhaps an avoidance of everyday life is the common theme that unites tales of extreme endurance. Irishman Sir Earnest Shackleton, who incredibly survived twenty-two months with his crew after the wreck of his ship the *Endurance* in the Antarctic, is quoted as saying, "If I had not some strength of will, I would make a first-class drunkard." As for those expecting any wisdom or insights from me, the reader has been warned.

Route 1A, the only road in and out of Key West, is up next. Connecting Key West to Stock Island, the highway bridge spans a narrow stretch of water known as Cow Key Channel. The name Stock Island is thought to come from the livestock that were raised on the island to feed Key West. Occasionally raising my head, I see a swimmer-kayak pair pass under the bridge. I have no inkling of my standing in the swim. Back at Fleming Island, Les had said I was doing really well, but I took his comment as no more than encouragement.

The freshwater Biscayne Aquifer near the Everglades National Park supplies fresh water to the Florida Keys. After a journey of some 130 miles, Key West's lifeblood passes through an eighteen-inch white pipe just above me.

Normally, swimming beneath this low four-lane bridge would be unnerving, but hours in the water have inured me. I remain calm as the concrete pilings glide by. The water is shallow here, and other than a can or two, the bottom is free of litter. Emerging from the dark, I enter Hawk Channel. The crystalline water in the channel reflects a light green tint. Up ahead lies the Atlantic Ocean. I will make a right turn there, and then it will be a straight shot back to Smathers Beach.

A woman about my age whom I remember from the pre-race meeting this morning passes me on the right. My competitiveness kicks in, and I give chase. I find, though, that I'm spent. Watching her strong stroke, I regret not pacing myself better. In cyclist terms, I've cracked. The last three miles will not be easy.

I look squint-eyed through the sun's reflection as a queue of swimmers executes flip turns. Don, an elderly swim coach, is tidying up the wreck of kickboards, swim noodles, and overturned chairs left by a passing storm. Standing between two starting blocks, I stare into the pool's deep blue water. "I always wanted to learn how to swim," I mutter as he passes by.

"I've taught older people than you. Stop by when you're ready."

Alone, I see myself gliding into the wall, somersaulting, and streaking off like a porpoise.

I wave my goggles about and boast to my classes that I'm going to learn to swim. Susan, our school's best girl swimmer, says my purple goggles are grotesque.

I walk out on the deck in my baggy, orange swimsuit, and Steve directs me to a vacant lane. "Swim ten lengths, with a thirty-second rest between each," he orders. My leaking goggles, gasps, and burning sinuses make me want to quit. I am overwhelmed by the aquamarine pool's deep water, the bottom's black elongated I-stripes, the water's mirror-like reflection, the yellow-green pool lights, the black, starry night sky, and the shouts from the deck. I grasp at Steve's mental images: rotate your body as if it were on a barbecue skewer; grip the water as if you were pulling yourself along a ladder; hold the water as if you were swimming through marbles. Once I am back on the deck, my head resonates like a melon; I clear my ears by bouncing stiff-legged on the pool deck. The chlorine dries my skin and makes it itch.

The winter solstice arrives. Cold air pours into the state. The surrounding palm trees rustle in the northwest wind. Gritting my teeth, I shiver while toweling off.

Don grumbles at me, "Let's clean this shit up."

Amanda, a swimmer and one of my students, stops by to watch my struggles. "You suck," she says before walking off.

Just before the New Year, a breakthrough occurs—I swim 400 consecutive yards. A week later, I total a mile for the session. I've crossed swimming's Rubicon.

I am swimming in spurts now. The saltwater has irritated the inside of my mouth and tongue. Over shallow spots, I switch to the breaststroke to avoid touching the bottom and escape the salt's sting. The tide is ebbing, but the water feels lifeless. Some low-lying vegetation grows on one side of the channel. On the other side is a seawall and behind it is Route 1A. I watch as tourists drive by comfortably ensconced in their tinted-glass sedans and SUVs. With day-to-day life so near, my struggle in the channel becomes absurd. I stop swimming for a drink.

"This is not fun anymore," I say between swigs.

"You're still moving. Just hang in there," says Les.

"Do I look sunburned?"

"Just a little," says Emery.

"Okay. Let's finish this damn thing," I say.

I feel a little renewed, but my nerves are on edge. My mind wanders; I wonder about the sun. Can you die from bad sunburn? Maybe, but then probably not. Haven't shipwreck victims survived days at sea despite suffering terrible burns? Oh, yeah, now I remember. Les and I were into reading outdoor survival books on mountaineering and sailing. He lent me *Adrift: Seventy-six Days Lost at Sea*. I can't remember the details now, other than the castaway was badly sunburned, yet survived. There is a great fear of the sun nowadays. Children can't go outside without Mom or Dad loading on the sunblock. It was not like that when I was growing up. My friends and I ran about every summer in our bathing suits. We became as brown as that Coppertone girl. "Don't be a paleface!" the ad said. I guess I was twelve or thirteen when my mother took me to a doctor to see about a small red, scaly rash on my face next to my ear. "He has lupus," said the doctor. My mother, who was a nurse, broke into tears. The doctor cauterized the lesion and told me to stay out of the sun. The rash never come back, and today there is only faint mark left.

"He didn't know what he was talking about," my mother said later.

Skin cancer is a problem, though, with ozone depletion and northern, fair-haired people migrating to lower latitudes. Growing up, we subscribed to *Reader's Digest*. Maybe because of my lupus scare and my mother fretting over us at the slightest cough or sneeze, I was always latching onto *Digest* pieces on melanoma—what the magazine called black mole cancer. It seemed as if every month it ran some story on it. I remember one article about a lawyer who while shaving came across a dark spot on his neck. He ignored it and was dead in three weeks when the cancer burned a hole in his throat. "No way something like that is going to happen to me," I thought. Sometimes I used to go crazy looking at this or that spot in the mirror until I saw a doctor. I'm still a little bit of the hypochondriac when it comes to my skin. A doctor removed a suspicious black spot from my calf a year ago. Guess what. It was scar tissue. I remembered later that I got a gash running through the woods. That doctor should have known better, but I convinced him there was something wrong. Anyone who frequents doctors knows they are always game to chase red herrings. Perhaps it's the money or the fear of a lawsuit.

Anyway, the water blocks the sun rays if you are deep enough. Too bad; I've been on the surface all day. I'm sure the saltwater has stripped off all the zinc oxide I smeared on. How bad will my burn be after this swim? And damn it! After all these years, I still don't know anything about that lupus thing.

The waves have picked up and the water shines with a bright green tint. My spirits lift, and I regain my composure. My attention returns to the swim. I am leaving the channel behind and swimming out into the ocean. We gradually bend around to the right with the shoreline. I stop for another drink. "Can you see the buoy? There is supposed to be a large orange buoy to mark the finish."

Emery and Les peer ahead, but they see nothing.

"What time is it?" I ask.

"A quarter to three," says Emery.

"Let's go," I say emphatically.

I have studied the route many times, and I know there is something like a mile and a half left to swim. I had hoped to break six hours, but I resign myself to it not happening.

I alternate between front crawl and breaststroke. I count the strokes off in sets of ten. The saltwater is repulsive to me. All I want is to be back on land and feel a cool breeze on my face. I wonder at those who have crossed the Channel. Just to endure the saltwater seems unreal. All along my right runs a three-foot-or-so-high concrete seawall. A little farther inland, across Route 1, is the Key West Airport. To ease my agony, I imagine myself flying down the runway.

I pause for moment and swim close to the kayak. "I'm done; I'm getting out over there and walking the rest of the way," I say.

"What? You can't do that!" shrieks Emery.

"Yeah, sure, just try it," Les says menacingly.

"I'm only kidding," I say with a laugh.

We approach a long line of weathered wooden pilings. I focus on reaching the first one. Flipping onto my back, I frog kick and simultaneously sweep my arms back. After gliding to a stop, I retract my legs and extend my arms up in preparation for the next stroke. Karma can be cruel. Here I am, the one who belittled marathon runners, struggling to finish with this half-ass stroke. I surprise myself, though, as the pilings glide by.

"You're really moving," I hear Les say.

Emery then shouts, "I see the buoy!"

Les looks ahead intently and agrees with her.

Feeling like a sailor who has heard, "Land ahoy!" I flip over and peer intently, but the afternoon sun's glare on the water obscures my view. Rolling over onto my back, I stroke on.

In the spring, my progress in the pool stalls. I turn to Peggy Lee Dean's book, Open Water Swimming *and Conrad Wenerberg's* Wind, Waves, and Sunburn: A Brief History of Marathon Swimmers. *I'm inspired, but my swimming is unimproved.*

Finding Terry Laughlin's, Total Immersion Swimming *is a revelation. Drawing parallels with tennis, he emphasizes technique over yardage. Most summer evenings, I bicycle thirteen miles south to a small beach on the Indian River Lagoon. I grow accustomed to warm brackish water, mossy bottom, and an occasional brush with a fish. Each evening I practice Laughlin's twelve stroke drills. Other than an occasional bather or two, I swim alone.*

A boiling school of baitfish halts my practice. Not knowing if a bull shark might be lurking about, I retreat to the shore and watch the parade pass.

Weeks go by. I become more relaxed and cease struggling. Becoming introspective, I focus Zen-like on my swimming. I equate each day's worth to the quality of my practices. A pattern of steady progress emerges. Cycling home with the sun setting, I rehash my small gains and new insights.

On weekends I bicycle to Humiston Park and swim a mile or more in the Atlantic. I stop at a citrus outlet on my cycle ride home. I devour one, two, sometimes three ruby red grapefruits. Every mariner knows vitamin C is not found in the sea.

Florida's two-day lobster season arrives. Emboldened by the swarms of divers hunting "bugs," my swim encompasses all three guard stations. I'm amazed.

My afternoon swim interrupted by a thunderstorm, I retreat to a private deck and watch as loggerhead turtles peek up from the rain-swept ocean.

I master breathing to my right. Ecstatic, I swim all morning until my tongue swells and burns.

I worry about sharks. "Of the fifty-one reported shark attacks in the world last year, nineteen occurred in Florida," I read. I feel exposed and vulnerable while swimming in the ocean, but I can't give it up. I talk to lifeguards, surfers, anybody, but no one knows anything. A guard painfully relates that a boy's body was found decapitated a few years back. "A twelve-foot tiger shark," he says. Believing there is safety in numbers, I selfishly swim in and about bathers.

My final summer in Florida, I travel to Siesta Key, Cypress Gardens, and North Palm Beach for open water swims.

The water off Fort Lauderdale's Central Beach is flat and clear as glass. Large cargo ships appear to be pasted on the blue horizon. I swim far out and float among the kayaks. We then walk down the beach for the swim start. White water, torsos, legs, and flailing arms; left at the green buoy, and then north, paralleling the beach—it is my last swim in Florida. I stroke madly.

The buoy is in sight, and I resume swimming freestyle. Emery readies her digital camera. I am determined to make a good show. The months of training; the miles in the pool; the hours of stretch cords, push-ups, pull-ups, and dips all is concentrated into these last fifty yards. Feeling rejuvenated, I swim fast toward the buoy. Reaching up with both hands, I slap the canvas hard. My ordeal over, I tread water lightly.

I swim behind Les and Emery as they paddle toward the beach. Reaching the shallows, I stand and walk slowly over the sea grass. Close to the shore, a young girl presents me with a medal. Before I can admire it, a wave of nausea overtakes me. Leaving Les and Emery, I walk over to a small bathhouse that is shaded by palm trees. Although not particularly thirsty, I take a sip from the fountain outside. When I walk into the house, my attention is drawn to a tall, elderly fellow with unkempt white hair. He stands behind a low door over in a corner stall. His shaking shoulders, hunched posture, and fervent face only add to my nausea. Turning around, I walk back outside. Near the fountain, I pass a young boy. I think of warning him, but decide instead to keep an eye on the house. Near a row of palms, I find Les and Emery unloading the gear from the kayak. Bill passes by and asks, "How did it go?" I thank him for organizing such a challenging swim.

Having almost forgotten the bathhouse, I feel relieved when the young boy walks over to join us. Wasting little time he says, "There is a weird guy in the bathroom."

Bill, apparently well acquainted with the boy, appears unperturbed and says in a happy, lighthearted manner, "What do you expect? This is Key West."

꙳꙳꙳

As I thought, Bill was again the winner for the fifty-and-older set. My pedestrian time, six hours and forty minutes, earned us a gift certificate to a waterside grill on Big Coppitt Key. We stopped off for lunch at the grill on our drive out the next day. There we shared our salads with a pair of stoic-faced three-foot-long iguanas.

Having viewed too many artifacts over the years—and both celebrities being deceased, they could not advise us—we opted to visit Ernest Hemingway's home over the Mel Fisher (discoverer of the sunken Spanish galleon *Atocha*) treasure museum the next morning. Almost anywhere else, Hemingway's two-story boxy home and lush tropical gardens would be unremarkable, but situated on cramped Key West, the home easily qualifies as an estate. Known more as a boxer than a swimmer, Hemingway nonetheless had an expansive thirty-yard pool dug in the island's solid coral, likely the site of many drunken poolside bashes in his day. I thought that with a couple of lane lines in place, the pool would be superb for lap swimming. I learned from our guide that the pool was last used when a group of college students visiting on spring break all jumped in while on tour.

By the time our guide had moved on to discussing Ernest's third wife, Janet and I excused ourselves and retreated to a well-shaded bench. "He didn't treat women very well," she lamented.

Not able to empathize with her, I turned to watch the numerous cats wander about. Noticing my interest, a rather intense, dark-haired, ponytailed staff member walked over and related that the grounds' polydactyl (six-toed) cats all descend from Hemingway's time. Hearing that the cats receive regular vet care and are well protected, I wondered aloud if Janet's cat ET might live out her sunset years here.

"Absolutely not," said the fellow. "The other cats would attack her and drive her out."

When Janet and I persisted in discussing ways in which we might introduce ET into the brood, the fellow became quite agitated and did all he could to dissuade us. Not to be too cruel, we ended our chat with assurances that ET would remain in Connecticut.

Having enjoyed Hemingway's writing when I was a teenager, but having no desire to read anymore, I nonetheless left Janet in the company of a couple of cats and walked over to the guest house, serving now as a gift shop and bookstore. I opened the shop door and was about to pick up a copy of the *Sun also Rises*, when a strong odor of cat urine spun me about. Back outside, I thought about poor Ernest, who in 1961 blew his brains out in Ketchum, Idaho, with the same shotgun his father had used to dispatch himself. A lover of bloody bullfights and a big-game hunter, the great man that he was saw that the 1960s were not going to be his time. He was not going to let himself become some wizened anachronism.

With Janet preferring to again rest at the motel, Les, Emery, and I went out in the evening after the swim to celebrate. Perhaps Emery was unable to relate to Les as she remembered having done years before, in college, because a palpable tension set in between the two after the first drink or two. I was too preoccupied with trying to quench my thirst to play peacemaker.

"He's changed," she confided.

Following Emery as she tracked Les from bar to bar, I wondered about my elevated pulse. Like an engine throttle set too high, my body continued to race. Emery thought I might be dehydrated. No matter the cause, I knew from previous long cycle rides that I would soon recover.

Our wanderings eventually led us to Mallory Square, where we joined the crowds to watch the acrobats, fire eaters, and odd musical acts. Growing bored, I strolled over to the water's edge. The sun had set, and a faint blue glow hugged the southern horizon. After tracing the red and green channel markers from the harbor out into the empty Atlantic, I tried to imagine how we must have appeared as we passed through the sunlit harbor this morning. Like after debarking from a boat, I still felt the waves' push and pull. With my back to the square, I peered intently and felt uplifted. A hum seemed to reverberate in the still air, and the vast expanse of water contracted. I stood there for a time, transfixed, but sensing darkness intruding, I soon turned and walked toward the square while hearing the sea's crash and thunder.

CHAPTER **12**

Crossings

Let us cross over the river, and rest under the shade of the trees.
—Stonewall Jackson

Stepping off the sand into the water, I wade in up to my waist. The cool water that chills my legs contrasts starkly with the hot Utah sun that warms my bare chest, shoulders, and face. The lake has bright aqua color today, much like a quarry lake. When I last swam here two years ago, the water did not have such a bright hue. I suppose the vibrant color comes from the lake level being so much lower this year.

After standing a while, I submerge my arms up to my elbows and splash water on my neck and face. When I was young, my mother would tell me to wet these pulse points to help overcome the initial shock of cold water. Never knowing if it was of any real use, I continue with the habit. Feeling ready, I step forward and hunker down, letting the water rise to my neck. Shaking off my initial shudder, I fit my swim cap and goggles. Waving to Janet, who is up on the beach, I start swimming parallel to the beach with a shallow breaststroke, not fully submerging my face.

Palisades Lake—located in a Utah State Park of the same name—is centrally located in the Mormon Corridor (a multistate region settled by Mormons in the nineteenth century.) Janet and I left Virginia and came west here to Utah for my new teaching position three years ago. Curiously, for most of these years, I have not been here in Utah; instead I have been living and teaching in Beijing, China.

Approaching a gray diving platform that is anchored a ways off the beach, I switch to a front crawl. I feel the cool water as it flows over my face, neck, and shoulders. The odd assortment of adults, teenagers, and children on the platform deck ignore me as I swim by. Back in the shallows, buoyed by brightly colored rings and rafts, a few families with young children loll about. Up from the beach, shaded by trees, other groups sit at picnic tables or on lawn chairs. Farther inland, numerous SUVs and campers with canopy tents set nearby fill the view. Adjacent to the beach, Janet walks along a paved drive paralleling my track.

Between breaths I gaze downward. The water now shines with a light green tint. Reaching up from lake bottom, tentacle-like vines occasionally entangle themselves around my arms and neck. After stopping a few times to rid myself of the stringy weeds, I veer off into deeper water.

This lake, at 6,000 feet above sea level, lies at the western base of the Wasatch Mountain Range. The surrounding steep, sand-colored hills dotted with blue-green sage, cypress, and scrub oak all make for spectacular scenery. Not too far off to the east, I can see peaks that rise to 8,000 feet. Returning from China on my summer breaks, I usually need a couple weeks of running, cycling, and swimming before I acclimate to Utah's elevation. Since I returned from Beijing only a couple of weeks ago, I expect this afternoon's swim to be sluggish.

The lake's western shore is not far now, maybe a football-field-length away. Upon reaching there, I will trace the shore's contour until it meets the dam at the lake's southern end. I see Janet again. She is waiting for me up ahead, a little ways up from the water. She will follow me along the dirt path that runs around the lake. Whenever I have swum here, this has been my favored route. Janet walks while I swim, and together we cross this lake.

How and why I came to be in Beijing after to moving to Utah is not terribly important. Suffice it to say that not long after I arrived in Utah, my employer found more value in my working over there than here. What is pertinent, though, is that I was able to swim for the years I was in China.

Indeed, it was only a few weeks ago that I was swimming in a dimly lit, cavernous Olympic-size pool. The pool, enclosed by high concrete walls broken only by a row of large, smudgy windows, sat adjacent to the school where I taught and lived in Beijing's Haidian District. The walls and the concrete-encased ceiling beams painted a light aqua color and peeling here and there gave the pool a forlorn, industrial feel. I would not complain, though, as the pool was free of charge and open from early morning to late at night during my stay.

It was not long after my first swim or two in the pool's head-high water that my high-elbow, boiling front crawl stroke caused me to feel out of place, for I saw the Chinese were inveterate breaststrokers. Men and women slowly undulating in the adjacent lanes, I watched as they methodically swam lap after lap in the same stolid, unwavering manner I had observed other Chinese ride their bikes. The sense of purpose, at times urgency, that I was so accustomed to back in States was absent from this pool. In this pool, each stroke counted for more than the entire swim.

Up on the pool deck, I later attracted the attention of an elderly lifeguard. Occasionally resting between laps, I smiled up at him as he happily laughed and waved while mimicking my stroke.

Swimming, like any physical activity removed from certain societal norms of behavior, gives a ready insight into a people's character. Through swimming, I learned the Chinese were invariably friendly, curious, and deferential. Those sharing a lane with me smiled pleasantly between laps, but knowing that I was a *wai guo ren*, a foreigner, they would discretely move over to swim in often-crowded lanes, thereby affording me a solitary, undisturbed swim.

Some weeks afterward, the elderly guard, without any prompting from me, began demonstrating to me what he thought my stroke should look like. Through a translator I learned he hoped to become my friend. In some months, when I could converse a little, I shared my age and learned his. The Chinese are keen on longevity, and one's age is usually among the first questions asked. We later exchanged phone numbers and small gifts.

Reaching the lake edge, I stop swimming and rest on the rocky bottom.

"How's the water?" asks Janet.

"Like heaven," I answer.

"The lake is so much lower this year," she says.

"I know, but last year the lake was drained. You couldn't even swim here," I say.

"We had more snow this winter," she says.

"Anyway, it feels good to be here," I add. "Quite a change from China," she says. "Unbelievable," I say.

"Are you ready?" she asks.

"Yeah. Let's go," I say before swimming off along the rocky shore.

Utah is ranked the second driest state in the nation after Nevada. Towns all along the Wasatch Mountains depend on the melting snows from the winter snow pack for their water. Lake-effect snow off the Great Salt Lake also allows the ski resorts north of here to back up their claim of having "The Greatest Snow on Earth."

Feeling my hands hit bottom, I swim farther out from the shore. Two summers ago, when the lake was full, I swam in close to the large boulders and sheer rock faces I am passing. That year's heavy winter snows allowed Utah ski resorts to stay open well into May. All the newspapers carried photos of girls in bikinis skiing down the slopes.

Farther south, where we reside, green bales of hay were seen stacked high in every rancher's field, and at a local Pioneer Day parade held in late July, Janet and I ducked as snowballs flew.

It feels good not to be returning to China. Arriving home in mid-July and then departing well before Labor Day made the last few summers all too short. All told, I made ten crossings of the Pacific during my three years teaching in Beijing. Janet, although spending a fair amount of time with me there the first two years, remained in Utah this past year. I have felt some remorse for contributing to the buildup of carbon dioxide in the atmosphere, but knowing that planes fly every day, with or without me, I have since rationalized away my guilt.

It seems odd—and I never would have expected in this, my last chapter—to be writing about China and the Chinese, and in truth, I was sent there for only one year, but when invited by my Chinese hosts to stay on, I saw the immense value in seeing my initial group of Chinese students through to their graduation. In but a few weeks, they too will depart China for college and university study here in the States.

In the end, neither Janet nor I really took to the insular expat lifestyle, centered as it is on work, dining, going to bars, and such. We also felt confined by Beijing city life. I missed open spaces, and Janet, although able to obtain locally grown organic foods, found living there too stifling. I do not mean to complain, though, because as I will elaborate below, we both took away much from our time in China.

No culture has been able to resist the West, and the same is true for China. The Chinese in the same breath will tell you that they have more than five thousand years of recorded history, but are still a developing country. A long suffering people—they most recently endured what they call a Century of Humiliation (from the first Opium War until the founding of the People's Republic of China in 1949)—today the Chinese are in a desperate game of catch-up with us.

Ever prideful, they wish to restore their country to what they view as its rightful place as the world's center of civilization. Despite the setbacks of the Great Leap Forward and the Cultural Revolution, the Chinese have made astounding progress. To help understand how far they have come, during the Roaring Twenties, when the West was embracing jazz, technology, suffrage, and a loosening of morals, the 180-acre Forbidden City (the emperor's residence) in central Beijing still harbored more than 1,000 eunuchs. Only in 1925, when the average life expectancy in China was less than twenty-five years, were these poor souls finally turned out to suffer life on their own.

China receives a good deal of coverage in the western press nowadays—much of it negative. It is true: intellectual property theft, air and water pollution, human rights abuse, economic chicanery, and political corruption all exist there. In fact, the air-quality index in Beijing went off the scale a few times this past winter. My Chinese colleagues, much in the way they deal with domestic political scandals, territorial disputes with Japan, or dissidents in the news, never showed much concern or alluded to the bad air in passing conversation. Of course, since I was not ever close to being fluent in Chinese, I was not totally clear on what was discussed in my presence. Concerns about the air quality, food, and water were what ultimately brought me back here to Utah, though.

Most of us here in the States are for the most part pleased and proud of our locale's environmental record. Air and water quality are certainly much better now than they were during the environmental crises of the 1960s and 1970s. We believe our lives and world are becoming healthier and "greener," and I wish this were true, but sadly, we here in the West are deluded. We have become complacent, have chased profits and shirked onerous tasks by unduly relying on the Chinese over the last thirty years or so. If we, in fact, have cleaned up our air and water, it is in part because we have shipped our factories, plants, and waste to places such as China. Powering their economy by burning coal, they are improving their own standard of living by following the same sooty route the U.S., England, and other developed countries took over the last couple of centuries. We here in the West rebuke them for their environmental degradation, while at the same time forgetting our own environmental catastrophes such as the Great Smog of London, which, caused by coal burning, killed thousands in the winter of 1952.

Way back in 1870, Mark Twain in his autobiographical *Roughing It* could have predicted our current state when he wrote:

> They [Chinese] are quiet, peaceable, tractable, free from drunkenness, and they are as industrious as the day is long. A disorderly Chinaman is rare, and a lazy one does not exist. So long as a Chinaman has strength to use his hands he needs no support from anybody; white men often complain of want of work, but a Chinaman offers no such complaint; he always manages to find something to do. He is a great convenience to everybody—even to the worst class of white men, for he bears the most of their sins, suffering fines for their petty thefts, imprisonment for their robberies, and death for their murders.

> They do not need to be taught a thing twice, as a general thing. They are imitative. If a Chinaman were to see his master break up a centre table, in a passion, and kindle a fire with it, that Chinaman would be likely to resort to the furniture for fuel forever afterward.

> All Chinamen can read, write, and cipher with easy facility—pity but all our petted voters could. In California they rent little patches of ground and do a deal of gardening. They will raise surprising crops of vegetables on a sand pile. They waste nothing. What is rubbish to a Christian, a Chinaman carefully preserves and makes useful in one way or another. He gathers up all the old oyster and sardine cans that white people throw away and

procures marketable tin and solder from them by melting. He gathers up old bones and turns them into manure. In California he gets a living out of old mining claims that white men have abandoned as exhausted and worthless.

I had a laugh when I read Twain's last paragraph above. Carting over cases at a time of sardine cans on my trips to Beijing, I can personally attest to the rapidity with which the empty cans continue to be made into marketable tin and solder.

Teaching Chinese students was a revelation to me. Where as in the States I had to contend with class interruptions from activities such as sports and play practice; harried, anxious administrators; whiny, excuse-making students; and at times, meddlesome parents, the focus at my 4,000-student Chinese public school was always on the classroom. Although I had some boys I took to calling—in good nature—*lan gui*, slackers, the level of academic achievement and respect for learning I found there was startling. During parents meetings (conducted in Chinese with a translator present) the question most often asked by parents was "How can my son or daughter improve?" Because of China's one-child policy, parents, grandparents, aunts, and uncles all treasured and would spare no expense to ensure their lone child had the brightest future. It is commonly believed (see Twain's "imitative" observation above) that Chinese students, because of their years of rote learning, are not very creative and tend to be unimaginative, but in working with Chinese students, I found this not to be the case. When allowed and encouraged, they were as creative as my best students back in the States.

While in China, I felt at times that the future of the human race was being worked out—decided—in China. The Chinese will soon overtake the U.S. in economic production. Their large population and the choices they make will have immense global impact. Whether this impact will be positive or negative remains to be seen. The Chinese have never been hampered by a creation myth that views work as punishment: "In the sweat of thy face shalt thou eat bread, till thou return unto the ground; for out of it wast thou taken: for dust thou art, and unto dust shalt thou return." Instead, they have always been eminently practical and never too much concerned about an afterlife. Today, they continue to adhere to the Confucian values of parental respect, obedience, loyalty, and diligence.

I have rounded the last rocky point. Janet is nearing the place where the end of the dam meets a small beach. I will take a break there, on the beach, before retracing my path on my swim back. My swim this afternoon has been languid and uninspired. Mixing in drills such as one-arm stroking, swimming on my side, and catch up, I have been searching for my stroke and trying to feel the water again.

Perhaps I have already written too much about the Chinese and our time there. In fact, I could write much more on topics such as *liu mianzi,* saving face; the ambivalence Chinese feel toward *lao wai,* foreigners and last-minute decision making; and how the rules on wiring money can seemingly depend on your teller's disposition, but I will leave these topics for some other time. I should note though that Janet and I never did any extensive traveling while in China. Other than day or overnight trips to city parks, nearby mountain resorts, or the Great Wall at Badaling and Mutianyu, we remained in Beijing. Never given to dromomania, I have always looked askance at those who like to travel. Travelers, upon their return, seldom seem particularly improved or changed to me. Surely mine is not a commonly held or popular view, but I have never seen much value in travel beyond diversion or relaxation. Although some of my western colleagues traveled to see Shanghai's historic waterfront region, the Bund, the Pandas in Sichuan, or the Wulingyuan Scenic Zone in Hunan where the world created in the movie *Avatar* Pandora took its inspiration, we never desired to do the like. Instead, our leisure hours in Beijing were spent mostly studying the Chinese language, or as the Chinese say, *Putonghua*, common speech.

Occupying the top shelves of a bookcase that is nestled in the corner of a small room in our modest duplex rental here in Utah is what Janet calls our Chinese corner. The bright-red tasseled ornaments, Chinese calendar, imperial-yellow teacup emblazoned with two *fenghuang* (Phoenix), miniature Beijing Opera masks and figurines, Chinese paper cuttings, antique snuff bottles, and hand-painted swallow kite from Weifang in Shangdong on display there are but a few of the keepsakes we received as gifts from my students and Chinese hosts. Although these mementos are pleasing to look at and commemorate our time in Beijing, it is the Chinese language and phrase books, graded readers, CDs, and general books on China shelved in the bookcase that we value most from our time in China.

Daniel Kane in his *The Chinese Language: Its History and Current Usage* wrote, "Undertaking the study of Chinese is a life sentence." Despite reading his caution, Janet and I began our study of Chinese not long after our arrival. There is no need to detail our struggles and difficulties during our first year there other than to say after several false starts, we found some materials and techniques that enabled us to move forward. Today (although our proficiency is not that great) we have a lifetime hobby on which we can spend an hour or two listening, reading, and discussing a page or two of Chinese. Someday we will perhaps return to China for a year or two of full-time language study, but whether we travel back or not—like with so many other Eastern arts or pursuits—there will be no end to our study.

Much like learning to play a musical instrument or making progress as a swimmer, mastering the tones of Chinese and its thousands of characters is a daunting task. For anyone hoping to learn Chinese, Kane points to the Chinese saying *ni shui xing zhou*, rowing a boat against the tide. In other words, if you cease applying yourself to your study, you will go backwards.

CROSSINGS

My hands finally hitting bottom, I stand in the shallows a short distance from the small beach. Janet stands up on the path to my west. The brilliant afternoon sun makes me squint to see her. Off to my left, a Great Pyrenees dog, having waded in to his shoulders, casually laps the water. He looks my way, and I think he might swim over, but he remains close to a young woman who keeps an eye on him from the path.

"How was the swim?" asks Janet. "Slow, but I'm here," I say.

"Don't worry. You will come around fast," says Janet.

"Yeah. Next time here will be better," I say.

I take my goggles off to survey the lake and the surrounding hills and mountains. The dry, desert-like aspect of the landscape seems incongruous with this lake. Coming across a pond, lake, or stream here in Utah can seem like a miracle at times.

"Are you ready?" asks Janet.

Refitting my goggles, I say, "Sure. Let's go."

Swimming off, I feel rejuvenated. Well accustomed to the water, I feel relaxed and my stroke feels strong. After five months in Beijing, I cannot imagine a more salutary place to swim than this lake in Utah. I will round the rocky point of land up ahead and then swim in a broad arc along the shore of the adjoining cove.

My progress, although steady, is not what it should be, but I should be patient and not be too hard on myself. *Ba miao zhu zhang*, do not pull the seedlings to make them longer, say the Chinese.

I wonder in what direction my swimming will head next. A fair number of years have passed since I made the open-water swims that I detailed in the previous chapters. The last five years, I have job hopped from Northeast Ohio to Richmond, Virginia; to Utah; and then on to China, always trying to stay ahead of our failing economy. In the years before moving to China, I focused on competing in triathlons and lowering my swim times over the mile-or-less distance required for the events. I have not been totally derelict, though, for when we lived in Delaware, I competed in a masters swim meet, and one of my events was the 200-yard individual medley. Swimming in succession the four strokes: butterfly, backstroke, breaststroke, and freestyle, albeit in not such a great time, I nonetheless felt that I had at last crossed over and finally become a swimmer.

The truth, though, is that water will eventually have its way with me. In time, I will no longer seemingly be able to turn back the pace clock when swimming hundred-yard repeats in a pool. Neither will I be able to bounce back from a hard pool workout with another spirited swim the next day. As with any sport or physical activity, my performances will inevitably decline with advancing age. I imagine my swimming will then take a more purposeful turn, where I aim at improving my form, technique, and feel for the water. In fact, I find myself now toying with a hesitation drill. Rolling side to side, I pause between strokes just long enough to take a few strong flutter kicks. Like when one takes long, reaching strides back on land, a sense of joyful power fills my body each time my hand grabs the water.

A swimmer can never spend enough time in the water. Water, forever an alien environment, will always hold some new facet of swimming to be discovered and mastered. Back in the pool over in China, to swim a lap slowly with exquisite form, rather than fast, was often enough for me. Years ago I found the same true when playing tennis. To execute a clean, polished shot could be more important to me than whether the point was won or lost. Never needing any opponent, and more balanced than tennis, swimming offers the same, only infinitely more often. For failing at a stroke, redemption can be had on the very next one.

The gains I accrue on this swim today, however, will soon be lost, for water demands our constant renewal. In the summers after crew season, I would sometimes run down to our dock on the Farmington River. Other than the heavy growth of vegetation all along the riverbank, what struck me was the calm stillness of the river. "Where have all the shouts, splashing oars, and droning boat engines gone?" I wondered. Walking out onto the pool deck before swim practices, or standing before an empty pond or lake, has also raised similar thoughts in me. Water, so soft and surrendering, is ultimately unyielding, as it always finds its way back to its own level. Does everything related to water need to be about loss? Can anything to do with water be preserved or retained? I suppose not. "And now why tarriest thou? Arise, and be baptized, and wash away thy sins," says the Bible. In truth, water abrogates all.

I am rounding into the cove. I forego the hesitation drill; my front crawl feels more secure and solid now. Janet, emerging from behind a rocky bluff, keeps pace on my left. Perhaps some have read and reflected on the F. Scott Fitzgerald quote, "All good writing is swimming underwater and holding your breath." Although I am now not able, like Fitzgerald, to define what good writing is, I believe I can recognize it when I read it. I can pause here, nose dive underwater, and gliding forward, sense the compression, the slow passage of time, and the silent isolation. Much like when a room light is suddenly extinguished, the light green water has sharpened my focus. Oddly, my determination to stay below the surface only increases with my growing sense of desperation. I might ask, then, have I achieved something of worth with my writing? Have I been able to hold my breath long enough, so to speak? Perhaps, but what interests more in this, my last chapter, is my writing's brooding and melancholy bent. Is it because of some fault of mine? Or does water deserve some of the blame? It is a silly question, of course—this is after all my work—which is a reflection of myself. I do believe, though, that water shares some responsibility. At best water is neutral, inert, and does little more than exist. At its worst, it is heavy, oppressive, and suffocating. It's little surprise that we have phrases such as "rain on my parade" or "dampens my spirits." There is nothing lighthearted about water. It is as sad as tears, and more, it is deadly serious. But not to despair; this all concerns down here, underwater, for surfacing, I see where the water froths, reflects the light, and rises with a passing wave. A swimmer lives simultaneously in two realms: one in heavy, sullen water and the other (but only smallest part) in light, cheery air. To swim well, one needs the proper balance between them. Is swimming then not a metaphor for life?

To be fair, I have overlooked the popular sport of underwater diving. Some years ago, back at the pool where I swam in Connecticut, a regular class met for those seeking their scuba certification. I stayed one evening to watch a class, but the cumbersome equipment and lack of physical activity put me off. More interesting for me is free diving. Minimalist in nature, freedivers dive underwater on a single breath. A while back, I purchased some books and watched videos on the Internet to learn more about the sport. Using breathing and relaxation techniques borrowed from yoga, competitive freedivers have dived to astounding depths. Sometimes after swimming in a pool, I would swim a length underwater or attempt to hold my breath for some target time. Although I never found these experiences very satisfying, I occasionally do practice some of the breathing techniques I picked up while walking or cycling.

Swimming well now, I have left the cove, and I am gliding by a section of sheared-off rock. I imagine when the lake is full, the top of the rock is a popular jumping-off place. Breathing for a time to my right, I can see a pair putting in a canoe on the other side of the lake. I can hardly look out over any body of water nowadays without entertaining thoughts of swimming across it, and now I feel the same urge to veer off into open water and make the not-too-far crossing, like a mountain to be climbed. Many others have felt the same, as almost every straight, channel, lake, and river has a record (even if unwritten) of those who swam across it. Perhaps apt here are the last words of Confederate General Stonewall Jackson quoted at the beginning of this chapter. Only eight days after being hit by friendly fire during the Battle of Chancellorsville in Virginia, his last vision also entailed a river to cross.

I have entered another shallow cove. After swimming through this cove, I will have a straight shot back to the lake's northern end. Upon reaching there, I will bend to my right, following the shore back to the beach.

Instead of following in the wake of those who swam across this lake or that river, I have often thought it might be more interesting and enjoyable to make what I might call a swim-tour. When we lived in Northeast Ohio, I swam all along the southern shore of Lake Erie while competing in triathlons. Back home, after swimming offshore from the towns of Maumee, Vermillion, Lorain, and Mentor-on-the-Lake, it was not these or other lakeside spots that interested me; rather it was the Lake Erie Islands, a chain of nearly thirty islands, that drew me. Set in the lake a few miles from Sandusky, Ohio, the Lake Erie Islands are popular with tourists during the warmer months. Somewhat like a vagabond, I often imagined myself accompanied with Janet and a friend or two in kayaks and stopping off at the islands and towns with curious names such as Middle Bass, Rattlesnake, Pelee, and Put-in-Bay for a time—meeting the locals and learning some history—before swimming on to the next one. I have thought this watery island hopping would make for a great adventure, although not likely ever to catch on.

The towns along the New Jersey Shore having figured much in my early years, I have also envisioned swimming the state's length. I see myself putting in at North Jersey Highlands and swimming south, staying just outside the surf zone. No more than a speck on the chest of some sleeping giant, I feel myself rise and fall with each passing swell. Again accompanied by a party of kayaks, I would swim past the resort towns of Sea Bright, Asbury Park, and Sea Girt, on down to Manasquan, encamping a day or two before swimming on. After mentally swimming the fifty of so miles from Manasquan to Atlantic

City, I can now feel the odd mix of nostalgia and euphoria as I mentally swim past the resorts from my childhood, Ocean City, Avalon, Stone Harbor, Wildwood, and Cape May. Always the outsider, I peer at those oblivious of me on the beach, boardwalks, or sitting outside the many nameless seafront homes and condos, but has anyone made or even tried such a swim? I now wonder. And what about sharks, places to stay, sunburn, and silly stuff, such as beach tags?

The beach is coming into view on my left. New groups of people have found their places on the beach to sunbathe. Those who were here when we arrived, perhaps having had enough sun or water, have moved on. The formerly empty picnic table next to ours is now occupied by a couple of women and their young children. As with any waterfront, this beach is in constant change, and after the park maintenance staff cleans and levels the beach at the end of the day, there will be no trace of the others or us who spent part of their day here. "Water's impermanence," I think.

The beach is not too far now, and my swimming feels effortless. My hands soon touching bottom, I rise to my feet. I trudge up the beach to meet Janet, who waits for me at the picnic table. She is looking forward to hiking with me on some of the trails that run up into the surrounding hills. Seeing again my quick, easy steps, she will no doubt recognize and compliment me for being the land mammal that I have always been.

Matawan Aberdeen Public Library
165 Main Street
Matawan, NJ 07747
(732) 583-9100